FUNDAMENTALS OF
STRUCTURED
PROGRAMMING
USING FORTRAN WITH
SF/k AND WATFIV-S

FUNDAMENTALS OF STRUCTURED PROGRAMMING USING FORTRAN WITH SF/k AND WATFIV-S

R. C. HOLT
J. N. P. HUME
Department of Computer Science
University of Toronto

RESTON PUBLISHING COMPANY, INC., Reston, Virginia
A Prentice-Hall Company

Library of Congress Cataloging in Publication Data

Holt, R   C
    Fundamentals of structured programming using
FORTRAN with SF/k and WATFIV-S.

    Bibliography: p. 337
    Includes index.
    1. FORTRAN (Computer program language)
2. Structured programming. I. Hume, J. N. P.,
joint author. II. Title.
QA76.73.F25H85   001.6'424   76-20593
ISBN 0-87909-303-X
ISBN 0-87909-302-1 pbk.

©1977 by
RESTON PUBLISHING COMPANY, INC.
Reston, Virginia 22090
A Prentice-Hall Company

10 9

Printed in the United States of America

PREFACE

This book is intended to form the basis of an introductory course in computing. No particular mathematical background beyond basic arithmetic is assumed; examples are taken largely from everyday life. In this way, the focus is on programming and problem solving, rather than on mathematics. It is our strong conviction that the foundation of computer programming must be carefully laid. Bad habits once begun are hard to change. Even for those who do not continue to study computer science, an experience in the systematic analysis of problems from the statement of "what is to be done" to the final algorithm for "doing it" can be very helpful in encouraging logical thinking.

The programming language presented here is Fortran, extended in such a way that it permits structured programming. This language is introduced in a series of subsets that we call SF/1, SF/2, SF/3, and so on. The SF stands for Structured Fortran. We hope that a student will learn the concepts of structured programming by following this step-by-step presentation of extended Fortran subsets.

Just as a program provides a list of instructions to the computer to achieve some well-defined goal, the methodology of structured programming provides a list of instructions to persons who write programs to achieve well-defined goals. The goals of structured programming are to get a programming job done correctly and in such a form that later modifications can be done easily. This means that programs must be understood by people other than their authors.

The Standard Fortran language is not a language that encourages structured programming but fortunately it has recently been extended to include several new features that are essential. One compiler that supports these extensions is the Watfiv-S compiler. All programs written in this book are compatible with Watfiv-S.

As each extended Fortran subset is learned, new possibilities open up. Even from the first subset SF/1, it is possible to write programs that do calculations and print. By the time the subset SF/4 is reached, a student has learned how to handle alphabetic information, as well as to do numerical calculations and structure the control flow of the program.

Extended Fortran was chosen because it contains control structures that make structured programming easy. It is, however, possible to produce the same result using Standard Fortran and this is described in detail. The reason that Standard Fortran is not used in the first place is that it obscures the elegance of the control structures and does not permit format-free input-output or direct character handling.

Structured programming is especially important when working on larger programs; a detailed discussion of the techniques of modular programming and top-down design accompanies the introduction of Fortran subprograms in SF/7.

Many examples in the book are from data processing. General concepts of data structures, searching, and sorting fit well into this important area that touches all our lives.

The book ends with examples of scientific calculations and the translation of a high-level programming language into machine language.

At all times we have tried to present things in easy to understand stages, offering a large number of program examples and exercises to be done by the student. Each chapter has a summary of the important concepts introduced in it.

The subsets of extended Fortran that we call SF/k are based on subsets for the PL/1 language called SP/k. THe SP/k subsets were designed by R. C. Holt and D. B. Wortman of the University of Toronto.

This book was prepared using a text editing system on a computer. Each program was tested using the Watfiv-S compiler. The job of transcribing the authors' pencil scrawls into the computer was done with great care and patience by Inge Weber. We are indebted to the many people who offered constructive criticism. In particular we would thank Jim Horning, Bob Cherniak, Brian Clark, Dave Barnard, Les Mezei, Rudy Schild, and Laurie Johnston for their detailed critiques. We have sprinkled through the book names of other people who have helped us.

The time taken to write a book comes at the expense of other activities. Since most of the time was in the evenings or on weekends we must end with grateful thanks to our wives Marie and Patricia.

R. C. Holt
J. N. P. Hume

CONTENTS

CHAPTER 1
INTRODUCTION
TO PROGRAMMING

The name of this book is somewhat of a mouthful! Perhaps it would help if we took it piece by piece and introduced you to the name slowly. We hope that it is no secret that the book has to do with computers and particularly with the use of computers rather than their design or construction. To use computers you must learn how to speak their language or a language that they can understand. We do not actually speak to computers yet, although we may some day; we write messages to them. The reason we write these messages is to instruct the computer about some work we would like it do for us. And that brings us to programming.

WHAT IS PROGRAMMING?

Programming is writing instructions for a computer in a language that it can understand so that it can do something for you. You will be learning to write programs in one particular programming language called Fortran. When these instructions are put on to some medium that a computer can read such as punched cards then they can be fed into the machine. They go into the part of the computer called its memory and are recorded there for as long as they are needed. The instructions could then be executed if they were in the language the computer understands directly, the language called machine language. If they are in another language such as Fortran they must first be translated, and a program in machine language compiled from the original or source program. After compilation the program can be executed.

Computers can really only do a very small number of different basic things. For example, an instruction which says, STAND ON YOUR HEAD, will get you nowhere. The repertoire of instructions that any computer understands usually includes the ability to

1

move numbers from one place to another in its memory, to add, subtract, multiply, and divide. They can, in short, do all kinds of arithmetic calculations and they can do these operations at rates of up to a million a second. Computers are extremely fast calculating machines. But they can do more; they can also handle alphabetic information, both moving it around in their memory and comparing different pieces of information to see if they are the same. To include both numbers and alphabetic information we say that computers are data processors or more generally information processors.

When we write programs we write a sequence of instructions that we want executed one after another. But you can see that the computer could execute our programs very rapidly if each instruction were executed only once. A program of a thousand instructions might take only a thousandth of a second. One of the instructions we can include in our programs is an instruction which causes the use of other instructions to be repeated over and over. In this way the computer is capable of repetitious work; it tirelessly executes the same set of instructions again and again. Naturally the data that it is operating on must change with each repetition or it would accomplish nothing.

Perhaps you have heard also that computers can make decisions. In a sense they can. These so-called decisions are fairly simple. The instructions read something like this:

IF JOHN IS OVER 16 THEN PLACE HIM ON THE HOCKEY TEAM
    ELSE PLACE HIM ON THE SOCCER TEAM

Depending on the condition of John's age, the computer could place his name on one or other of two different sports teams. It can decide which one if you tell it the decision criterion, in our example being over sixteen or not.

Perhaps these first few hints will give you a clue to what programming is about.

WHAT IS STRUCTURED PROGRAMMING?

Certain phrases get to be popular at certain times; they are fashionable. The phrase, "structured programming" is one that has become fashionable recently. It is used to describe both a number of techniques for writing programs as well as a more general methodology. Just as programs provide a list of instructions to the computer to achieve some well-defined goal, the methodology of structured programming provides a list of instructions to persons who write programs to achieve some well-defined goals. The goals of structured programming are, first, to get the job done. This deals with how to get the job done and how to get it done correctly. The second goal is concerned with having it done so that other people can see how it is done, both

for their education and in case these other people later have to
make changes in the original programs.

Computer programs can be very simple and straightforward but
many applications require that very large programs be written.
The very size of these programs makes them complicated and
difficult to understand. But if they are well-structured, then
the complexity can be controlled. Controlling complexity can be
accomplished in many different ways and all of these are of
interest in the cause of structured programming. The fact that
structured programming is the "new philosophy" encourages us to
keep track of everything that will help us to be better
programmers. We will be cataloguing many of the elements of
structured programming as we go along, but first we must look at
the particular programming language you will learn.

WHAT IS FORTRAN?

The name Fortran is short for FORmula TRANslation and Fortran
is a language that has been developed to be independent of the
particular computer on which it is run and oriented to the
problems that persons might want done. We say that Fortran is a
high-level language because it was designed to be relatively easy
to learn and use. As a problem-oriented language it is
particularly concerned with problems of numerical calculations
such as occur in scientific and engineering applications but it
has been extended so that it can be useful in alphabetic
information handling required by business and humanities
applications.

Fortran as it has been extended is a very extensive language,
so that although each part is easy to learn, it requires
considerable study to master. Many different computer
installations have the facilities to accept programs written in
Fortran. This means that they have a Fortran compiler that will
translate programs written in Fortran into the language of the
particular machine that they have. Also many programs have
already been written in Fortran; in some installations a standard
language is adopted, and Fortran is often that standard language.

It has been the experience over the past years that a high-
level language lasts much longer than machine languages, which
change every five years or so. Fortran began its existence
nearly twenty years ago and it has had numerous extensions. As
each new version of Fortran was created an attempt was made to
keep it compatible with previous versions. This is because once
an investment has been made in programs for a range of
applications, an installation does not want to have to reprogram
when a new Fortran compiler is acquired.

Because of the long life-span of programs in high-level
languages it becomes more and more important that they can be

adapted to changes in the application rather than completely reconstructed. A high-level language has the advantage that well-constructed and well-documented programs in the language can be readily modified. It is our aim to teach you how to write such programs. To start your learning of Fortran we will study subsets of the extended Fortran language called SF/k. SF/k was developed at the University of Toronto.

WHAT IS SF/k?

The name SF/k stands for <u>Structured</u> <u>Fortran</u> <u>subset</u> k. There really is a series of subsets beginning at SF/1, then SF/2, and going on up. The first subset contains a small number of the language features of extended Fortran, but enough so that you can actually write a complete program and try it out on a computer right away. The next subset, SF/2, contains all of SF/1 as well as some additional features that enlarge your possibilities. Each subset is nested inside the next higher one so that you gradually build a larger and larger vocabulary in the extended Fortran language. At each stage, as the special features of a new subset are introduced, examples are worked out to explore the increased power that is available.

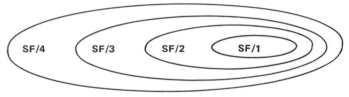

THE SF/k SUBSETS

In a sense, the step-by-step approach to learning Fortran is <u>structured</u> and reflects the attitude to programming that we hope you learn.

There is no substitute for practice in learning to program, so as soon as possible and as often as possible, submit your knowledge to the test by creating your own programs.

WHY LEARN JUST A SUBSET?

The Fortran language is very extensive; some features are only used rarely or by a few programmers. If you know exactly what you are doing, then these features may provide a faster way to program; otherwise they are better left to the experts. A beginner cannot really use all the features of the complete Fortran language and will get lost in the complexity of the language description. With a small subset it is much easier to pick up the language and then get on with the real job of learning programming.

For learners we need a fast compiler because, for many
programs, compiling is nearly all that happens; the execution is
sometimes omitted or is very short because there are errors in
the program. A special compiler might be used for the SF/k
language and this could be small enough to run on some very
inexpensive computers often called minicomputers. But it is not
necessary to have an SF/k compiler to use the SF/k language since
it is a subset of the extended Fortran language of the Watfiv-S
compiler.

But perhaps most important, the SF/k language has been
selected from the extended Fortran language so as to provide
features that encourage the user to produce well-structured
programs. This is why it is appropriate as a means of learning
structured programming.

CORRECTNESS OF PROGRAMS

One of the maddening things about computers is that they do
exactly what you tell them to do rather than what you want them
to do. To get correct results your program has to be correct.
When an answer is printed out by a computer you must know whether
or not it is correct. You cannot assume, as people often do,
that because it was given by a computer it must be right. It is
the right answer for the particular program and data you provided
because computers now are really very reliable and rarely make
mistakes. But is your program correct? Are your input data
correct?

One way of checking whether any particular answer is correct
is to get the answer by some other means and compare it with the
printed answer. This means that you must work out the answer by
hand, perhaps using a hand calculator to help you. When you do
work by hand you probably do not concentrate on exactly how you
are getting the answer but you know you are correct (assuming you
do not make foolish errors). But this seems rather pointless.
You wanted the computer to do some work for you to save you the
effort and now you must do the work anyway to test whether your
computer program is correct. Where is the benefit of all this?
The labor saving comes when you get the computer to use your
program to work out a similar problem for you. For example, a
program to compute telephone bills can be checked for correctness
by comparing the results with hand computations for a number of
representative customers and then it can be used on millions of
others without detailed checking. What we are checking is the
method of the calculation.

We must be sure that our representative sample of test cases
includes all the various exceptional circumstances that can occur
in practice, and this is a great difficulty. Suppose that there
were five different things that could be exceptional about a
telephone customer. A single customer might have any number of
exceptional features simultaneously. So the number of different

types of customers might be 32, ranging from those with no exceptional features to those with all five. To test all these combinations takes a lot of time, so usually, we test only a few of the combinations and hope all is well.

Because exhaustive testing of all possible cases to be handled by a program is too large a job, many programs are not thoroughly tested and ultimately give incorrect results when an unusual combination of circumstances is encountered in practice. You must try to test your programs as well as possible and at the same time realize that with large programs the job becomes very difficult. This has led many computer scientists to advocate the need to prove programs correct by various techniques other than exhaustive testing. These techniques rely on reading and studying the program to make sure it directs the computer to do the right calculation. Certainly the well-structured program will be easier to prove correct.

CHAPTER 1 SUMMARY

The purpose of this book is to introduce computer programming. We have begun in this chapter by presenting the following programming terminology.

Program (or computer program) - a list of instructions for a computer to follow. We say the computer "executes" instructions.

Programming - writing instructions telling a computer to perform certain data manipulations.

Programming language - used to direct the computer to do work for us.

Fortran - a popular programming language. PL/1, Cobol, Basic and APL are some other popular programming languages.

SF/k - the programming language used in this book. SF/k is a subset of the extended Fortran programming language, meaning that every SF/k program is also an extended Fortran program, but some Fortran programs are not SF/k programs. SF/k is itself composed of subsets SF/1, SF/2 and so on. This book teaches SF/1, then SF/2, and so on up to SF/8.

High-level language - a programming language that is designed to be convenient for writing programs. Fortran is a high-level language.

Structured programming - a method of programming that helps us write correct programs. The SF/k language has been designed to encourage structured programming. This book teaches a structured approach to programming.

Watfiv-S - a compiler developed at the University of Waterloo
    to support the extended Fortran language. The language
    SF/k is a subset of the language supported by the
    Watfiv-S compiler.

Standard Fortran (also called ANSI Fortran) - this is the
    Fortran language as specified by the American National
    Standards Institute. The Watfiv-S compiler supports
    Standard Fortran along with a number of extensions, and
    SF/k uses some of these extensions. In a later chapter
    we will show how an SF/k program can be modified to make
    it into a Standard Fortran program.

CHAPTER 2
THE COMPUTER

"The time has come," the walrus said, "to talk of many things" - Lewis Carroll.

And the things we want to talk about in this chapter have to do with getting to know a little bit about computers and how they are organized. A computer is a complex object composed of wires, transistors, and so on, but we will not be trying to follow wiring diagrams and worrying about how to build a computer. What we will be interested in is the various main parts of a computer and what the function of each is. In this way your programming will be more intelligent; you will understand a little of what is going on inside the computer.

PARTS THAT MAKE THE WHOLE

We have already mentioned a number of things about computers. They have a <u>memory</u> where numbers and alphabetic information can be recorded. They can add, subtract, multiply, and divide. This means they have a part called the <u>arithmetic unit</u>. They can read information off certain media, like punched cards, and print results on printers. The printer may print a whole line at a time or just one character at a time, like a typewriter. We say they have an <u>input</u> (for example, a card reader) and an <u>output</u> (a printer). The input-output unit is often referred to as the I/O. Computers execute instructions in sequence. The part of the machine that does this is called the <u>control unit</u>. The arithmetic unit and the control unit are usually grouped together in a computer and called the <u>central processing unit</u> or CPU. So then the computer is thought of as having three parts, memory, I/O and CPU.

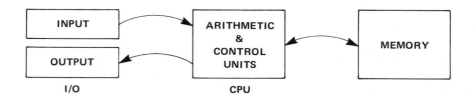

MAIN PARTS OF A COMPUTER

We will look at these different parts in turn and see how they work but first we must see how numbers and alphabetic information can be represented in a computer.

CODED INFORMATION

You are all familiar with the way that information used to travel over telegraph wires in the form of Morse Code. Perhaps you know that each letter or number is coded as a pattern of dots and dashes. For example, the letter A is a dot followed by a dash, E is one dot, V is three dots and a dash. The letters are separated from each other by a pause with no dots or dashes. The famous signal SOS is

... --- ...

This is an easy one to remember in emergencies. The Morse Code was designed so that the signal could activate some noise-making device and the listener could then translate the coded message back into letters. Modern teletype machines can send messages much faster because the machines themselves can be used to decode the messages. For these, a character is represented by a pattern of pulses, each pattern being of the same length. Instead of dots and dashes, which are two different lengths of electric pulses, they use one basic time interval and in that time interval have either a pulse or a pause. Each character requires 5 basic time intervals and is represented by a sequence of pulses and pauses. We often write down a pulse as a 1 and a pause as 0, and then the pattern for B is 10011, I is 01100, L is 01001. The word BILL would be transmitted as

10011011000100101001

Strings of ones and zeros like this can be associated with numbers in the <u>binary system</u>. In the decimal system the number 342 means

$$3 \times 10^2 + 4 \times 10^1 + 2 \times 10^0$$

where 10^2 stands for 10 squared, 10^1 for 10 to the first power, that is 10, and 10^0 for 10 to the power zero, which has a value 1. In the binary system of numbers 1101 means

$$1 \times 2^3 + 1 \times 2^2 + 0 \times 2^1 + 1 \times 2^0$$

In the decimal system this binary number has a value 8+4+0+1=13. We say that this number in the decimal system requires 2 decimal digits to represent it. In the binary system it requires 4 binary digits. We call a binary digit a bit. So the binary number representing the word BILL has 20 bits, each letter requiring 5 bits. Sometimes we take the number of bits required to represent a character as a group and call it a byte. Then the word representing BILL has four bytes. In a computer we must have a way of recording these bits, and usually the memory is arranged into words, each capable of holding a whole number of bytes.

In some machines a single letter is represented by a byte of six bits and the word length is 6 bytes or 36 bits. There are many different combinations of byte length and word length in different computers. This is something the machine designer must decide.

MEMORY

Most machines record letters and numbers in the binary form because it is possible to have recording devices that can record, read, and hold such information. Most recording devices involve a recording something like that on the tape of a magnetic tape recorder. There is a big difference, though, in the recording. On audio tape we have a magnetic recording that varies in intensity with the volume of the sound recorded. The frequency of the variations gives the pitch of the sound. For a computer, the recordings vary between two levels of intensity which you might think of as "on" and "off". If in a particular region there is an "on" recording it could indicate the binary digit one and if "off" the digit zero. So on a strip of magnetic tape there would be designated areas that are to hold each bit of information.

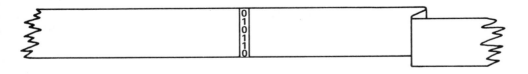

BITS RECORDED ON MAGNETIC TAPE

Binary digits can thus be recorded on reels of magnetic tape. In a similar way they can be recorded on tracks of a magnetic

disk and these disks can be stacked one above the other on a
spindle that is kept constantly spinning. To read or record
information on a magnetic disk the recording/reading head moves
to the correct track of the correct disk.

MAGNETIC DISK MEMORY

This kind of memory is called a magnetic disk pack and is
commonly used when large amounts of information are to be stored
in the computer and requested randomly. If information is to be
retrieved in a particular sequence or order then a magnetic tape
reel can be used to store it. Tape reels and disk packs can be
removed from the machine and stored if you need to keep
information for long periods of time.

Neither tape nor disks are as fast to read and write as
another type of magnetic recording on the surface of a constantly
spinning cylinder called a drum.

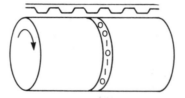

MAGNETIC DRUM MEMORY

All these devices require the movement of objects, a reel of
tape, a spinning disk or drum, and sometimes read/write heads.
These mechanical devices can never give really high-speed access
to information. We need memory devices with no moving parts so
we can perform operations at rates of the order of a million a
second. The only things that move in a really high-speed memory
device are the electric signals in the wires. As you know,
electric signals can move very rapidly, at nearly the speed of
light. A very common form of high-speed memory is the magnetic
core memory. A magnetic core is a tiny doughnut-shaped piece of
material that can be magnetized. When magnetized it is like a
bar magnet bent around in a circle.

MAGNETIC CORE

There are two directions in which a core can be magnetized, clockwise and counter-clockwise, and these can represent the two binary digits. To form a memory the cores are threaded on to wires in two directions just like a fly screen, with a core around every intersection of the wires. When signals pass through the wires thay can record information in the cores or read out information from the cores, and it can all happen extremely rapidly.
"DIAGRAM(7) HERE"

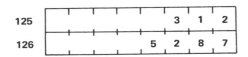

MAGNETIC CORE MEMORY

The main memory of the computer can be made of magnetic cores grouped into words. To find any particular word you need to know where it is located in the array of cores. You need to know its address. Every word (which, remember, is just a group of bits, one bit in each core) has its own address which is a number. An address may, for example, be 125. Words that are neighbors in the array have consecutive addresses, such as 125 and 126, just like houses on a street. The addresses themselves do not have to be stored in the computer. You can tell what address a word has from its location in the array. This is not always possible for houses on a street where the numbering is not completely systematic.

| 125 | | | | | | 3 | 1 | 2 |
| 126 | | | | | 5 | 2 | 8 | 7 |

THE CONTENTS OF WORDS IN MEMORY

ARITHMETIC UNIT

All computers have a part where arithmetic can take place. This is the arithmetic unit. When a new number is written in a memory location, the old number stored there is automatically erased, just as any old recording is erased as a new recording is made on a magnetic tape recorder. Just reading a number, like playing an audio recording, does not damage the recording no matter how often you do it. If you want to combine numbers, say add them, it must be done in a special location in the arithmetic unit called the accumulator. On some machines, the size of the accumulator is the same as the size of a word in memory. Words, or rather the information stored in memory locations, can be loaded into the accumulator. In a simple machine language, the instruction

> LOAD 125

would cause the number recorded in location 125 to be placed in the accumulator. Whatever was recorded in the accumulator before would be erased before the load takes place. If we want to add another number we would write

> ADD 126

This would add the number stored in 126 to what was already in the accumulator and the sum of the two numbers would then be in the accumulator. This total could be recorded in the memory for later use by the instruction

> STORE 127

The result of the addition would now be in location 127 but would also remain in the accumulator.

The accumulator can also be used for subtraction, multiplication, and division. In a high-level language like Fortran you never need to think about the accumulator. You merely indicate that you want numbers in two locations, say A and B, to be added and name the location, say C, where you want the answer to be stored. You write this all in one statement, namely

> C=A+B

This Fortran statement says: add the number stored in location A to the number stored in location B and place the result in location C. In the machine all location addresses are numbers. In Fortran we give the locations names which are called identifiers. The compiler changes these names to numerical locations and changes the single instruction

> C=A+B

to the three machine instructions.

> LOAD   A
> ADD   B
> STORE C

You have just seen examples of machine language instructions. They each consist of two parts: the operator part, for example LOAD, and the address part, A. Each part can be coded as a binary number, then the whole instruction will just be a string of bits. Suppose that you have a machine with a word length of 36 bits. Then an instruction might be itself stored in such a word with, say, 18 bits for the operation part and 18 bits for the address part. With 18 bits you can represent binary numbers that go from 1 to 2 to the power 18, which is 262,144. You can refer to any one of over a quarter of a million different memory locations.

Consecutive instructions in a machine language program are stored in consecutive locations in the memory and are to be executed one after the other. The control unit does two things. It uses a special location called the instruction pointer to keep track of what instruction is currently being executed. It places the instruction to be executed in a special location called the control register. In the control register the instruction is decoded and signals are issued to the different parts of the computer so that the operation requested is actually carried out. As each instruction is executed, the instruction pointer is increased by one to give the address of the next instruction in the program. This next instruction is then fetched from the memory, placed in the control register, and executed. This process continues, with instructions being executed sequentially unless a special instruction is encountered, which resets the instruction pointer and causes a jump from the normal sequence to a different part of the program.

In brief, the control unit controls the sequence of execution of instructions and determines the effect that execution has on the information stored in the memory.

Computers were originally referred to as stored program calculators because the instructions as well as the numbers or characters they operate on are stored in the memory. They were also referred to as sequential machines, because normally they followed a sequence of instructions one after another unless a jump instruction directs them to do otherwise.

INPUT AND OUTPUT

We have spoken of having both data and instructions in the memory of the machine and changing the data by the execution of instructions. But how do we get data or instructions into the computer, and how do we get data out of the machine after it has been operated on? That is the function of the <u>input</u> and <u>output</u> <u>units</u>. We must have instructions that cause the machine to <u>read</u> information into its memory and to <u>print</u> information out from its memory. And we must have parts of the computer, the input and output units, that respond to these instructions. One reading device commonly used is a punched card reader. You are all familiar with the standard punched card with 80 columns in which punching can take place.

80-COLUMN PUNCHED CARD

For digits, a single hole is made in a column in the position corresponding to the digits 0 to 9. Each alphabetic character requires two holes in a column, one in a digit position and the other in one of the three positions at the top of the card called the 0, 11, and 12 positions. Special characters like dollar signs require that three holes be punched in a column. The actual representations in terms of punched holes for each character or digit can be fixed into a card punch <u>keyboard</u> so that when the key on the keyboard for the character is pressed, the correct punching occurs on the card. Many <u>keypunches</u> also interpret the punching by printing the corresponding characters at the top of the card above the column where the punching is. This is so that you can read what is punched on the card. The machine can only read the punching.

Sometimes cards are prepared by marking them with a soft black pencil in certain designated areas. These marks are then

read by a reader that senses their presence, just as the punched
card reader senses holes. On mark sense cards digits require a
single mark, alphabetic characters and special characters require
two marks in the same column. Keywords in the Fortran language
can be obtained by marks in the first column.

MARK SENSE CARD

For some input units there is no medium, like cards, outside
the computer where information is first recorded.   Instead, a
keyboard is attached directly by a line, such as telephone line,
to the input unit. This eliminates the card and the card reader
but the result is similar.

When a mistake is made in punching cards, the card is to be
ejected from the punch and removed. A second attempt is then
made to produce a correctly punched card. One of the good things
about cards is that they can individually be replaced or removed
and new cards inserted in a card deck without having to repunch
the entire deck. Since instructions are placed in sequence,
usually one to a card, this sequence must be maintained. If you
drop a deck of cards they can get out of sequence and it is
difficult to get them arranged correctly again. Keep an elastic
band around your card decks to prevent accidents. The elastic is
removed as they are placed into the card reader then replaced
immediately after they are read.

The keyboard of a card punch or online computer input
terminal is similar to that of a standard typewriter, so it helps
if you can type. But hunt-and-peck methods will get you there
too. In addition to the ordinary typewriter keys, there are
special keys for indicating the end of the input for that card or
line.

The output units can be line-at-a-time printers or typewriters. The typewriters are the same as those used for input with online terminals. When card decks are the form of input, the output usually comes on the fast printers. Printers can have very high speeds. A speed of 1000 lines a minute is common, but some printers go faster. Most printers are slower.

Across a printed page there are often positions to print 120, 132 or more characters although some printers print only 72 characters on a line. The paper is continuous but may be divided by perforations into pages, each capable of holding about 60 lines of printing. Your output will probably be limited to a few pages for each run on the computer. Because users' jobs are run one after another each must be careful to put an identification on the program so that the appropriate output can be claimed. You have to tear the pages apart by hand as the machine feeds paper continuously, piling the printer output on the other side of the printer from the blank paper supply.

PROGRAM TRANSLATION

We have said that three machine language instructions, namely,

```
LOAD  A
ADD   B
STORE C
```

correspond to what is written in Fortran as

```
C=A+B
```

Instructions in the high-level language Fortran are very much simpler to write than instructions in machine language. For one thing, you do not have to be aware of the accumulator; for another, the notation is very similar to the one used in simple mathematical expressions and should be easy for you to get used to. The Fortran language is more powerful in that a single Fortran instruction can correspond to many machine language instructions. We will see later that if you are working in a high-level language, the machine can detect when you make certain kinds of mistakes in your program.

In short, high-level languages are designed to suit you rather than suit a computer. And in being that way they make the job of programming less difficult.

A Fortran program cannot execute directly on a computer but must be translated into the language for the particular computer you have. This is accomplished after the Fortran program has been read in, or loaded into, the memory. The translation is performed by another program, called the compiler, that is already stored in the computer memory. The compiler reads your

Fortran program and forms the appropriate sequence of machine language instructions from your Fortran statements. After compilation, execution of the machine language program begins automatically, provided you have not made any errors in your Fortran program that the compiler can detect but cannot repair. The kind of errors that are detectable are mostly in the <u>form</u> of the statements. If they are not proper or grammatical statements in the Fortran language the compiler will report an error to you in your printout. Errors in grammar are called <u>syntax</u> <u>errors</u>. In English you know there is an error in the sentence,

THE BOYS IS WALKING.

A machine can spot this kind of error but it cannot easily spot an error in meaning. It might never determine that the sentence,

THE HOUSE IS WALKING.

is not a meaningful sentence; it would accept it as syntactically correct.

Well, that is enough of an introduction now; let us get down to actually writing programs.

CHAPTER 2 SUMMARY

In this chapter we presented the main parts of a computer and showed how information is stored in the memory. We explained briefly how a high-level language such as Fortran is translated, or compiled, to machine language before being executed by a computer. The following important terms were introduced.

Memory - the part of a computer that stores information, such as data or a program. Magnetic tapes, disks, and drums are called secondary memory; they require mechanical motion to access information stored on them. Main memory can be immediately accessed by the computer; main memory may be composed of magnetic cores. The computer can transfer information between secondary memory and main memory.

CPU (central processing unit) - composed of the arithmetic unit and the control unit. The arithmetic unit carries out operations such as addition and multiplication. The control unit directs other parts of the computer, including the arithmetic unit, to carry out a sequence of instructions that is in the main memory.

Input and Output - ways of getting information into and out of a computer. The punch card, or IBM card, can be used to prepare input for a computer. An input device called a card reader is used to sense the holes in punch cards and transmit the encoded information to the main memory.

An output device called a printer takes information from main memory and prints it on paper.

Coded information - before information can be entered into a computer, it must be coded in a convenient form for the computer's circuitry. The circuitry recognizes "off" and "on" which we can think of as 0 and 1. The smallest unit of information is a binary digit, 0 or 1, called a bit. Letters are represented in a computer by a sequence of bits, called a byte. Bytes are arranged into words, typically four bytes to the word. The main memory of the computer is a sequence of words. These words can hold data and programs.

Translation (or compilation) - before a program written in a language like Fortran can be executed by a computer, it must be translated into machine language. The program as written in Fortran is called the source program. The translated program is placed in words in the main memory and is executed by the computer's CPU.

CHAPTER 3

SF/1: PROGRAMS THAT CALCULATE AND PRINT

This is the chapter where we set the stage for programming and you meet the cast of characters in the play. Nothing very much is going to happen in this first subset, SF/1, but you will be able to go through the motions of writing a complete program, submitting it to a computer and having it executed. This will let you get used to the mechanics of handling cards, learn how to arrange a card deck, and find out what you must do with it to get it read by the computer. Also you will see what kind of printed output to expect. Things will happen, though what the computer is actually doing for you will not be very exciting yet. But remember you will go through the same motions as are necessary when your programs do have more content.

CHARACTERS

We will be learning the programming language Fortran a little bit at a time. Any language consists of words and the words are made up of <u>symbols</u> that we call <u>characters</u>. These characters are put together in <u>strings</u>. In English the word

ELEPHANT

is a string of characters of length eight. It contains only seven different characters, the character E being used twice. We can tell that it is a word because it has a blank in front of it and one at the end. In a way the blank is also a character, but a <u>special</u> <u>character</u> for separating words. We sometimes denote the blank by b when we print programs in this book so that you can see how many blanks are present.

In English, we group words into sentences and we can tell the end of a sentence because of a special mark, the period. We also have a different kind of sentence that ends with a question mark, don't we? In addition to periods and question marks, we have other <u>punctuation marks</u> which serve to make sentences in the language easier to read. They also serve to remove ambiguity in a sentence. There is some doubt about the meaning of the sentence,

THE STUDENT CLAIMS THE TEACHER UNDERSTANDS.

The doubt is removed if it is written with commas, as,

THE STUDENT, CLAIMS THE TEACHER, UNDERSTANDS.

It is important that statements in a programming language be <u>unambiguous</u>, so punctuation is used a great deal. Instead of a sentence, the basic unit in the main part of a program is a <u>statement</u>. Statements are separated from each other by starting each statement on a new card for input. In some other high-level languages, statements are separated by having a semicolon between them. This serves to separate them just as periods separate sentences in English. In most high-level languages the comma is used to separate items in any list of similar items, and parentheses are used to enclose things that belong together.

We will have words in Fortran that are made up of letters of the alphabet and might also have digits in them. Although there are definite rules governing the way that Fortran statements are formed, we want them to be understandable. This means the words should be like English words. We use words like NAME, COST, INCOME, TAX, SUM, or words like PAGE1, TABLE6, ITEM35, and so on. Most of these words are invented by you. You are not allowed to use words that do not start with a letter. If the Fortran compiler sees a digit at the beginning of a word it assumes that it is a <u>number</u>. For example, the word 317 is taken as a number. This means that words like 3RD are illegal and will not be accepted by the Fortran compiler. The words that you make up must not be longer than six characters. So words like INVOICE, ACCOUNT, SURNAME and DIRECTION are illegal.

Before we leave characters we should perhaps list them all. A <u>character</u> is a letter, or a digit, or a special character. The <u>letters</u> are

A B C D E F G H I J K L M N O P Q R S T U V W X Y Z

The <u>digits</u> are

0 1 2 3 4 5 6 7 8 9

The special characters are

```
+  -  *  /  (  )  =  .  ,  $
b  (blank)
'  (apostrophe or single quote)
```

NUMBERS

Computers can do arithmetic calculations and they can do them extremely rapidly. When you learned arithmetic you first learned to handle numbers that are whole numbers, or integers. You learned that 5+6=11 and 2x3=6. In Fortran numbers like 2, 3, 512, 809, and 46281 are called integer constants. Any string of digits is an integer constant. You will remember that we will be storing numbers in the computer and representing them as a string of bits in some coded representation. The largest number we can represent will be limited by the length of the string of bits that are in a word in our computer. Word lengths vary from one computer to another and different Fortran compilers have different maximum lengths for the digit strings that represent integers. You will probably be safe in expecting at least nine decimal digits to be within the maximum.

If you have integers requiring longer digit strings, say for instance the population of the world, you must use the other form of numbers which is the real form.

If you have a large number like

635,642,000

you can write it as

6.35642×10^8

Perhaps you recognize this as what is called scientific notation. In Fortran the form of a real constant such as our example is

0.6356420E9

The first part is called the mantissa, the second part the exponent. The exponent is the letter E followed by the power of 10 that is to multiply the mantissa. Maybe you learned this notation before in a science course where very big numbers, like the mass of the moon, often occur. Real notation is also used for numbers that are not integers. These are either fractions or mixed numbers. We write either of these in decimal notation where a point called the decimal point separates the integer from the fraction part. Examples of fractions are

.5   .0075   .0000023

Mixed numbers are

5.27   889.6   6.0216

When we write fractions in scientific notation we usually standardize the form by putting the first non-zero digit followed by a decimal point then the remaining digits. Then the power of 10 is computed to make it right. The fraction .0000023 is written as 2.3×10^{6}. In Fortran we standardize the form as a zero followed by the decimal point followed by the digits so that our number would be 0.2300000E-05. This is the way it appears in the standard printed form. For input or in a program it can also be written as .23E-5, or 23.E-7.

An integer constant must <u>not</u> have a decimal point; a real constant <u>must</u> have a decimal point, an exponent or both. The exponent is the letter E followed by an optional plus or minus sign followed by one or more digits. Many compilers allow up to seven digits in the fraction of a real number, and exponents up to E+76 and down to E-78. If the mantissa of a real constant is an integer it need not have a decimal point provided that the exponent is present.

CHARACTER STRINGS

We have said that computers can handle both numbers and strings of characters. We have seen that there are two forms for numbers, the integer and the real.

A character string can consist of any of the characters that we have specified: letters, digits and special characters. Very often, when printing the results of a computer calculation, we want the results labeled. What we want is to print a string of characters on the page. In the statement that specifies that we want the computer to print, we include the actual string that we want printed enclosed in single quotation marks. These strings enclosed in quotation marks are called <u>literals</u> or <u>character string constants</u>.

Examples of literals are

'BILL JONES', 'BALANCE IN ACCOUNT', 'X='

If the literal you want to give contains a quotation mark or an apostrophe, which is the same character, then you must put two quotes rather than a single quote. For example, the literal corresponding to the short form of 'CANNOT' is 'CAN''T'.

We will see how to use these literals in a program when we learn what the instruction is that causes printing.

EXPRESSIONS

One of the important concepts we have in Fortran is that of an <u>expression</u>. The way that we explain what a word like expression means is basically to give examples and then generalize these examples.

First of all 32, 5, 6.1E2 and 58.1E6 are all expressions. So the general statement is that integer constants and real constants are expressions. Any expression may be enclosed in parentheses and still be an expression. For example (32) and (6.1E2) are also expressions. The expressions that are integer or real constants can be combined into compound expressions using the signs of arithmetic for adding, subtracting, multiplying, and dividing. These expressions are called <u>arithmetic expressions</u>. We use the standard signs for adding and subtracting, namely the plus and minus. For multiplication we use the asterisk (*) because there is no times sign. For division we use the slant or slash symbol (/). Examples of arithmetic expressions are

2+3, 5.2E1*7.8E5, 6./2., 10-15

Integer and real values may be combined in a single expression, and when they are the result is a real value. For example, 2+3.0E1 has the value 3.2E1.

If two numbers are to be divided, one of them must be a real number. Instead of writing 13/2 you write 13/2. and get the correct result 6.5E0. Make a habit of using a decimal point to make the divisor a real number for the division in any integer division and all will be well.

A very complicated arithmetic expression is

2*5+8-3*5/2.+6

In evaluating this you have to know what to do first because you really can only add, subtract, multiply or divide numbers two at a time. The rule is to do the multiplications and divisions first, then the additions and subtractions. Also you start at the left-hand side of the expression and work to the right. We are using here <u>rules of precedence</u>, that the operations multiply and divide have precedence over add and subtract. Parentheses can be used to guide the sequence of evaluation. For example, you write 3*(5+8) instead of 3*5+8 if you want the addition to take place before the multiplication. Expressions in parentheses take precedence.

Numbers may be raised to a power by means of the <u>exponentiation</u> operator which is written as **. For example, the value of 5 cubed is 5**3, this being the same as 5*5*5. Non-integer powers may also be computed. For example, we can write

10.**.5 to mean the square root of 10. We will later see that a
more efficient way of computing square roots is to use the built-
in function SQRT and write SQRT(10.) to get this same result.

The   exponentiation   operator   has higher precedence than the
other arithmetic operators so that in the expression

        5+3**2

the 3 is first squared to give 9 then added to 5 to give 14. If
two   or   more   exponentiation   operators   appear   in   the   same
expression they, unlike other arithmetic operators, are evaluated
from the right to the left-hand side of the expression.

EXAMPLES OF ARITHMETIC EXPRESSIONS

The   following   examples   illustrate the rules for performing
arithmetic in the Fortran programming language.

72+16   Value is 88.

8*5+7   Value is 47. Note that * means multiply.

2+10*4   Value is 42. Note that multiplication is done before
               addition.

(2+10)*4   Value is 48. The parentheses cause the addition to
               be done before the multiplication.

1/3   This division is not advisable because neither 1
               nor 3 is a real number. Instead, you could
               write 1/3. (3. is the real equivalent of 3).

1/3.E0   Value is 0.3333333E0, which is approximately one
               third. Note that the result of combining an integer
               such as 1, and a real number, such as 3.E0,
               is a real number. The value 0.3333333E0 can be
               written in other forms such as 3.33333E-1 and
               3.33333E-01.

72.E0+16.E0   Value is 88.E0, which can be written in other forms
               such as 8.8E1 and 8.80000E+01.

(9.83E0+16.82E0)/2.935E0

               This expression is equivalent to the following
                    $$\frac{9.83+16.82}{2.935}$$
               The parentheses were used so the division would
               apply to the sum of 9.83E0 and 16.82E0 (and not just
               to 16.82E0).

PRINTING

Our main purpose in subset number one is to introduce you to
Fortran and to get you to write your first program. The program
is not going to do very much but it has to do something so that
you can see that it is working. The most it can do is to print
numbers or character strings on the printer. Then you can see
that some action is taking place.

The statement that we will use in the program is like this

    PRINT, 3, 5.1E1, 'BILL'

Printing produced by the PRINT statement is placed in successive
fields across the print line. The size of the field depends on
the type of value that is being printed. The print line has
spaces for a certain number of characters. An integer value is
printed in a field of width 12 characters; a real value in a
field of 16 characters. The items that are after the PRINT are
placed in fields going from left to right with a blank separating
each pair of fields. Literals are printed, without the quotation
marks, in fields that have the same number of character spaces as
the literal has characters including blanks. When real numbers
are printed, their exponents are given, and they appear in a
standard form, for example

    0.2500000E-01

If two PRINT statements are given one after another then the
printing of the second goes to a new line. A blank line can be
left by using

    PRINT,' '

since here the literal consists of a blank. This is also useful
for skipping character spaces, and any number of blanks may be
printed.

Expressions   other   than   integer   and   real constants and
literals may also be placed in a PRINT statement. The statement

    PRINT, 2+3, 4/2.

will result in a 5 being printed on the right side of the first
field of width 12 and 0.2000000E 01 in the second which will be
of width 16. An interesting statement might be

    PRINT,'2+3=',2+3

It would print

2+3=   5

There would be twelve spaces between the equal sign and the 5 in the actual printing because the 5 is printed in a field 12 wide and a blank separates the two fields. Note that the quotes around the literal are not printed.

In printing expressions it is not legal to have a expression that begins with a parenthesis. It is illegal to write

```
PRINT,(2+3)*5
```

Instead you write the legal expression

```
PRINT,+(2+3)*5
```

It is not legal to have two arithmetic operators, together, so this is not allowed:

```
PRINT,5/-3.
```

Instead you write the legal expression

```
PRINT,5/(-3.)
```

THE PROGRAM

Now that you know a statement that will give some action, you must learn what is necessary to make a complete program. Then you can try the computer for yourself. The shortest program you can write consists of one statement followed by the two words

```
RETURN
END
```

The keyword END indicates to the Fortran compiler that this is the end of the program during translation. The keyword RETURN causes control to return to the operating system at the end of the execution of your program.

Now comes the big moment for a complete program.

```
PRINT,'2+3=',2+3
RETURN
END
```

There it is, our first Fortran program.

But wait, something is still needed, namely, two control cards. On one you identify yourself, so that the output printing can be returned to you, and not someone else, and also you tell the computer what compiler to use.

CONTROL CARDS

The beginning control card that is used is different in different installations. The one we use is of the form

```
$JOB      PAT HUME          $ COMPILE
```

The $ sign is punched in column 1 of the card followed immediately, starting in column 2, by the word JOB. You put your own name starting at a particular column of the card that varies from installation to installation. One place we know uses column 9. Your name then appears on your output exactly as you wrote it. Often control cards are prepunched with things like $JOB on them and you must add your own name. In our examples we will just use $JOB and a name and you can find out what is required by your own compiler.

When you punch the cards for the program use columns 1-72 of the card. Column 1 is used for the special $ sign which indicates control cards. Punching beyond column 72 is ignored by the Fortran compiler. The punching of a statement begins in column 7 or later. Any number of blanks can be left before the first word or between words. Later on we will be showing you how to indent the statements in your program to make it easier to read. If a statement is too long to fit on a card it may be continued on the following card by placing a + sign in column 6.

There is another control card required at the end. It has $ENTRY in the first six columns. Some computer installations may require $DATA instead of $ENTRY. $ EXECUTE.

AN EXAMPLE PROGRAM

The following is a complete job for the computer. This job illustrates the use of the PRINT statement.

```
1    $JOB      RIC HOLT
2              PRINT,'Z     G         Z     G'
3              PRINT,' I  A          I  A '
4              PRINT,'  GZ            GZ   '
5              RETURN
6              END
7    $ENTRY
```

The program causes the following pattern to be printed.

```
    Z     G         Z     G
     I  A          I  A
      GZ            GZ
```

As you can see, the top line of the pattern is printed by the PRINT statement numbered 2. Statements 3 and 4 cause the printing of the second and third lines of the pattern.

CHAPTER 3 SUMMARY

In this chapter, we explained how to write very simple computer programs. These programs are written in a small subset of the Fortran language which is called SF/1. The following important terms were presented.

Character - is a letter: ABC...Z, digit: 0123456789 or special character: +-*/()=.,$ and blank.

Integer constant - is an integer (whole number) such as 78 and 2931. There may be a minus sign in front of the integer. An integer constant must not contain commas or a decimal point. The following should <u>not</u> be used: 25,311 125.00.

Real constant - is a number such as 3.14159E0 (equal to 3.14159×10^0 or simply 3.14159). Real constants consist of a mantissa (3.14159) and an optional exponent part (E0). The exponent can be absent when there is a decimal point.

Literal (or character string constant) - is a sequence of characters enclosed in quotes, such as 'WHY NOT'.

Arithmetic expression - composed of either a single number or a collection of numbers combined using addition, subtraction, multiplication, division and exponentiation (+,-,*,/ and **). Parentheses may enclose parts of the expression. If arithmetic expressions appear in a PRINT statement they must not begin with a left parenthesis. Place a + sign in front of the parenthesis to avoid the problem. Two operators (*,-,*,/,**) cannot appear next to each other.

Rules of precedence - specify the order for applying +,-, * and / to find the value of an arithmetic expression. Parenthesized expressions are evaluated first. Next, any ** operators are applied from right to left. Finally, proceeding from left to right, * and / are applied first and then + and -.

Control Cards - a card with $JOB precedes a Fortran program. A card with $ENTRY must follow the program cards.

PRINT statement - this statement is of the form:

PRINT, list of items separated by commas

The items to be printed must be literals or arithmetic expressions. Each PRINT statement starts a new print line.

Field   -   the   PRINT statement causes printing in fields across a
        line. The size of the fields depends on what is being
        printed.   Integers appear in 12-character fields, real
        numbers in 16-character fields, and literals in fields of
        their own length.   Each pair of fields is separated by a
        blank.

Output (or printout) - printing which the computer does at your
        request.   The PRINT statement produces output from the
        computer.

END   -   the   last line of every Fortran program. It is used as a
        signal to stop compiling.

RETURN   -   the   signal that control is to be returned to the
        operating system of the computer because the execution is
        finished.

SQRT   -   the built-in function for obtaining the square root of a
        number. For example to print the square root of 2 we write

```
    PRINT,SQRT(2.)
```

Note that the function SQRT gives the square root of a real
number so that we must include the decimal point.

CHAPTER 3 EXERCISES

1. What will the following program cause the computer to print?

```
    PRINT,'*   *'
    PRINT,'** **'
    PRINT,'* * *'
    PRINT,'*   *'
    RETURN
    END
```

Can you rearrange the lines in this program to print a different
letter?

2. Consider the following program.

```
    PRINT,'H   H   A    L     '
    PRINT,'H   H   A A  L     '
    PRINT,'HHHHH  AAAAA L     '
    PRINT,'H   H   A   A L     '
    PRINT,'H   H   A   A LLLLL'
    RETURN
    END
```

    (a) What will the program cause the computer to print?
    (b) Which lines do <u>not</u> cause any printing?

3. Write programs to print the following:

(a)

```
        SEESEE       YOU   YOU      PEAPEAPEA
    SEE    SEE       YOU   YOU      PEA   PEA
    SEE               YOU   YOU      PEA   PEA
    SEE               YOU   YOU      PEAPEAPEA
    SEE               YOU   YOU      PEA
    SEE               YOU   YOU      PEA
    SEE    SEE       YOU   YOU      PEA
        SEESEE       YOUYOUYOU      PEA
```

(b)

```
    T
    TR                 M         SQUARE
    TRI              A O         Q   R          A
    TRIA             I   N       U   A        R M
    TRIAN           DIAMOND      A   U       Y   I
    TRIANG           I   N       R   Q      PYRAMID
    TRIANGL          A O         ERAUQS
    TRIANGLE           M
```

(c)

```
       T  T
       I  I
       C  C                                       PLUS
    TICTACTOE        Z   G   Z    G               PLUS
       A  A            I  A    I  A           PLUSPLUSPLUS
       C  C             GZ       GZ           PLUSPLUSPLUS
    TICTACTOE                                     PLUS
       O  O                                       PLUS
       E  E
```

(d)

```
       H           STAIR          CH  EC  KE  RS
      O P            S               CH  EC  KE  RS
       S             T            CH  EC  KE  RS
       C             E               CH  EC  KE  RS
      O T            P            CH  EC  KE  RS
       C           STAIR             CH  EC  KE  RS
       H             S            CH  EC  KE  RS
                     T               CH  EC  KE  RS
                     E
                     P
```

4. What do the following cause the computer to print?

```
(a) PRINT,2,'PLUS',3,'IS',2+3
(b) PRINT,'23424+19872+36218=',23424+19872+36218
(c) PRINT,'2 FORMULAS:',2+3*5,+(2+3)*5
(d) PRINT,'SUBTRACTION',20-10-5,20-(10-5)
```

5. Write   statements to calculate and print the following:

   (a) The sum of 52181 and 10032.
   (b) 9213 take away 7918.
   (c) The sum of 9213, 487, 921, 2013 and 514.
   (d) The product of 21 times the sum of 816, 5 and 203.
   (c) 343 plus 916 all multiplied by 82.
   (f) 3.14159 (pi) times 8.94 divided by 2.
   (g) 3.14159 times the square of 8.94 (Note: X^2 can be written
       as X*X or as X**2).

6. Write programs to calculate and print the following with the
   appropriate labels:

   (a) The area of a triangle whose base is 10.5 cm and whose
       altitude (or height) is 8.7 cm.
   (b) The volume a cylinder whose circumference is 9.2 cm and
       whose height is 5.3 cm.
   (c) The distance between two points in a plane whose co-
       ordinates are (3,2) and (5,8).
   (d) The value of the polynomial $y=x^2-2x+3$ at the three values
       x=1,2,3.

CHAPTER 4

SF/2: VARIABLES
AND ASSIGNMENTS

In this subset you will learn how to read numerical information into the computer, how to perform arithmetic calculations on the numbers you read in, and how to print the answers out. You will learn, as well, how to make your programs understandable to others (as well as to yourself) by careful choice of words that you can make up and by comments that you can add to your program. The principal concept to learn in this subset is the idea of a variable.

VARIABLES

We have said that a computer has a memory and that in the memory there are locations where information can be stored. Each location has its own unique address. In a high-level language like Fortran we do not ever refer to an actual machine address. Instead we use a name to identify a particular location. It is like referring to a house by the name of the owner rather than by its street address. We use the word variable to stand for the memory location. It is named by an identifier.

The identifier for a variable must begin with a letter and contain no blanks or special characters. If you think of the variable as the store location and its name as the identifier then you will realize that the value of the variable will be the actual information that is stored in the memory location. Locations are arranged to hold only one type of information or data. We speak of the data type of a variable. A variable may hold integers, in which case we say it is an integer variable. It could also be a real variable or a character variable. If a variable is an integer variable its value can be any integer. The value may be changed from time to time in the program but its

type attribute can never change; once an integer variable, always
an integer variable.

Examples of variable identifiers are

FACTOR, TAX, TOTAL, MARK

Identifiers for variables can be up to 6 characters long.

It is very important to choose identifiers that relate to the
kind of information that is stored in the corresponding
locations. Well-chosen identifiers make a program easier to
understand.

DECLARATIONS

We must make the words we want to use as variable identifiers
known to the compiler and associate them with memory locations
suitable for the particular data type they will hold. This is
accomplished by means of "declarations" that are placed at the
beginning of the program.

We will not, at the moment, show how character variables can
be declared but look only at integer and real variables. To
declare that SUM is to be an integer variable we write

INTEGER SUM

The identifier is placed after the keyword INTEGER. This
establishes SUM as having the type INTEGER. To declare WIDTH to
be a real variable use

REAL WIDTH

If a number of INTEGER variables are required they can all be
listed separated by commas, for example

INTEGER SUM,MARK,NUMBER

Putting declarations in a program is like phoning ahead for hotel
reservations; when you need it, the space is there with the
right name on it. Also the compiler can substitute the actual
machine address whenever it encounters a variable in the program.
It does this by keeping a directory showing variable identifiers
and corresponding memory locations. This directory is set up as
the declarations are read by the compiler.

You should not use as variable identifiers any of the words
that are Fortran keywords. These are INTEGER, REAL, PRINT,
RETURN, END, and so on. Sometimes it would cause no trouble to
do this; often it would.

ASSIGNMENT STATEMENTS

In addition to declarations, you will be learning two kinds of Fortran statements that cause things to happen as the program is executed. We say that they are <u>executable</u> <u>statements</u>. The PRINT statement is an executable statement; it causes printing to take place. One of the two new executable types we will have is the statement that <u>reads</u> cards, the READ statement, but first we will look at the <u>assignment</u> <u>statement</u>.

There are no keywords in an assignment statement but it has a very definite form. The form is

    variable identifier = expression

There is an <u>equal</u> <u>sign</u> and on the left of it is a single word, a variable identifier. This identifier must have been declared to be either integer or real. On the right hand of the equal sign there is an expression. We have looked at expressions that contained integer or real constants; now expressions can also contain integer or real variable identifiers. We have expressions like

    5+10/3.E0   (8+9)*7

but now we can have expressions like

    SUM+1   TOTAL/1.00E2   SUM-MARK

We will not use variable identifiers in the expression on the right-hand side of an assignment statement to begin with but instead use a simple expression, an integer constant. For example,

    AGE=5

is an assignment statement. It has the result of storing the number 5 in the memory location identified by the name AGE. If AGE has appeared in the declaration

    INTEGER AGE

then the number will be stored as an integer and would be printed out by

    PRINT,AGE

as 5. If, on the other hand, it were declared REAL AGE it would be stored and printed as 0.5000000E 01.

Assignments look like equations and this is misleading. When we write

    AGE=5

we are not stating something that is true when you encounter it
in a program. You mean by the statement that the value 5 is to
be assigned to the variable AGE. Some programming languages try
to keep assignments from looking like equations by using an arrow
pointing left instead of an equal sign, and write

        AGE <- 5

    This way of writing the assignment indicates the action that
is to take place. We are stuck with Fortran's equal sign and you
must just learn to think of the action.

    So far the expression on the right-hand side of the
assignment has just been an integer constant, but we can have
more complicated expressions.

        AGE=1976-1966

Here we are subtracting the year of birth, 1966, from the year
1976 to get the age in 1976. This instruction would assign the
value 10 to the variable AGE. We could get the same result as
follows

        BORN=1966
        NOW=1976
        AGE=NOW-BORN

Here we have two additional variables BORN and NOW which are
given values in assignment statements and then used in an
expression on the right-hand side of another assignment
statement. We could have another statement

        NEWAGE=AGE+1

which would give the age the following year to the variable
NEWAGE. Remember, if we use identifiers in a program they must
all appear in declarations. We would need the declaration

        INTEGER AGE,BORN,NOW,NEWAGE

A variable may be assigned values over and over during a program.
For example, we might have

        SUM=2+3
        PRINT,SUM
        SUM=3+4
        PRINT,SUM

and so on. Now we come to perhaps the most confusing type of
assignment statement. Suppose in a program you were making
calculations year by year and needed to keep a variable AGE that
held the value of the current age for the calculation. We might
change the value at the end of the year by the assignment:

        AGE=AGE+1

Now you can see that the assignment statement is certainly not an equation, or this would be nonsense. What happens when this statement is executed is that the value stored in the variable AGE is added to the integer 1 and the result of the addition stored back in the same location.

In machine language, if the memory location of AGE is 336 and if there is a constant 1 stored in location 512, then the Fortran assignment statement

        AGE=AGE+1

could be translated as

        LOAD   336
        ADD   512
        STORE   336

                        TRACING EXECUTION

We have seen that variables are associated with locations in the memory of the computer. We can assign values to variables and, during a program, we can change the values as often as we want. The values can <u>vary</u> and that is why the locations are called variables. The location stays the same but the value can change.

Sometimes it is helpful when getting used to writing programs, to keep track of values stored in the memory locations corresponding to each variable. This can help us to understand the effect of each statement. Some statements change a value; others do not. We call this <u>tracing the execution</u> of instructions.

We do not need to know the numerical, or machine address of the locations. As far as we are concerned the identifier is the address of the variable. For example, if before execution of

        AGE=AGE+1

we had
        AGE is 9
then after
        AGE is 10

We will trace now a slightly more complicated program by writing the values of all the variables involved after each instruction is executed. Here we will use some meaningless names like X, Y, and Z because the program has no particular meaning. We just want to learn to trace execution. We will write the tracing on the right-hand side of the page and the program on the left. The labels over the right-hand side give the names of the locations; their values are listed under the names, opposite each

instruction. When the value of a particular variable has not yet
been assigned we will write a dash.

LINE		X	Y	Z
1	INTEGER X,Y,Z	-	-	-
2	X=5	5	-	-
3	Y=7	5	7	-
4	Z=X+Y	5	7	12
5	X=X+5	10	7	12
6	X=Z	12	7	12
7	Y=Z	12	12	12
8	X=X+Y+Z	36	12	12
9	Y=Y*Z	36	144	12
10	Z=(X+Y)/12.	36	144	15
11	X=X/5.	7	144	15
12	PRINT,X,Y,Z	7	144	15
13	RETURN			
14	END			

The lines of the program are numbered so that we can make
reference to them. You will have found that the computer numbers
the lines in your program so that it can refer to errors in
specific lines.

First notice that the locations X, Y, and Z do not get
established until the declaration INTEGER X,Y,Z. They have no
values assigned at this point though. All is straightforward
until line 5 when X appears on both sides of the assignment
statement. The values shown at the right are, remember, the
values after execution of the statement on that line. In line 10
note that since a division is not reliable unless either the
divisor or dividend has a real value, we add a decimal point to
the integer 12. When the division yields an integer the answer
is exact but in line 11 you can see that the fractional part of
the division is dropped. We say it is <u>truncated</u>. The true
answer is 7.2 but the integer 7 is stored in location X because
it is of the type INTEGER. To get the fractional part of the
result in a division we must store the answer in a REAL variable
location.

The output statement in line 12 is different from the output
statements in SF/1 because now we can include the names of
variables in the list. We have

        PRINT,X,Y,Z

The machine can tell the difference between variable identifiers
and literals because identifiers have no quotes. There is no
possible confusion between numbers and identifiers because an
identifier may not begin with a digit. You can see now why
Fortran has this rule.

In this example we showed a division with truncation. Sometimes we want to round off the results of a division, say in determining costs to the nearest cent. If COST is the value in cents of a 2-kilogram package of soap flakes then the cost of one kilogram to the nearest cent KGCOST is produced by

      KGCOST=COST/2.+.5

The variable KGCOST has been declared to be integer so it will accept only whole number values. This method of rounding is to add .5 to the answer, which is computed with the proper fractional part. Then, after addition, the fractional part is truncated because the value is assigned to the integer variable KGCOST. Adding .5 has the effect that if the right answer has a fractional part below .5 then it is rounded by truncation of the fraction. If it is .5 or over , it is rounded up to the next integer. Try it yourself for 88.3 and 88.7.

                          INPUT OF DATA

     Now we will learn how to read data from cards into the computer. We did not learn this at the same time as we learned to print data because the idea of a variable is essential to input. It is not essential to output because we can have numbers and literals, that is, integer and real constants and constant character strings. If we write

      READ,X,Y,Z

we will read three numbers off a card and store them in the three variables X, Y, and Z. The card with the three numbers is called a data card and is placed in the card deck immediately following the $ENTRY control card. We need to have a $ENTRY control card whether or not there are any data cards. On the data card, the numbers need not be arranged in any set fields, but must be separated from each other by at least one blank. Here is a sample program, including control cards, that reads information in and prints it out.

```
$JOB    PAT HUME
        INTEGER X,Y,Z
        READ,X,Y
        Z=X+Y
        PRINT,Z,Y,X
        RETURN
        END
$ENTRY
  5   7
```

The printed output for this program would be

      12   7   5

On input, the first number on the data card, namely 5, is associated with the first variable X and stored in that location. The number 7 is stored in location Y.

When punching real numbers for input, you do not have to put any more significant figures than necessary in either the mantissa or exponent; you need not punch

    0.2000000E+01

You can have only 2.E0 or 2E0. If the exponent is zero, you may omit it completely as long as a decimal point is present. Thus numbers like

    35.8   3.14159   0.025   2.

are all acceptable as real numbers.

CONVERSION BETWEEN INTEGER AND REAL

Conversions between integer and real form will occur automatically whenever required by the type of the variable that is to hold the number. If a data item is on a card as an integer and is read into a location defined by a variable that has been declared as REAL, then it will be converted to real. A real constant cannot be read into a location defined by a variable that has been declared as INTEGER. For example:

```
$JOB    RIC HOLT
        INTEGER X,Y
        REAL Z
        READ,X,Y,Z
        PRINT,X,Y,Z
        READ,X,Y,Z
        PRINT,X,Y,Z
        RETURN
        END
$ENTRY
    22      36        25
     2     181        5.E4
```

The output for this program will have two lines with the printing

```
    22      36      0.2500000E 02
     2     181      0.5000000E 05
```

Each READ statement begins reading on a new card, and that is why each set of three values of X, Y and Z was on a separate data card.

Within a program it is often necessary to convert between integer and real. This can be accomplished by assigning the

integer to a real variable and vice versa. For example, suppose
that AVMARK is a real variable holding the average mark in a term
examination.   You would like the average to the nearest mark.
Declare another variable MARK as integer and write in the program

        MARK = AVMARK+.5

MARK will then be an integer, the rounded average mark.

COMMENTS

     One of the main aims of structured programming is that your
programs be easily understood by yourself and by others.
Choosing variable names that suggest what is being stored is an
excellent way to make programs readable. We have shown several
programs with just X, Y, and Z as variable names. This is
because these are meant to show you what happens in assignment
statements and READ and PRINT statements and are not about real
applications. It is not advisable to use such meaningless names.
We want your programs to look more like English than like algebra
when you are finished.   Unfortunately the six character
limitation on variable names leads to some unavoidable
abbreviating.

     One other thing that you can do to make a program
understandable is to include comments in English along with the
program. We have been providing comments to some of our examples
in the accompanying text but you can write comments right into
the program. To accomplish this, simply precede the comment by a
C in column 1 of the input card. In that way the comment is not
mistaken for a program statement. For example

C   THIS IS A COMMENT

could be placed at the beginning of a program or between
statements or between declarations <u>anywhere</u> in the program.

     Comments should not be split between cards, or be put in the
data. From now on we will be including comments in our examples.

AN EXAMPLE JOB

     We now give a job (control cards, program and data values)
which illustrates the use of variables, assignment statements,
READ statements, and comments. The program reads in the length,
width and height of a box (as given in inches) and then prints
the area of the base of the box (in square centimeters) and the
volume of the box (in cubic centimeters). Lines 1 and 18 are
control cards, lines 2-17 are the program and lines 19 and 20
give the data.

```
 1    $JOB     MARIE GUINDON
 2    C READ BOX LENGTH, WIDTH AND HEIGHT IN INCHES
 3    C      THEN CONVERT TO CENTIMETERS AND CALCULATE
 4    C      THE BOX'S BASE AREA AND VOLUME
 5            REAL LENGTH,WIDTH,HEIGHT,AREA,VOLUME,INTOCM
 6            INTOCM=2.54
 7            READ,LENGTH,WIDTH
 8            LENGTH=INTOCM*LENGTH
 9            WIDTH=INTOCM*WIDTH
10            AREA=LENGTH*WIDTH
11            PRINT,' AREA=',AREA
12            READ,HEIGHT
13            HEIGHT=INTOCM*HEIGHT
14            VOLUME=HEIGHT*AREA
15            PRINT,'VOLUME=',VOLUME
16            RETURN
17            END
18    $ENTRY
19       2.6    1.2
20       6.92
```

This program will print the following

```
    AREA=      0.2012898E 02
    VOLUME=    0.3538030E 03
```

where the area is in square centimeters and the volume is in cubic centimeters. The area and volume printed depend on the three values on the data cards; the data values 2.6, 1.2 and 6.92 could be replaced by the dimensions of a different box.

Lines 2, 3 and 4 are comments intended for you, the reader of the program, and are ignored by the computer.

Line 5 of the program sets up memory locations for variables called LENGTH, WIDTH, HEIGHT, AREA, VOLUME and INTOCM (the conversion factor from inches (IN) to centimeters (CM)). These variables have the REAL type, instead of the INTEGER type, because they have non-integer values (such as 2.6). Line 6 sets the value of INTOCM to 2.54. Line 7 causes the data values 2.6 and 1.2 to be read into variables LENGTH and WIDTH.

Line 8 takes the value 2.6 from the LENGTH variable, multiplies it by INTOCM, and then returns the result to LENGTH. The multiplication sign (*) is required; we could not write simply

```
    LENGTH=2.54 LENGTH
```

Line 9 is similar to line 8.

Line 10 takes the values in LENGTH and WIDTH, multiplies them together, and places the result in AREA. Line 11 then prints:

```
AREA=      0.2012898E 02
```

Notice that we have put two blanks ahead of AREA= in the literal. This is to make it line up with VOLUME= printed by line 15.

As of line 10, the variables HEIGHT and VOLUME have not been used. An attempt to print HEIGHT or VOLUME in line 11 would be an error because those variables have not yet been given a value.

Since the READ statement of line 7 reads the first data card with 2.6 and 1.2, the READ statement of line 12 reads the next card, placing the value 6.92 into HEIGHT. The computer does not know that 6.92 represents the height of a box. It only knows that it is instructed to read the next data value into the variable named HEIGHT.

Line 13 converts to centimeters, line 14 computes the volume and line 15 prints the volume. Line 16 tells the computer to stop working on this program.

This job would print the same thing if we made the following changes.

(1) Replace line 7 by the two assignment statements:

```
LENGTH=2.6
WIDTH=1.2
```

(2) Replace line 12 by the assignment statement:

```
HEIGHT=6.92
```

(3) Delete lines 19 and 20, the data values.

These three changes result in a program which is given the dimensions of the box by assignment statements rather than by input statements (READ statements). The advantage of the original program, which uses READ statements, is that the program will work for a new box simply by replacing the data cards.

LABELING OF OUTPUT

Just as comments help to make a program more understandable, output that is properly identified by labels is self-explanatory. What you are trying to do is to prepare documents that need no further explanation from you when you show your computer printout to others.

The compiler always lists your program, including comments, but the output data should also be labeled so the reader is in no doubt about what the numbers are, without reading the program.

Very often you present results without showing how you got them, that is, you do not include the program.

There are two basic ways to label results. If different values of the same set of variables are listed in columns on the output, then a label can be placed at top of each column. For example, the output for comparing costs of boxes of soap flakes might be

```
COST (CENTS)  WEIGHT (KGS)   COST PER KG
       125             1          125
       200             2          100
       260             3           87
```

There is no reason to use exactly the same labels as the variable names, since the literals printed at the top of the columns can be longer and contain blanks. If you are labeling columns of integers the labels should be 12 characters long; for real numbers 16 character labels fit over the columns. Blanks can be inserted to make them come out to the right length. The program that produces this table might be

```
$JOB    DICK SWENSON
C COMPUTE AND TABULATE COST PER KG
        INTEGER COST,WEIGHT,KGCOST
C       PRINT HEADINGS OF TABLE
        PRINT,'COST (CENTS)','WEIGHT (KGS)',' COST PER KG'
C       PROCESS DATA FOR FIRST BOX
        READ,COST,WEIGHT
        KGCOST=COST/(WEIGHT*1.)+.5
        PRINT,COST,WEIGHT,KGCOST
C       PROCESS DATA FOR SECOND BOX
        READ,COST,WEIGHT
        KGCOST=COST/(WEIGHT*1.)+.5
        PRINT,COST,WEIGHT,KGCOST
C       PROCESS DATA FOR THIRD BOX
        READ,COST,WEIGHT
        KGCOST=COST/(WEIGHT*1.)+.5
        PRINT,COST,WEIGHT,KGCOST
        RETURN
        END
$ENTRY
      125   1
      200   2
      260   3
```

You can see how comments can be inserted, how the column headings are printed, and how each line of the table is calculated and printed. We multiplied WEIGHT by the real constant 1. because this produces the real number equivalent of WEIGHT; this is done to avoid dividing an integer by another integer. In the program we have repeated three statements, without change, one set of three for each box. If we had 100 boxes, this would have been a little monotonous. When we want to repeat statements we do <u>not</u> do it this way; a more convenient way is possible with a new kind of statement that will cause this repetition. But that comes in the next subset, SF/3.

A second kind of output labeling was already used in the previous example but can be illustrated by a program segment

```
COST=5
PRINT,'COST=',COST
```

This would result in the printing

```
COST=           5
```

This method is easier when just a few numbers are being printed, and saves the problem of making labels of a precise number of characters.

It is often a good idea to print out the input data as it is being read in. Although the computer automatically lists the program it does not list the data following the $ENTRY control card. In our example, the cost and weight were printed out along with the cost per kilogram so that there was not a need to echo the input data as it was read.

PROGRAM TESTING

It is easy to make mistakes in programming. The first thing you should do to test a program is to read over your program carefully to spot errors. It is valuable to trace the execution yourself before you submit it to the computer. Your goal should always be to produce programs that you <u>know</u> are correct without testing, but this is not always possible. You could ask someone else to read it too. If he cannot understand your program it may show that your program is poorly written or has errors. Next you put your program on cards and proofread your cards to see that they match your intentions. Check that the control cards are present. Next you submit your deck.

If you have made errors in your program that involve the form of statements, the compiler spots these during compilation and reports them on the output. It refers to an error of a certain type in line so and so of the program. It has been careful to give numbers to each line so that it can make these references. Errors in form are called <u>syntax errors</u>. Examples of common syntax errors are

1. leaving out the comma after READ or PRINT
2. forgetting the END or RETURN
3. misspelling a keyword

In a way, a syntax error is a good error since it is detected for
you by the computer. But it is frustrating to have to correct it
and resubmit the deck. It wastes time. Some people say that
having syntax errors is a symptom of sloppy programming and a
sure indication that there are other errors.

When there are simple syntax errors, some compilers attempt
to repair them and go on. Their repairs are just guesses at what
you intended and some of the guesses are pretty wild. They
always give the programmer a warning if a repair has been
attempted. Some errors cannot be repaired and, as a result, no
execution takes place. Your printout has only the program
listing and error messages. Very sad! Back to the drawing board.
Be sure to proofread the entire listing of your program, looking
for unreported errors.

If there are no unrepairable syntax errors, execution takes
place right after compilation. This does not, however, mean that
all is well.

If answers are printed, they should be checked against hand
calculated answers. If they agree, it is possible that your
program is correct. If they disagree it is possible that your
hand calculations are incorrect or that your program has errors.
The errors now are usually of a kind called semantic errors. You
are asking for a calculation that you did not mean to ask for.
It has a different meaning from your intentions. For instance,
you are adding two numbers and you meant to subtract them.

To find semantic errors you must look at the program again
and try to trace what it must be doing rather than what you
thought it would do. To help in the tracing it is often good to
insert additional PRINT instructions between other statements and
print out the current value of variables that are changing. In
this way you can follow the machine's activity. These extra
PRINT instructions can be removed after the errors have been
found.

Sometimes there is no output printing from the PRINT
instructions that give the final results. This might happen in
many ways, for instance, if you ask in the READ statements for
more data items than you have on the data cards. The computer
will tell you it reached the END OF FILE so the error is spotted.
It is important that the data items match the variables in the
READ statements, or answers can be ridiculous.

Care must be taken about the INTEGER and REAL distinction
between numbers as the computer converts automatically and will
not warn you if things are going wrong.

COMMON ERRORS IN PROGRAMS

When you try running a program on a computer, the computer may detect <u>errors</u> in your program. As a result, <u>error messages</u> will be printed. Since the computer does not understand the purpose of your program, its error messages are limited to describing the specific illegalities which it detects. Unfortunately, the computer's error messages usually do not tell you how to correct your program so that it will solve the problem you have in mind.

In order to help you avoid such errors, we list some of the errors which commonly occur in students' programs.

Missing commas – Do not forget to put commas after the READ and PRINT keywords.

Too many commas – Do not put commas after the keywords INTEGER or REAL.

Parentheses – For every left parenthesis in a expression there must be a balancing right parenthesis.

Missing END at the end of the program.

Missing $ENTRY.

Missing quotes, especially the last quote, for example

      PRINT,'COST OF LIVING

Uninitialized variables – When a variable is declared, a memory location, or cell, is set aside, but no special value is placed in the cell. That is, the cell is not yet initialized. A variable must be given a value, via an assignment statement or a READ statement, before an attempt is made to use the value of the variable in a PRINT statement or in an expression.

Undeclared variables – Before a variable is used in a statement (assignment, READ or PRINT) the variable must be declared. All declarations must precede all other statements.

Mistaking I for 1 – The characters I and 1 look similar, but are entirely different to the computer.

Mistaking O for 0 – The characters O (oh) and 0 (zero) look similar, but are entirely different to the computer.

Mistaking 1 (one) for l (the letter "ell").

Attempt to read beyond end-of-file – Sometimes a program reads all of its data, and then tries to read more (non-existent) data. That is, READ statements consume all the data values

following $ENTRY, and then a READ statement tries to read
another (non-existent) data value. Either the program or the
data is in error. Remember that each READ statement starts
reading a new card just as each PRINT statement starts a new
line of printing.

CHAPTER 4 SUMMARY

This chapter introduced <u>variables</u>, as they are used in
programming languages. Essentially, a variable is a memory
location, or cell, which can hold a <u>value</u>. Suppose X is the name
of a variable; then X denotes a cell. If X is a variable having
the INTEGER type, then the cell for X can hold an integer value
such as 9, 291, 0 or -11.

The following important terms were discussed in this chapter.

Identifier - can be used as the name of a variable. An
    identifier must begin with a letter; this letter can be
    followed by additional letters or digits. It cannot be
    longer than six characters. The following are examples of
    identifiers: X, I, WIDTH, INCOME and A1.

Type (or attribute) - Each variable has a type; in this chapter
    we introduced the INTEGER and REAL types. The type of a
    variable is determined by its declaration.

Declaration - establishes variables for use in a program. For
    example, the declaration

        INTEGER I

    creates a variable called I which can be given integer
    values. Declarations must be at the beginning of a program
    before any READ, PRINT or assignment statements. A
    declaration can be one of the forms:

        INTEGER list of identifiers separated by commas
        REAL list of identifiers separated by commas

Assignment - means a value is assigned to a variable. For
    example, the following is an assignment statement which gives
    the value 52 to the variable I:

        I=52

Truncation - throwing away the fractional part of a number. When
    a real number is assigned to a variable with type INTEGER,
    the variable is given the truncated value.

Number conversion - changing an integer number to a real number or vice versa. Conversion from real to integer causes truncation of the result.

Data (or input data) - values which a program can read. The data values follow the $ENTRY card.

READ statement - this statement is of the form:

READ, list of variable names separated by commas

If a READ statement contains a list of several variables, reading will automatically proceed to the next data card when the values of one card have all been read. Each new READ statement will start reading a new card. If unread values exist on the previous card they are ignored.

Comments - information in a program which is intended to assist a person reading the program. The following is a comment which could appear in a Fortran program:

C THIS PROGRAM PRINTS GAS BILLS

The initial C of a comment must be in card column one. Comments do not affect the execution of a program.

Documentation - written explanation of a program. Comments are used in a program to document its actions.

Keyword - a word, such as READ or RETURN, which is an inherent part of the programming language. Keywords must not be used as identifiers.

Errors - improper parts of, or actions of, a program. For example, the statement

PRINT,5*(2+3

has an error in that a right parenthesis is missing. If the computer detects an error in your program, it will print an "error message".

CHAPTER 4 EXERCISES

1. Suppose that I, J and K are variables with the integer type and they presently have the values 5, 7 and 10. What will be printed as a result of the following statements?

```
PRINT,I,I+1,I+J,I+J*K
K=I+J
PRINT,K
J=J+1
PRINT,J
I=3*I+J
PRINT,I
```

2. RADIUS, DIAMTR, CIRCUM and AREA are REAL variables. A value
has been read into RADIUS via a READ statement. Write statements
which do each of the following.

    (a) Give to DIAMTR the product of 2 and RADIUS.
    (b) Give to CIRCUM the product of pi (3.14159) and DIAMTR.
    (c) Give to AREA the product of pi and RADIUS squared.
        (RADIUS squared can be written as RADIUS*RADIUS.)
    (d) Print the values of RADIUS, DIAMTR, CIRCUM and AREA.

3. Suppose I is a variable with the INTEGER type. I has already
been given a value via an assignment statement. Write statements
to do the following.

    (a) Without changing I, print out twice the value of I.
    (b) Increase I by 1.
    (c) Double the value of I.
    (d) Decrease I by 5.

4. M, N and P are variables of integer type. What will the
following statements cause the computer to print?

```
M=43
N=211
P=M
M=N
N=P
PRINT,M,N
```

5.(a) What will be printed by the following job?

```
 1   $JOB     ANN MORLEY
 2           INTEGER FIRST,SECOND
 3           READ,FIRST,SECOND
 4           PRINT,FIRST+SECOND
 5           READ,FIRST,SECOND
 6           PRINT,FIRST+SECOND
 7           RETURN
 8           END
 9   $ENTRY
10      22   247   -16
11      52    12
```

(b) Which lines of this job are control cards? Which are program
and which are input data?

6. (a) What will be printed by the following job?

```
 1  $JOB     FRED LEE
 2  C        CALCULATE TERM MARK
 3           REAL GRADE1,GRADE2
 4           INTEGER MARK
 5           READ,GRADE1,GRADE2
 6           MARK=(GRADE1+GRADE2)/2+.5
 7           PRINT,GRADE1,GRADE2,MARK
 8           RETURN
 9           END
10  $ENTRY
11      81.7
12      85.9
```

(b) Which lines of this job are control cards; which are program and which are input data?

7. Trace the execution of the following program. That is, give the values of the variables SIZE, LENGTH, WIDTH, and ABOUT and give any output after each line of the program.

```
$JOB     JOE MURPHY
         REAL SIZE,LENGTH,WIDTH
         INTEGER ABOUT
C        READ SIZES AND CONVERT FEET TO YARDS
         READ,SIZE
         WIDTH=SIZE/3.
         READ,SIZE
         LENGTH=SIZE/3.
         ABOUT=WIDTH*LENGTH+.5
         PRINT,'LENGTH AND WIDTH ARE',LENGTH,WIDTH
         PRINT,'AREA IS:',LENGTH*WIDTH,
      +     'THIS IS ABOUT',ABOUT,'(SQUARE YARDS)'
         RETURN
         END
$ENTRY
      9.60
      15.9
```

8. Write a program which reads three values and prints their average, rounded to the nearest whole number. For example, if 20, 16 and 25 follow the $ENTRY card then your program should print 20. Make up your own data for your program.

9. Write a program which reads a weight given in pounds and then prints out the weight in (1) pounds, (2) ounces, (3) kilograms and (4) grams. Note: 16 ounces equal one pound, 2.2046 pounds equal one kilogram and 1000 grams equal one kilogram.

10. Write a program which reads a distance given in miles and prints the distance in (1) miles, (2) yards, (3) feet, (4) inches and (5) meters. Note: 1760 yards equal one mile and 1 kilometer equals 0.62137 miles.

CHAPTER 5

SF/3: CONTROL FLOW

In the first two subsets of Fortran we have learned to write programs with statements that cause the computer to read cards and assign values to variables, evaluate arithmetic expressions and assign the values to variables, and print results with labels. In all programs the statements were executed in sequence until the RETURN was reached, at which time the program execution was terminated. In this subset we will learn two ways in which the sequence of statements may be altered. One involves the repetitious use of statements; the other involves alternate paths in the flow of statements. The first is called a loop, the second a branch. We speak of the flow of control since it is the control unit of the computer that determines which statement is to be executed next by the computer.

COUNTED LOOPS

The normal flow of control in a program is in a straight line. We can, however, give a statement that will cause a set of statements to be repeated. In the last chapter, in the example where we were reading information about boxes of soap flakes, we had to write the statements over and over to get repetitions. A statement that will produce repetition is the counted DO loop. For our example we could have written

```
      DO label I=1,3
          READ,COST,WEIGHT
          KGCOST=COST/(WEIGHT*1.)+.5
          PRINT,COST,WEIGHT,KGCOST
label     CONTINUE
```

The three statements that we had to repeat three times are prefaced by

```
    DO label I=1,3
```

and followed by CONTINUE. The word label in small letters appears
twice; for the moment we will ignore it.

    The variable I is an index, which must be declared as an
integer variable, and which counts the number of repetitions.
First the index I is set to 1, then the three statements are
executed. When the CONTINUE is reached, control is sent back to
the DO. At this time the index I is increased by 1, making it 2.
A test is made to see if this value of the index is greater than
the 3 which appears in the DO statement. The 3 is called the
test value. Since 2 is not greater than 3 we will proceed. The
three statements are again executed and, at CONTINUE, back we go
to the DO. This time I becomes 3 which is not greater than the
test value and a third execution of the three statements in the
DO loop takes place. When control returns to the DO, this time I
would become 4 and this is found to be larger than the 3 which is
the upper limit of the count. When this happens, control goes
out of the loop to the next statement after the CONTINUE.

    We must now look at the "labels" that we have ignored so far.
In order that the computer may perform the looping operation it
is necessary in Fortran to tell, at the beginning of the counted
DO loop where the end is located in the program. This is done by
giving to the CONTINUE statement, which is the end of the loop, a
label. The label of a statement is any number from 1 to 99999.
The label of a statement must be placed in columns 1 to 5 of the
card for input. We always start the label in column 1. The
CONTINUE statement is the only statement we have looked at so far
that needs a label. We can choose any number we like in the
allowed range. Of course if there are several CONTINUE
statements in the same program each must have its own individual
label.

    Suppose we choose (in an arbitrary way) to use 10 for the
label, our program would be written as

```
    DO 10 I=1,3
        READ,COST,WEIGHT
        KGCOST=COST/(WEIGHT*1.)+.5
        PRINT,COST,WEIGHT,KGCOST
10      CONTINUE
```

    A counted or indexed DO loop is used whenever we know exactly
how many repetitions we want to take place. We do not need to
count by ones or start the count at 1. We could, for example,
have

```
    DO label COUNT=12,24,2
```

Here we have called the index COUNT and are starting at 12 and
going by 2s up to, and to include, 24. If the increment by which
you are counting is not 1 it is included in the DO following the
test value. Each of the initial value, the test value, and the

increment must be positive non-zero integers or variables which
have positive integer values. This means for instance, that
counting backwards (by -1) is impossible. Sometimes the initial,
test, and increment will be referred to as start, limit, and step
respectively.

The other kind of loop statement is the WHILE...DO statement
but we cannot introduce it until we look at conditions. The
WHILE...DO is a loop statement that causes repetition as long as
a certain condition is true. The condition concerned is written
in parentheses after the word WHILE.

CONDITIONS

There are expressions in Fortran that are called logical
expressions and these have values that are either true or false.
The following is a list of logical expressions with their value
written on the same line. The symbol .GT. means greater than,
.LT. means less than, the symbol .EQ. means is equal to, .LE.
means less than or equal to, .GE. means greater than or equal to,
and .NE. means not equal to.

logical expression	value
5.EQ.2+3	true
7.GT.5	true
2.LT.6	true
5+3.LT.2+1	false
6.NE.10	true
5.GT.5	false
5.GE.5	true

You can see how these work.

There are compound conditions formed by taking two single
conditions and putting either the logical operator .AND. or the
logical operator .OR. between them. With .AND. both conditions
must be true or else the compound condition is false. For
example, (8.GT.7.AND.6.LT.3) is false since (6.LT.3) is false.
With .OR., if either or both of the single conditions is true,
the compound condition is true. For example, (8.GT.7.OR.6.LT.3)
is true since (8.GT.7) is true. It is possible to have multiple
compoundings. For example,

(8.GT.7.AND.2.EQ.1+1).AND.(6.GT.7.OR.5.GT.1)

is true. The parentheses here show the sequence of the
operations. There is a rule of precedence if there are no
parentheses, namely, the .AND. operator has higher precedence
than the .OR. operator. This means that .AND. operations are
done before .OR. operations.

LOGICAL VARIABLES

If you want to assign a logical value to a variable, it must be typed by a declaration as LOGICAL. In Fortran we write .TRUE. to indicate true, and .FALSE. to indicate false. Logical variables can be assigned logical values, but cannot be printed, read, or used in arithmetic expressions. For example, if you want a logical variable SWITCH assigned the value true you must include the declaration and the assignment.

```
LOGICAL SWITCH
SWITCH=.TRUE.
```

The variable SWITCH may be used in a condition.

CONDITIONAL LOOPS

We have introduced the notion of a condition; now we will actually use it. One of the major uses of conditions is in the WHILE (condition) DO loop. The repetition is to take place as long as the condition stated in parentheses after the word WHILE is true. Once it is false, the control goes to the statement following the END WHILE that terminates the loop. The counted DO loop was terminated by a CONTINUE. The WHILE...DO is terminated by END WHILE.

So far we have discussed only conditions involving integer constants. These we labeled as true or false. The condition in the WHILE...DO loop cannot be like this, because if it is always true we would loop forever and if always false we would not loop at all. The condition must involve a variable whose value changes during the looping.

In the following example the WHILE...DO is used to accomplish exactly what the counted DO loop did for the soap flakes boxes.

```
1          I=1
2          WHILE(I.LE.3)DO
3              READ,COST,WEIGHT
4              KGCOST=COST/(WEIGHT*1.)+.5
5              PRINT,COST,WEIGHT,KGCOST
6              I=I+1
7          END WHILE
8          PRINT,I
```

In statement 1 the value of the variable I appearing in the condition is set initially to 1, then we enter the loop. This stage is called <u>initialization</u> and is always necessary in conditional loops. In line 2 we begin the loop. The condition

in parentheses is true since I is 1, which is less than 3. Thus
the next four statements are executed. These constitute the <u>body</u>
of the loop. In the body, statement 6 <u>alters</u> the value of the
variable appearing in the condition. This means that it is
changing each time around the loop. At the end of the first loop
it becomes 1+1=2. The END WHILE causes control to return to the
start of the loop. The condition is then examined and since it
is true (2.LE.3) the body is executed a second time. It will be
true also on the third time but on the fourth round, I will be 4
and (4.LE.3) is false. When I is printed by statement 8 it is 4.
This printing is not part of the original example, but was
included here to show you what happens to the index I. It is
best not to concern yourself with the value of a counting
variable outside the loop since for a counted DO the value of the
index is undefined outside the loop.

The various phases of a WHILE...DO loop are:

Phase 1. Initialization, especially of the variable in the
condition.

Phase 2. Test condition and if true then continue to next
statement, if false go to statement following END WHILE.

Phase 3. Execute body of loop which includes altering the
variable in the condition.

Phase 4. At the END WHILE return to phase 2.

READING CARDS

As an example of the two types of DO loops we will look at a
very simple example of reading data from cards and printing it
out, assuming that each card produces one line of printing. The
only real problem will be to stop when we reach the last card.
There are two distinct ways of doing this. One is to count the
cards by hand, prepare a card with this count on it, and place it
in front of the data cards. Then we use a counted DO loop to
read them. The other method is to place a card at the end of the
data cards with a piece of data that is impossible as an actual
entry. We call it a <u>dummy</u> <u>card</u>. Sometimes it is called an <u>end-
of-file</u> <u>marker</u>. Suppose, to talk specifically, that each data
card has on it a student number and a grade received in an
examination. To illustrate we will have only three data cards,
but you can see how it will work with more.

Method 1. Counting the cards

```
$JOB    GORDY PROCTOR
        INTEGER IDENT,MARK,COUNT,I
        PRINT,'STUDENT NO. ','MARK IN EXAM'
        READ,COUNT
        DO 25 I=1,COUNT
            READ,IDENT,MARK
            PRINT,IDENT,MARK
25          CONTINUE
        RETURN
        END
$ENTRY
    3
    1026    86
    2051    90
    3163    71
```

Notice that we took the trouble to label the output.

In the second method we will place a dummy card with two
zeros on it at the end of the deck.

Method 2. Testing for the dummy card

```
$JOB    JIM CORDY
        INTEGER IDENT,MARK
        PRINT,'STUDENT NO. ','MARK IN EXAM'
        READ,IDENT,MARK
        WHILE(IDENT.NE.0)DO
            PRINT,IDENT,MARK
            READ,IDENT,MARK
            END WHILE
        RETURN
        END
$ENTRY
    1026    86
    2051    90
    3163    71
       0     0
```

In this example you will notice that the initialization
involves reading the first card outside the loop, in order to get
a value for the variable IDENT appearing in the condition of the
WHILE...DO. Since the first card has already been read, it must
be printed before a new card is read. This means that the
sequence is PRINT then READ, rather than the way it is in the
first method. As soon as the new card has been read, we return

to the WHILE...DO where the condition is tested. These two
techniques for dealing with a variable number of items, like
cards, are used again and again in programming. The WHILE...DO
is more difficult to program but probably more useful, since if
there are many cards, it is easier for the user to stick in an
end-of-file card than to count cards. Notice that the CONTINUE
of the counted DO needs a label but that the END WHILE does not
use a label.

EXAMPLES OF LOOPS

     We will now give example programs to illustrate details about
loops. The examples each draw a zigzag. Here is the first
example:

```
1    C THIS PROGRAM IS CALLED WIGGLE
2          INTEGER J
3          DO 55 J=1,3
4              PRINT,'*   '
5              PRINT,'  *  '
6              PRINT,'    *'
7              PRINT,'  *  '
8    55        CONTINUE
9          RETURN
10         END
```

This program, appropriately called WIGGLE, prints the following
pattern:

```
        *
          *
            *
          *
        *
          *
            *
          *
        *
          *
            *
          *
```

The WIGGLE program causes the body of the loop, statements 4
through 7, to be executed three times. The variable J is 1
during the time the first four stars are printed. J is 2 during
the time the next four stars are printed, and J is 3 while the
last four stars are printed. After the last star is printed, J
would be set to 4 and since this exceeds the test value, 3, of
the loop, the loop is terminated.

Notice that in this program the variable J is used for only one purpose: to see that the loop is repeated the desired number of times. Line 3 means, essentially, "Repeat this loop three times." If we replaced line 3 by the following line

        DO 55 J=9,13,2

then the program would still print the same pattern. The only difference is that J would have the values 9, 11 and 13 during the printing of the stars. Similarly, the same pattern would be printed if we replaced line 3 by the line:

        DO 55 J=9,14,2

Here again, J would be 9, 11 and 13 during the printing of the stars. In this case the test value, 14, does not actually match 13, the last value of J within the loop. However, the loop still stops after three times through because when 2 is added to 13, the result of 15 exceeds the limit of 14. Although our two replacements for line 3 do not change the pattern printed, they should not be used because they make the program more confusing for people to understand. This is because people more naturally think of "repeat this loop three times" as running through the loop with values 1, 2, and 3, rather than values 9, 11, and 13.

As you have seen from these examples, as a Fortran counted DO loop completes, the final value of the counting variable is not equal to the test value. The value should never be used outside the loop as it is only defined while control is inside the loop.

There is another possible problem in counted DO loops. The Fortran language does not permit you to change the value of the counting variable or index inside a counted DO loop.

We will now rewrite our WIGGLE program using WHILE...DO instead of a counted DO. We will call our new program WAGGLE. (Did you know that in German "wiggle waggle" means "waddle" like a duck? Well it does.)

```
 1   C THIS PROGRAM IS CALLED WAGGLE
 2         INTEGER J
 3         J=1
 4         WHILE(J.LE.3)DO
 5            PRINT,'*  '
 6            PRINT,' * '
 7            PRINT,'  *'
 8            PRINT,' * '
 9            J=J+1
10         END WHILE
11         RETURN
12         END
```

This WAGGLE program works like our previous WIGGLE program.
Lines 3, 4, and 9 of WAGGLE are equivalent to line 3 of WIGGLE.
Since it is easier to see that line 3 of WIGGLE means, "Repeat
this loop three times," the WIGGLE version is preferable. We
will, however, use WAGGLE to illustrate a few more points about
loops.

In the WAGGLE program, consider moving line 9, which is

        J=J+1

up to between lines 4 and 5. This change does not alter the
printed pattern. It simply changes the point at which J has its
value increased. J will have the value 2 while the first four
stars are printed, then 3 while the next four stars are printed
and finally 4 while the last four stars are printed. J ends up
with the value of 4. Even though J is set to 4 before the last
four stars are printed, the loop is not stopped. This is because
J is not compared to the limit value 3 until control returns to
line 4. This illustrates the fact that in a WHILE...DO loop, the
condition is tested only once - at the top - each time through
the loop.

Now let us look back at the unchanged WAGGLE program.
Suppose that you prepared this program for the computer and
mistakenly made line 9 into

        J=J-1

The mistake is that the plus sign was changed to a minus sign.
Such a small mistake! Surely the computer will understand that a
plus was wanted! But it will not do so. The computer has a habit
of doing what we <u>tell</u> it to do rather than what we <u>want</u> it to do.
Given the WAGGLE program, with the mistake, the computer will do
the following. With J set to 1 it will print the first four
stars. Then, as a result of the erroneous line 9, it will set J
to 0 and will print another four stars. Then it will set J to -1
and print four more stars. Then it will set J to -2 and print
four more stars and so on and so on. In theory, it will <u>never</u>
<u>stop</u> printing stars because the condition J.LE.3 will always be
true. This is called an <u>infinite loop</u>. Luckily, the computer
will eventually stop your program when your program has printed
too much or when your program has executed too many statements.
When it stops your program, it will print an error message
complaining about the excessive printing or running of your
program. Unfortunately, the error message will not tell you that
you should have had a plus sign instead of a minus sign, because
the computer will not know what you were thinking when you
prepared the program.

64
FUNDAMENTALS OF STRUCTURED PROGRAMMING

BRANCHES IN CONTROL FLOW

We have learned how to change from a flow of control in a straight line, or <u>linear</u> sequence, to flow in a loop, either counted or conditional. Now we must look at a different kind of structure in the sequence of control. This structure is called branching. It is a little like a fork in the road where there are two paths that can be followed. The road branches into two roads. When you come to a fork in a road you must <u>decide</u> which of the two branches you will take. Your decision is based on where you are heading. Suppose one sign at the fork gives the name of your destination and the other road sign gives some other name. Suppose your destination is Toronto; an instruction for deciding which branch to take might be

```
IF(LEFT.EQ.'TORONTO')THEN DO
    take the left branch
ELSE DO
    take the right branch
```

We have written this decision in the form you use in your programs for branching in the sequence of control. The main difference is that the part we have written as "take the left branch" must be replaced by Fortran statements to do something. The same is true of the other branch which follows the keywords ELSE DO.

Suppose that there is a variable called CLASSA which contains the number of students in a class called A. Students are to be assigned to Class A if their mark in computer science (CSMARK) is over 80; otherwise they are to be assigned to Class B (CLASSB). The statement that decides which class to place the student in, and counts the number going into each class, is

```
IF(CSMARK.GT.80)THEN DO
    CLASSA=CLASSA+1
ELSE DO
    CLASSB=CLASSB+1
    END IF
```

Notice that the IF...THEN DO...ELSE DO (which we refer to briefly as IF...THEN...ELSE) has after it END IF. This terminates the statement just as END WHILE terminates WHILE...DO.

The IF...THEN...ELSE statement causes control to split into two paths but, unlike forks in roads, you will notice that it immediately comes back together again. This means that we are never in any doubt about what happens; after the execution of one or the other of the two branches, the control returns to the normal sequence following the END IF. One way of looking at the IF...THEN...ELSE statement is that it provides two possibilities,

only one of which is to be <u>selected</u>, depending on whether the
condition following the IF is true or false. After one or other
path is executed the normal control sequence is resumed.

     Notice that in the IF...THEN...ELSE there are parentheses
around the condition just as there are in the WHILE...DO.

     You must always have at least one statement after the THEN.
If there is nothing that you want to do in the ELSE DO branch you
must leave out the ELSE DO entirely. For instance, you may have
the statement which would eliminate the balance in a bank account
if it were less than or equal to 10 cents.

```
     IF(BALNCE.LE.10)THEN DO
        BALNCE=0
     END IF
```

> *WHILE*
> *~~IF~~ (BALNCE .LE. 10) DO*
> *BALNCE = 0*
> *END WHILE.*

Here there is no ELSE DO statement, but this just means that if
the balance is larger than 10 cents we do <u>not</u> make it zero.

THREE-WAY BRANCHES

     We have seen how a linear control structure can be split up
into two branches and then brought together again. What do we
write if we have a situation where more than two branches are
required? We will do a three-way branch and then you will see
how any number of branches can be achieved. This can also be
viewed as selecting one of three alternatives.

     As an example, we will write a program that counts votes in
an election. Suppose that there are three political parties
called Right, Left, and Middle, and that to vote for one of these
parties you punch a 1, or a 2, or a 3 respectively on a card.
Here is the program that reads the vote cards and counts each
party and the total. The last card has -1 on it.

```
$JOB     MARJORIE DUNLOP
C THIS PROGRAM COUNTS VOTES
        INTEGER VOTE,RIGHT,LEFT,MIDDLE,COUNT
        RIGHT=0
        LEFT=0
        MIDDLE=0
        READ,VOTE
        WHILE(VOTE.NE.-1)DO
            IF(VOTE.EQ.1)THEN DO
                RIGHT=RIGHT+1
            ELSE DO
                IF(VOTE.EQ.2)THEN DO
                    LEFT=LEFT+1
                ELSE DO
                    IF(VOTE.EQ.3)THEN DO
                        MIDDLE=MIDDLE+1
                        END IF
                    END IF
                END IF
            READ,VOTE
            END WHILE
        COUNT=RIGHT+LEFT+MIDDLE
        PRINT,'RIGHT COUNT ','LEFT COUNT  ','MIDDLE COUNT','TOTAL COUNT'
        PRINT,RIGHT,LEFT,MIDDLE,COUNT
        RETURN
        END
$ENTRY
(vote cards with either 1, or 2, or 3 on them)
-1 (dummy card for end-of-file)
```

In this program we have two different things happening. One is a three-way branch, which is accomplished by a series of three IF...THEN statements, one for each value of VOTE. It may startle you to see the three END IFs one after the other. Each IF requires its own END IF. You will notice that an invalid vote does not get counted anywhere. If we wanted notification that there was an invalid vote we could have inserted the following in the program right after MIDDLE=MIDDLE+1

```
        ELSE DO
            PRINT,'INVALID VOTE',VOTE
```

This then makes it a four-way branch.

The minimum program needed for a three-way branch would be one IF...THEN...ELSE statement nested inside another:

```
IF(VOTE.EQ.1)THEN DO
   RIGHT=RIGHT+1
ELSE DO
   IF(VOTE.EQ.2)THEN DO
      LEFT=LEFT+1
   ELSE DO
      MIDDLE=MIDDLE+1
      END IF
   END IF
```

If there are any invalid votes, they are given to MIDDLE.

   There is no fixed way of doing the job. Here is another try
at it.

```
IF(VOTE.LT.3)THEN DO
   IF(VOTE.LT.2)THEN DO
      RIGHT=RIGHT+1
   ELSE DO
      LEFT=LEFT+1
      END IF
ELSE DO
   MIDDLE=MIDDLE+1
   END IF
```

Again we have nesting of two IF...THEN...ELSE statements, but in
a different sequence. Notice that we put the ELSE that goes with
an IF vertically beneath it so that the nesting of the statements
is clear.

EXAMPLE IF STATEMENTS

   We will now give a series of examples of IF statements which
might be used in a government program for handling income tax.
Let us suppose that the program is to write notices to people
telling them whether they owe tax or they are to receive a tax
refund.   The amount of tax is calculated and then the following
is executed.

```
IF(TAX.GT.0)THEN DO
   PRINT,'TAX DUE IS',TAX,'DOLLARS'
ELSE DO
   PRINT,'REFUND IS ',-TAX,'DOLLARS'
   END IF
```

Notice that it was necessary to change the sign of "tax" when printing the refund.

Unfortunately, our program, like too many programs, is not quite right. If the calculated tax is exactly zero, then the program will print REFUND IS 0 DOLLARS. We could fix this problem by the following.

```
IF(TAX.GT.0)THEN DO
    PRINT,'TAX DUE IS',TAX,'DOLLARS'
ELSE DO
    IF(TAX.EQ.0)THEN DO
        PRINT,'YOU OWE NOTHING'
    ELSE DO
        PRINT,'REFUND IS',-TAX,'DOLLARS'
        END IF
    END IF
```

We have used a <u>nested</u> IF statement to solve the problem, that is, an IF statement which is inside an IF statement. In general, we can nest any kind of statement inside an IF statement including assignment statements, READ and PRINT statements, DO statements and IF statements.

Now suppose that when tax is due we wish to tell the taxpayer where to send his check. We can expand the program as follows:

```
IF(TAX.GT.0)THEN DO
    PRINT,'TAX DUE IS',TAX,'DOLLARS'
    PRINT,'SEND CHECK TO DISTRICT OFFICE'
ELSE DO
    IF(TAX.EQ.0)THEN DO
        PRINT,'YOU OWE NOTHING'
    ELSE DO
        PRINT,'REFUND IS',-TAX,'DOLLARS'
        END IF
    END IF
```

We will now change the order of tests and slightly change the problem in order to illustrate another point. Suppose that when the "tax" is zero, we do not want to print anything. We can start out by checking for zero, and if we do not find zero, we can print an appropriate "tax due" or "refund" message.

```
IF(TAX.NE.0)THEN DO
    IF(TAX.GT.0)THEN DO
        PRINT,'TAX DUE IS',TAX,'DOLLARS'
    ELSE DO
        PRINT,'REFUND IS ',-TAX,'DOLLARS'
        END IF
    END IF
```

Since we did not want to print anything when the tax is zero, we omitted the ELSE part of the initial IF statement. There is a possible point of confusion in that we must be sure that the computer will consider the single ELSE clause to be part of the second IF. There is no difficulty, because this ELSE clause appears before the END IF belonging to the second IF. Thus, the message about the refund is printed when the condition (TAX.GT.0) is found to be false. To help people understand our program, we have indented the ELSE clause to the level of its corresponding IF statement. However, this indentation is ignored by the computer.

PARAGRAPHING THE PROGRAM

In order to follow the structure of the nesting of IF...THEN...ELSE statements we have indented the program so that the IF and ELSE that belong to each other are lined up vertically. The statements following the THEN DO and the ELSE DO are indented. This is called paragraphing the program, and is analogous to the way we indent paragraphs of prose to indicate grouping of thoughts. Paragraphing makes a valuable contribution to understandability and is a must in structured programming. The END IF that belongs to an IF is indented to the same level as the statements that go with the THEN DO or ELSE DO of that IF.

Also, if you examine the programs with DO loops you will see that the loop has been indented starting right after the DO and going down to the CONTINUE or END WHILE that belongs with the DO.

In the next chapter we will be examining the situation where DO loops are nested just as our IFs are nested here, and then we will use two levels of indentation for these too.

There are no set rules about how much indentation you should use or exactly how, for instance, an IF...THEN...ELSE statement should be indented; but it is clear that being systematic is an enormous help. When you are writing programs, decide how many blanks you will use for each level of indentation and stick to this. We use three blanks for indentation.

CHAPTER 5 SUMMARY

In this chapter we introduced statements which allow for (a) repetition of statements and (b) selection between different possibilities. We introduced conditions which are used to terminate the repetition of statements and to choose between different possibilities. Comparisons and logical operators are used in specifying conditions. The following important terms were discussed in this chapter.

Loop (or DO loop) - a programming language construct which causes repeated execution of statements. In SF/k, loops are either counted DO loops or WHILE...DO loops.

Counted DO loop - has the following form:

```
        DO label index variable=initial,test [,increment]
        statements
label      CONTINUE
```

The index variable, or counting variable, must have the INTEGER type. The square brackets shown around increment indicate that it can be omitted. If it is omitted, an increment of 1 is assumed. Each of initial, test and increment must be integer constants or variables, whose values are strictly positive. Sometimes we refer to start, limit and step instead of initial, test and increment. The initial value should not be larger than the test value. A counted DO loop is always executed once before a test is made.

WHILE...DO loop - has the following form:

```
        WHILE(condition)DO
           statements
        END WHILE
```

The condition is tested at the beginning of each pass through the loop. If it is found to be true, the statements inside the loop are executed and then the condition is again tested. When the condition finally is found to be false, control is passed to the statement which follows the END WHILE. Any variables which appear in the condition must be given values before the loop begins. Notice that the condition is in parentheses.

Loop body - the statements that appear inside a loop.

Comparisons - used in conditions. For example, comparisons can be used in a condition to determine whether or not to execute a loop body. The following are used to specify comparisons.

```
        .LT.    less than
        .GT.    greater than
        .LE.    less than or equal
        .GE.    greater than or equal
        .EQ.    equal
        .NE.    not equal
```

Conditions - are either true or false. Conditions can be made up of comparisons and the following three logical operators.

```
        .AND.
        .OR.
        .NOT.
```

End-of-file (or end-of-data) detection - When a loop is reading a series of data items, it must determine when the last data item has been read. This can be accomplished by first reading in the number of items to be read and then counting the items in the series as they are read. It can also be accomplished by following the last data item by a special dummy card which contains special, or dummy data. The program knows to stop when it reads the dummy data.

IF statement - has the following form:

```
IF(condition)THEN DO
   statements
[ELSE DO
   statements]
   END IF
```

The square brackets are shown around the ELSE DO clause to show that it can be omitted. If the condition is true, the first statement or statements are executed. If the condition is false, the second statement or statements, if present, are executed. In either case, control then goes to the next statement after the END IF. Any statement, including another IF statement, can appear as a part of an IF statement.

Paragraphing - indenting a program so that its structure is easily seen by people. The statements inside loops and inside IF statements are indented to make the overall program organization obvious. The computer ignores paragraphing when translating and executing programs.

CHAPTER 5 EXERCISES

1. Suppose I and J are variables with values 6 and 12. Which of the following conditions are true?

```
(a)   2*I.LE.J
(b)   2*I-1.LT.J
(c)   I.LE.6.AND.J.LE.6
(d)   I.LE.6.OR.J.LE.6
(e)   I.GT.0.AND.I.LE.10
(f)   I.LE.12.OR.J.LE.12
(g)   I.GT.25.OR.(I.LT.50.AND.J.LT.50)
(h)   I.NE.4.AND.I.NE.5
(i)   I.LT.4.OR.I.GT.5
(j)   .NOT.(I.GT.6)
```

2. The following program predicts the population of a family of wallalumps over a 2-year period, based on the assumption of an initial population of 2 and a doubling of population each 2 months. What does the program print?

```
C THIS PROGRAM SHOWS POPULATION EXPLOSION
      INTEGER MONTH,NUMBER
      NUMBER=2
      PRINT,'    MONTH    ','POPULATION'
      DO 12 MONTH=2,24,2
         PRINT,MONTH,NUMBER
         NUMBER=2*NUMBER
12       CONTINUE
      RETURN
      END
```

3. Suppose you have hidden away 50 dollars to be used for some future emergency. Assuming an inflation rate of 12 per cent per year, write a program to compute how much money, to the nearest dollar, you would need at the end of each of the next 15 years to be equivalent to the buying power of 50 dollars at the time you hid it.

4. Trace the following program. That is, give the values of the variables together with any output after the execution of each statement.

```
     $JOB     S. OMENYI
 1   C THIS PROGRAM HANDLES EXAMINATION MARKS
 2         INTEGER NUMBER,GRADE,SUM
 3         SUM=0
 4         READ,GRADE
 5         NUMBER=0
 6         WHILE(GRADE.NE.-1) DO
 7            IF(GRADE.GE.0.AND.GRADE.LE.100)THEN DO
 8               SUM=SUM+GRADE
 9               NUMBER=NUMBER+1
10            ELSE DO
11               PRINT,'**ERROR:GRADE=',GRADE
12               END IF
13            READ,GRADE
14            END WHILE
15         PRINT,'AVERAGE IS',1.*SUM/NUMBER
16         RETURN
17         END
     $ENTRY
     95
      110
     85
     -1
     75
```

5. Write a program that reads the following data cards and calculates the average of (a) each of the two columns of data, and (b) each row of the data. You should either precede the data with a number giving the count of the following data cards or add a dummy card following these data cards.

92	88
75	62
81	75
80	80
55	60
64	60
81	80

6. Write a program which reads in a sequence of grades (0 to 100) and prints out the average grade (rounded to the nearest whole number), the number of grades and the number of failing grades (failing is less than 50). Assume that a "dummy" grade of 999 will follow the last grade.   See that your output is clearly labeled. Answer the following questions:

(a) What will happen if the grade 74 is mispunched as 7 4?

(b) What will happen if the dummy grade 999 is left off? (You can try this.)

(c) What will your program do if there are no grades, i.e., if 999 is the only data item?

(d) What will happen if the two grades 62 and 93 are mispunched as 6293?

Test your program using the following data:

          85   74   44   62   93   41   69   73   999

7. Write a program which determines the unit price (cents per ounce) of different boxes of laundry soap. Round the unit price to the nearest penny. Each box will be described by a card of the form:

          pounds   ounces   price in cents

             5   0   125

This box of soap has a rounded unit price of 2 cents per ounce. Make up about 10 data cards describing soap boxes; if you like, use real examples from a supermarket. You are to precede these cards with one data card containing a single integer giving the number of soap box cards. Do not use a dummy card to mark the end of the data. Print a nicely labeled table giving weights, prices in cents and unit costs. Answer the following questions:

(a) What would your program do if the above example data card were mispunched as

          50   125

(b)   Would it be possible to make your program "smart enough" to
detect some kinds of mispunched data? How or why not?

8.   Write a program that tabulates y for values of x=.1, .2, ...
1.0 given that y is the sum of terms for n=1, 2, ... 10 where the
term for n=3 is $x^3/3!$.   The 3! is factorial 3, namely 3*2*1.
Remember that 0! has a value 1.

9.   Write a program to find and print the integers from 1 to 100
that are perfect squares.

10. Write a program that will read real values for the lengths of
the three sides of a triangle, calling them A, B and C, and
determine which of the following is true:

   (a) no triangle is possible,
   (b) triangle is isosceles,
   (c) triangle is equilateral,
   (d) triangle is right-angled,
   (e) triangle is neither isosceles, nor equilateral, nor
       right-angled.

CHAPTER 6

STRUCTURING CONTROL FLOW

In the last chapter we introduced the two kinds of statements that cause an alteration from the linear flow of control in a program. One type caused looping, the counted DO or the WHILE...DO; the other caused branching, or selective execution, the IF...THEN...ELSE. Learning to handle these two kinds of instructions is absolutely essential to programming. And learning to handle them in a systematic way is essential to structured programming.

BASIC STRUCTURE OF DO LOOPS

It is hard to appreciate, when you first learn a concept like loops, that all loops are basically the same. They consist of a sequence of statements in the program that:

1. initialize the values of certain variables that are to be used in the loop. These consist of assigning values to

   (a) variables that appear in the condition of a WHILE...DO

   (b) variables that appear in the body of the loop on the right-hand side of assignment statements.

2. indicate that a loop is to commence and give the information that is to control the number of repetitions. Both types of loops contain a control phrase. The control phrase may be of two types:

   (a) for the counted DO, it is, for example

       I=1,20,1

(b) for the conditional DO, it is, for example

WHILE (I .LE. 20)

The condition should contain at least one variable.

3. give the list of statements, called the body of the loop, that
are to be executed each time the loop is repeated. If   the   loop
is controlled by a WHILE (condition), then within the body of the
loop there must be some statements that assign new values to   the
variables   appearing   in the condition.   Usually there is only one
variable and its value may be changed by either

(a) an assignment statement or

(b) a READ statement.

4.   indicate   the   end   of   the loop.   This is the CONTINUE for a
counted DO or the END WHILE for   a   conditional   loop.   At   this
point   control   is returned to the beginning of the loop with its
control phrase.

5.   give   the   next statement to be executed once the looping has
been   carried   out   the required numbers   of   times.   Control   goes
from the DO to this statement when

(a) the condition of the WHILE...DO is found to be false or

(b)   the   value   of the index controlling the counted DO plus
the increment is beyond the test value   indicated   after   the
first comma in the DO.

It   is   to be noted very carefully that there is no _exit_ from
the loop, except from the DO itself, and this exit goes   to   the
statement   immediately   after the CONTINUE or END WHILE.   In this
way we keep track of control flow and never have the   possibility
of   getting   confused   about   its   path.   The   complete   Fortran
language offers   a   statement   called   the   GO   TO   statement   for
altering   the   path   of   control.   It permits you to send control
anywhere in your program.   Since   computer   scientists   came   to
recognize   the importance of proper structuring in a program, the
freedom offered by the GO TO statement has been recognized as not
in keeping with the idea of structures in control flow.   For this
reason we will _never_ use it.   It is _not_ a member of any subset of
SF/k.   If you are using the Watfiv-S compiler, you will find that
the GO TO statement is permitted.   But do not use it.

For   many   good   programmers   it   has   long become a habit to
restrict the use of the GO TO to that of leaving the body of a DO
loop   somewhere   in   the   middle   and   exiting   to   the statement
following the end of the loop.   _We_ will only   exit   from   the   DO
itself.   An   exit inside the body is usually related to a second
condition.   This second condition   can   be   incorporated   in   the
condition   of the DO by having a compound condition.   We will look
at examples of this later in the chapter.

FLOW CHARTS

A flow chart is a diagram made up of boxes of various shapes, rectangular, circular, diamond and so on, connected by lines with directional arrows on the lines. The boxes contain a description of the statements of a program and the directed lines indicate the flow of control among the statements. The main purpose of drawing a flow chart is to exhibit the flow of control clearly, so that it is evident both to the programmer and to a reader who might want to alter the program.

A method of programming that preceded the present method of structured programming found that drawing a flow chart helped in the programming process. It was suggested that a first step in writing any program was to draw a flow chart. It was a way of controlling complexity.

When we limit ourselves to the two standard forms of altering control flow, the DO loop and the IF...THEN...ELSE, there is little need to draw these flow charts. In a sense, especially if it is properly paragraphed, the program is its own flow chart; it is built of completely standard building blocks.

Perhaps it would be helpful to show what the flow charts of our two basic building blocks would be like in case you wanted to draw a flow chart for your whole program.

The flow chart for an IF...THEN...ELSE statement is shown.

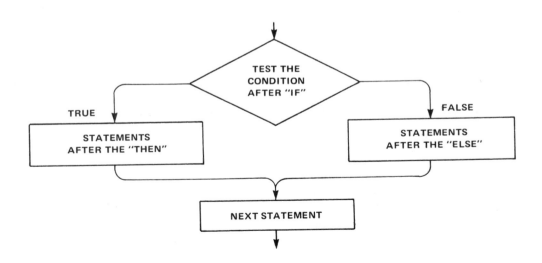

FLOW CHART FOR IF...THEN...ELSE

For the WHILE...DO loop that we described, the flow chart would be as shown. The various phases are numbered.

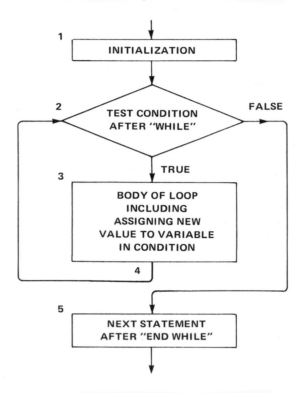

FLOW CHART FOR CONDITIONAL DO

The flow chart for the counted DO would be similar except that box 2 would initialize the index to its first value, then on successive loops increment it by the required amount and test to see if it has gone beyond the test value.

With these basic diagrams and the ordinary straight line sequence, flow charts for all SF/k programs can be built. In a way, because they are so obviously related to the program, they do not really need to be drawn. Any one of the rectangular boxes in these diagrams may be replaced by a sequence of rectangular boxes, or either one of the two basic diagrams themselves.

PROBLEMS WITH LOOPS

Certain errors are very common with loops. With counted loops the likelihood of errors is much smaller, since the initialization and alteration of the index are done by the DO itself. You can, however, forget to initialize a variable that is used in the body of the loop. Another problem comes if by chance the index that is used to count the loop is altered in the loop body. This is strictly illegal in Fortran. The letters I, J, and K are often used as indexes, and you might forget to declare them or accidentally use them again. This can happen when one DO loop is nested inside another and the index I is used by mistake for both loops. You might write

```
DO label I=1,N
```

and forget to initialize N. You should trace the execution of all loops by hand to see if the first iteration is working alright. Then you should also check the last one.

Another important limitation on counted DO loops in Fortran is that each of the initial, test, and increment values must be positive; counting backwards by a negative increment is impossible.

NESTED LOOPS

We will now look at the more complicated loops. In the following example, subsidiary output has been inserted for testing purposes. The program sums the marks of students in 4 subjects and prints these with the average, to the nearest mark. There are a number of cards, one for each student. A card with the total number of students precedes the mark cards.

```
$JOB     BOB CHERNIAK
C THIS PROGRAM COMPUTES THE OVERALL AVERAGE FOR EACH STUDENT
         INTEGER NUMBER,I,SUM,AVRAGE,MARK,J,IDENT
         READ,NUMBER
         DO 50 I=1,NUMBER
            SUM=0
            READ,IDENT
            DO 40 J=1,4
               READ,MARK
               SUM=SUM+MARK
               PRINT,MARK,SUM
40             CONTINUE
            AVRAGE=SUM/4.+.5
            PRINT,IDENT,AVRAGE
50          CONTINUE
         RETURN
         END
$ENTRY
(the following data items are punched one to a card, not as shown)
   3
   205    55    60    65    70
   208    83    81    96    90
   209    72    68    78    81
```

The program is being tested with the extra printing of

    PRINT, MARK, SUM

    Here is the output produced by the computer in addition to
the usual program listing:

```
        55          55
        60         115
        65         180
        70         250
       205          63
        83          83
        81         164
        96         260
        90         350
       208          88
        72          72
        68         140
        78         218
        81         299
       209          75
```

Since we were now satisfied that all was well, we removed the
card with PRINT,MARK,SUM and ran the program with the full number
of data cards. You will notice that when we have one DO loop
nested inside another we use two levels of indentation to
indicate the control structure.

AN EXAMPLE PROGRAM

    We will illustrate some details about loops with another
program. Like some of our previous examples, this program prints
a zigzag. However, our new program is smarter than the old ones
in that it can print out different sizes of and numbers of zigs
and zags, depending on the input data.

```
$JOB    IRA GREENBLATT
C WE CALL THIS PROGRAM PICKZIG
        INTEGER MAJOR,MINOR,COUNT,SIZE
        READ,COUNT,SIZE
        DO 250 MAJOR=1,COUNT
           PRINT,'****'
           DO 200 MINOR=1,SIZE
              PRINT,'*      '
200           CONTINUE
           PRINT,'****'
           DO 225 MINOR=1,SIZE
              PRINT,'    *'
225           CONTINUE
250        CONTINUE
        RETURN
        END
$ENTRY
  3   2
```

This program, given the data values 3 and 2, prints the following
pattern. We have shown in parentheses values of MAJOR and MINOR
during the printing of each of the single star lines.

```
                                    (MAJOR,MINOR)
    ****
    *                                   (1,1)
    *                                   (1,2)
    ****
        *                               (1,1)
        *                               (1,2)
    ****
    *                                   (2,1)
    *                                   (2,2)
    ****
        *                               (2,1)
        *                               (2,2)
    ****
    *                                   (3,1)
    *                                   (3,2)
    ****
        *                               (3,1)
        *                               (3,2)
```

The first data value, 3, caused the sub-pattern

to be printed three times. The second data value, 2, was used in determining the height of this sub-pattern.

As you can see in the program, there are two separate loops inside the main DO loop. Both of these loops use the variable MINOR as a counting variable. There is no difficulty using MINOR in this way. Each time one of these two loops is entered, MINOR is set back to have the value 1. When you are writing a program, you must see that an appropriate CONTINUE is supplied for each DO loop. It is good practice to number the CONTINUE statements so that the sequence of numbers corresponds to the sequence of the CONTINUE statements in the program although this is not essential. In our example, the CONTINUE labeled 200 comes before that labeled 225.

We can change the pattern printed by changing the data card. For example, the following pattern is printed for data values 1 and 1.

```
                        (MAJOR,MINOR)
****
*                           (1,1)
****
     *                      (1,1)
```

In this case, the loops are each executed only once.

In Fortran there is no way of having a counted DO loop executed less than once since the test is not performed until the body of the loop has been executed once. If you want the possibility of no execution at all, that is zero executions of a loop, then you must use a WHILE...DO.

The data values were used by this program to determine the pattern to print. You could write other programs which print different pictures for different data. For example, your program could print a face which is smiling or frowning, or bald or with frizzy hair, depending on the data.

LOOPS WITH MULTIPLE CONDITIONS

Sometimes we must terminate a loop if something happens that is unusual. One of the conditions controlling the loop is the standard one; the other is the unusual one. All loops with double-headed conditions must be WHILE...DO loops, since the counted loop does not allow for the possibility of a second condition. We have seen that compound conditions can be formed from two or more simple conditions using the .AND. and .OR. operators.

As an example, we will write a program to look for a certain number in a list of numbers on cards. If you find it in the list, print the position it occupies in the list; if it is not in the list, print NOT IN LIST. The list will be positive integers terminated by an end-of-file marker -1.

```
$JOB      MARY SEEDHOUSE
C THIS PROGRAM LOOKS FOR A CERTAIN NUMBER IN A LIST
        INTEGER NUMBER,LISTNO,I
        READ,NUMBER
        READ,LISTNO
        I=1
        WHILE(LISTNO.NE.NUMBER.AND.LISTNO.NE. -1)DO
           READ,LISTNO
           I=I+1
           END WHILE
        IF(LISTNO.EQ.NUMBER)THEN DO
           PRINT,'I=',I
        ELSE DO
           PRINT,'NOT IN LIST'
           END IF
        RETURN
        END
$ENTRY
(the following data items are placed one to a card)
 35
 12    16    25    35    40   51   -1
```

The output for the program with this data is

```
        I=    4
```

Notice that in the body of the loop the variable LISTNO in the condition can be changed by the READ,LISTNO statement; it is initialized outside the loop. Since an index I is required to give the position of the number in the list, it must be incremented in the statement I=I+1 and initialized to 1 outside the loop.

IF STATEMENTS WITH MULTIPLE CONDITIONS

Just as WHILE...DO statements can have multiple conditions, so also can IF statements. These can be used very effectively to avoid nesting of IF statements. Suppose you want to count people in a list who fall into a particular age group, say 18-65, as ADULTS. The following program will count the number in the category ADULT in the list. The list of ages is terminated by a -1.

```
$JOB    ANGIE BLONSKI
C THIS PROGRAM COUNTS THE NUMBER OF ADULTS IN A LIST
      INTEGER ADULT,AGE
      READ,AGE
      ADULT=0
      WHILE(AGE.NE. -1)DO
        IF(AGE.GE.18.AND.AGE.LE.65)THEN DO
          ADULT=ADULT+1
          END IF
        READ,AGE
        END WHILE
      PRINT,'NUMBER OF ADULTS=',ADULT
      RETURN
      END
$ENTRY
(the following data items are placed one to a card)
 16 25 31 12 28 69 -1
```

The output is NUMBER OF ADULTS= 3. The IF with the compound condition could have been replaced by the more awkward construction with a nested IF statement:

```
    IF(AGE.GE.18)THEN DO
      IF(AGE.LE.65)THEN DO
        ADULT=ADULT+1
        END IF
      END IF
```

but this is not advisable.

CHAPTER 6 SUMMARY

 In this chapter we have taken a closer look at loops and IF constructs. We discussed flow charts and the GO TO statement as they relate to the SF/k subset of extended Fortran. We presented more complex examples of loops and conditions. The following important terms were discussed.

Flow chart - a graphic representation of a program. A flow chart consists of boxes of various shapes interconnected by arrows indicating flow of control. SF/k programs can be represented by flow charts.

Exit from a loop - means stopping the execution of a loop. Exit from a WHILE...DO loop occurs where the loop's condition is found to be false.

GO TO statement (not in SF/k) - transfers control to another part of a program. The GO TO statement is available in full Fortran and is sometimes used to exit from a loop by transferring control to the statement following the loop. Careless use of GO TO statements leads to complex program structures which are difficult to understand and to make correct.

Nested statements - means statements inside statements. For example, DO loops can be nested inside DO loops.

Multiple conditions - conditions which use the .AND. or .OR. logical operators. Both WHILE...DO loops and IF statements can have multiple conditions; counted DO loops may not.

CHAPTER 6 EXERCISES

We will base all the exercises for this chapter on the same problem, which we now describe. A meteorologist keeps records of the weather for each month as a deck of punched cards. The first card of the deck gives the number of days of the month, its length. The following cards give the rainfall, low temperature, high temperature and pollution count for each day of the month. For example, the data for a month could be as follows:

```
31
   0    33    37    3
 1.2    34    39    3
   0    35    40    .5
   0    34    38    2
etc.
```

Each of the following exercises requires writing a program which reads one month's weather and answers some questions about the month's weather. To make things easier for you, answers for the first two exercises are given.

1. Find the first rainy day of the month. (The following program finds the required day.)

```
C THIS PROGRAM FINDS THE FIRST WET DAY OF THE MONTH
      REAL RAIN,LOW,HIGH,POLLUT
      INTEGER DAY,LENGTH
      READ,LENGTH
      DAY=0
      RAIN=0
      WHILE(RAIN.EQ.0.AND.DAY.LT.LENGTH)DO
         READ,RAIN,LOW,HIGH,POLLUT
         DAY=DAY+1
         END WHILE
      IF(RAIN.GT.0)THEN DO
         PRINT,'DAY',DAY,'WAS RAINY'
      ELSE DO
         PRINT,'NO RAINY DAYS'
         END IF
      RETURN
      END
```

2. See if the data cards for the days of the month are reasonable. Verify that the rainfall does not exceed 100 and is not negative. Verify that the temperature lies between -100 and 200 and that the high is at least as large as the low. Verify that the pollution count is neither above 25 nor below zero. (The following program validates the month's data and is a solution for this exercise.)

```
C THIS PROGRAM VALIDATES THE WEATHER DATA
      REAL RAIN,LOW,HIGH,POLLUT
      INTEGER DAY,LENGTH
      READ,LENGTH
      DO 10 DAY=1,LENGTH
         READ,RAIN,LOW,HIGH,POLLUT
         IF(RAIN.LT.0.OR.RAIN.GT.100) THEN DO
            PRINT,'DAY',DAY,'HAS WRONG RAIN:',RAIN
            END IF
         IF(LOW.LT.-100.OR.LOW.GT.HIGH.OR.HIGH.GT.200)THEN DO
            PRINT,'DAY',DAY,'HAS WRONG TEMPERATURES:',LOW,HIGH
            END IF
         IF(POLLUT.LT.0.OR.POLLUT.GT.25)THEN DO
            PRINT,'DAY',DAY,'HAS WRONG POLLUTION:',POLLUT
            END IF
10       CONTINUE
      RETURN
      END
```

3. What was the warmest day of the month, based on the high?

4. What was the first rainy day having a high temperature above 38?

5. What were the days of the month with more than a 5-degree difference between the high and low temperatures?

6. What were the two warmest days of the month?

7. Did the pollution count ever exceed 5 on a day when the temperature stayed above 35?

8. What three consecutive days had the most total rainfall?

9. Was it true that every rainless day following a rainy day had a lower pollution count than the rainy day?

10. Using the first 10 days' data, "predict" the weather for the 11th day. Compare (either by hand or within the program) the prediction with the data for the 11th day.

CHAPTER 7

SF/4: ALPHABETIC INFORMATION HANDLING

We have said that computers can handle alphabetic information as well as perform numerical calculations. But most of the emphasis so far, except for labeling our tables of numerical output, has had very little to do with alphabetic data handling. It is true that we have been dealing with words, like identifiers, but these have been in the Fortran programs rather than being handled by them as data. We have, in fact, never had anything but numbers, either real or integer, on the data cards following the $ENTRY control card. In this chapter we will learn how to read in alphabetic data from data cards, how to move it from one place to another in the memory of the computer and how to search for a particular piece of information.

CHARACTER STRINGS

The term "alphabetic information" that we used in the last section is really not general enough to describe what we will learn to handle in this subset of Fortran. It is true that we will be able to handle what you normally mean by alphabetic information, things like people's names

SARAH MARIE WOOD

but we also want to handle things like street addresses. For example, an address like

2156 CYPRESS AVENUE

includes digits as well as letters of the alphabet. This kind of information we call alphanumeric or alphameric for short. But that is not all; we want to handle any kind of English text with words, numbers, and punctuation marks, like commas,   semicolons, and question marks.

    THIS TEXT CONTAINS 7 WORDS; DOESN'T IT?

We have defined a word as being a string of one or more characters preceded and followed by a blank or a punctuation mark, other than an apostrophe. This definition makes 7 a word.

    The information we want to handle is any string of characters that may be letters, digits, punctuations marks or blanks.   We tend to think of a blank as being not a character, but a string of blanks is quite different from a string with no characters at all. We call the special string with no characters at all a null string. We often write b for the blank character so that you can count how many blank characters are in a string.

    HEREbISbAbCHARACTERbSTRINGbSHOWINGbTHEbBLANKSbEXPLICITLY.

In Chapter 3 we introduced the characters in the Fortran language.   In that listing there are more than we have referred to so far in this chapter.   The list of special characters includes symbols we need for arithmetic operations +, -, /, *, as well as the equal sign, comma and parentheses.

    One reason we want to be able to handle strings of any of these characters is to be able to work with Fortran programs themselves as data. This is the kind of job a compiler must do, and a programming language similar to Fortran should be suitable for writing a compiler program. This is one of the reasons it has been extended to include the ability of handling character strings.

CHARACTER STRING VARIABLES

    Just as we had to set aside space in the computer memory for storing real and integer numbers, we must have space for storing strings of characters.   Character strings can be declared with different lengths.

    We might declare a character string variable named TEXT by the declaration

    CHARACTER*50 TEXT

We know it is a character string variable because of the keyword CHARACTER. The amount of memory reserved for the variable TEXT is enough for 50 character spaces. This will be a number of machine words as each character requires about 6 bits to represent it. When a character string of less than 50 characters in length is placed in this character string variable it is placed on the left-hand side of the available space and padded on

the right with blanks. If an attempt is made to place a longer
string into the space it is truncated on the right.

READING AND PRINTING STRINGS

We learned in the first subset how to print a string of
characters that was in the form of a literal such as 'COST=', and
we have been using this for printing labels on our numeric
output. We just put the literal, which is a string of characters
enclosed in single quotes, in the list of a PRINT statement. The
string would be printed, in a field of its own size and with the
quotation marks removed.

Now that we can have character string variables we can read
information into them from cards and print them out.   For
example, this program reads and prints character strings.

```
$JOB      STEVE POZGAJ
C READ AND PRINT A TEXT
        CHARACTER*78 TEXT
        READ,TEXT
        PRINT,TEXT
        RETURN
        END
$ENTRY
  'HERE IS A SAMPLE TEXT'
```

The output printing would be

    HERE IS A SAMPLE TEXT

Notice that the input data must have quotes around the character
string and that these quotes are not printed since they are not
part of the string. The largest string that can be put on an 80-
column card is 78 characters, since the quotation marks take two
columns.   It is best to limit variables that are input to those
that will fit on to a card. On output the size is limited by the
length of a print line. Variables that go from card to card or
line to line are difficult to manage.   Some compilers limit
string variables to being at most 255 characters.

Character string variables may also be given values in an
assignment statement. In the example

```
    CHARACTER*10 NAME
    NAME='CORLEY PHILLIPS'
    PRINT,NAME
```

the character string to be assigned to NAME has more characters
than the maximum 10 that are declared.   This means that the
leftmost 10 characters are stored in NAME and the rest are lost.

The output would be

    CORLEY PHI

This is a string of length 10. Remember the blank is a
character.

COMPARISON OF STRINGS FOR RECOGNITION

We need to be able to compare one string with another for two
purposes. One purpose is for the recognition of strings. In
this we are concerned with whether two strings are the same or
not. String comparisons are made in logical conditions since
their result is either true or false; the strings are the same or
they are not. Here is a program that reads and prints words
until it reaches the word STOP:

```
$JOB    JOHN GUTTAG
C THIS PROGRAM STOPS WHEN IT IS TOLD
       CHARACTER*10 WORD
       INTEGER COUNT
       COUNT=0
       READ,WORD
       WHILE(WORD.NE.'STOP')DO
          PRINT,WORD
          COUNT=COUNT+1
          READ,WORD
          END WHILE
       PRINT,COUNT
       RETURN
       END
$ENTRY
(the following data items are placed one to a card)

 'SOUP' 'SLOW' 'SIP' 'STOP' 'SIT'
```

The output will be

```
SOUP
SLOW
SIP
      3
```

The logical condition (WORD.NE.'STOP') controls the WHILE...DO.
It is true until the WORD read is STOP. Note that the last word,
SIT, is never read. If there were no word STOP in the program
the computer would inform you of an end-of-file error, as you
would just run off the end of the list of words.

SEQUENCING STRINGS

The other use of string comparisons is to sequence strings, to put them in order. Usually we speak of alphabetic order for alphabetic strings.

ABCDEFGHIJKLMNOPQRSTUVWXYZ

The alphabet and digits have the normal order among themselves: 0 comes before 9, A comes before Z. Blanks have the lowest value. The operators .GT. and .LT. are used to compare the strings. If the two strings being compared are of unequal lengths, blanks are added on the right of the shorter string to make them equal in length. The following comparisons are labeled as true or false:

Comparison	Value
('JOHN' .GT. 'JIM')	true
('JOHN' .LT. 'JOHNSTON')	true
(' A' .LT.'A')	true because blank.LT.A
('MCLEOD' .GT. 'MACKAY')	true
('22' .GT. '156')	true because 2.GT.1

The following program reads in 10 names and prints out the one that is the last alphabetically.

```
$JOB     LAURIE JOHNSTON
C LOOK FOR ALPHABETICALLY LAST NAME
         CHARACTER*15 NAME,LAST
         INTEGER I
         LAST='AAAAA'
         DO 18 I=1,10
            READ,NAME
            IF(NAME.GT.LAST)THEN DO
               LAST=NAME
            END IF
18       CONTINUE
         PRINT,LAST
         RETURN
         END
$ENTRY
(The following data items are placed one to a card)

'HUME' 'HOLT' 'HULL' 'SEVCIK' 'PHILLIPS' 'WORTMAN'
'HORNING' 'TSICHRITZIS' 'GOTLIEB' 'SWENSON'
```

This program will output

        WORTMAN

Notice that the variable LAST is initialized to the string AAAAA.
This is to provide a beginning value for use in the IF statement.
Because it is alphabetically low in value it will undoubtedly be
replaced by the first name read. We could instead have read the
first name into LAST and reduced the count in the DO loop by one.

CHAPTER 7 SUMMARY

    In this chapter we have given methods of manipulating strings
of characters. We introduced character string variables and
showed how they can be used to read and print strings, recognize
strings, or sequence them alphabetically. The following
important terms were presented:

Length of a literal - a literal (character string constant) must
    have a length of at least one, as in 'Q'. Note that the
    literal 'DON''T' has length 5 because it represents DON'T.

Length of a character string variable - given in the declaration
    of the variable. The length of the variable never changes.
    If a character string shorter than the declared length is
    assigned to the variable then the string is padded with
    blanks on the right up to the declared length.

Null string - The string of length zero, that is, the string with
    no characters. In SF/k programs the null string, written as
    '', is not legal.

String truncation (or chopping) - throwing away characters from
    the right-hand end of a character string. Suppose a
    character string is assigned to a character string variable
    S, and the length of the string exceeds the length of S; then
    S takes the value of the string as truncated to the length of
    S. (An error message may be printed.)

String comparisons - used to test character strings for equality
    and for ordering. Strings can be compared using the
    following operators:

                    .LT. comes before (less than)
                    .GT. comes after (greater than)
                    .LE. comes before or is equal (less than or equal)
                    .GE. comes after or is equal (greater than or equal)
                    .EQ. equal
                    .NE. not equal

Blank padding - extending a character string on the right with
    blanks so it can be compared with or assigned to a longer
    string. For example, in SF/k, the comparison

        'JONES'.EQ.'JONES '

is true because the shorter string is temporarily extended on the right with blanks.

CHAPTER 7 EXERCISES

1. Which of the following comparisons of strings are true?

    (a) 'DAVID BARNARD'.EQ.'DAVID BARNARD'
    (b) 'E. WONG'.EQ.'EDMUND WONG'
    (c) 'MARK FOX'.EQ.'MARK FOX'
    (d) 'JOHNSTON' .GT. 'JOHNSON'
    (e) '416 ELM ST' .LT. '414 ELM STREET'
    (f) 'HUME,PAT' .GT. 'HOLT,RIC'
    (g) 'ALLEN' .NE. 'ALAN'

2. Write a program that reads a list such as the following and prints a list of all persons named Jones:
    'JONES, A.B.'
    'YOUNG, A.C.'
    'JONES, R.M.'
    'COLLINS, R.A.'
    'ZZZZ' (dummy value)

Hint: Use one string that is .LE. the alphabetically first Jones and another string that is .GE. the alphabetically last Jones.

3. Write a program that reads in ratings for movies and prints out titles for those rated 'X'. For example, the data might be:

    'THOR AND THE AMAZON WOMEN' 'ADULTS ONLY'
    'BULLETS, GORE AND SEX'   'X'
    'ALICE IN WONDERLAND'   'CHILDREN'
    'THE GODFATHER, PART VIII'   'X'
    'ZZZ'   'NONE'

4. Write a program which looks up Nancy Wong's telephone number and prints it. You are given a set of data cards, each containing a name and a phone number. For example, the first card of this deck might be

    'JOHN ABEL'   '443-2162'

The last data card is the dummy card

    'ZZZ'   '000-0000'

5. You are to write a program which prints "personalized" appeals for contributions to the annual fund drive of the Loyal Order of Wallalumps, an exclusive men's club.

    Each club member is recorded on a card. Each member is to be sent a letter of the following form:

```
Dear XXXXXX,
    Thank you so much for your last year's
contribution of CCCCCCC dollars.
    Since your contribution last year was
PPPPPPPPPPPP
to help us meet our quota this year.
                    Yours sincerely,
```

Each data card contains the member's last name, his nickname if known (if not, '?' is used), his last year's contribution and his estimated salary.

The field XXXXXX should be filled in with the member's nickname, if known, but otherwise with Mr. YYYYYY, where YYYYYY is the member's last name. The phrase PPPPPPPPPPPP should be either

        so generous, we are counting on you

or

        not as large as hoped, we need you

Phrase PPPPPPPPPPPP is picked according to whether last year's contribution was more or less than .1% of the member's estimated salary.

    The following is an example data card:

    'LAZOWSKA' 'FUNK'   15   12000

CHAPTER 8

SF/5: ARRAYS

So far in our programming, each memory location for data had its own special name; each variable had a unique identifier. In this chapter we will introduce the idea that groups of data will share a common name and be differentiated from each other by numbering each one uniquely.

Suppose that we have a list of names of persons. We could give the list the name PERSON and identify the first name as PERSON(1), the second as PERSON(2), and so on. We call the number that is enclosed in parentheses the index of the list or array. The reason why we should use this method of identifying variables is not clear. We will have to do an example so that you can see the power of the new method. As an example, suppose you wanted to read in a list of names of 50 PERSONs and print them out in reverse order, that is, last first. We would need to read in the entire list before we could begin the printing. This means we must have a memory location for each name. We must be able to reserve this space by a declaration.

DECLARATION OF ARRAYS

For the list of names of persons we would use a declaration

    CHARACTER*20 PERSON(50)

Each name is a character string variable whose length is 20. The fact that the variable identifier PERSON is a list is shown by having something in parentheses after it. And what is shown is the fact that it is a list numbered, or indexed, from 1 to 50. What actually is shown in parentheses is the number of entries in the list.

HANDLING LISTS

We are now ready for the program that reverses the order of a list of names. Here the array index is an integer variable I.

```
$JOB    LES MEZEI
C THIS PROGRAM REVERSES THE ORDER OF A LIST OF NAMES
        CHARACTER*20 PERSON(50)
        INTEGER I,J
C       READ LIST OF NAMES
        DO 5 I=1,50
           READ,PERSON(I)
5          CONTINUE
C       PRINT REVERSED LIST
        J=50
        DO 15 I=1,50
           PRINT,PERSON(J)
           J=J-1
15         CONTINUE
        RETURN
        END
$ENTRY
   (list of 50 names, each in quotes, one to a card)
```

Now, perhaps, you can see what a powerful programming tool the indexed variable can be. In the first DO loop the index I that is counting the loop can be used to refer to the different members of the list. In the first DO loop the names are read; the first is stored in the variable PERSON(1), the second in PERSON(2), and so on. In contrast, we want the printing loop to output PERSON(50), next PERSON(49), and so on. Since a counted DO cannot have a negative increment we must use a separate index J to pick out the elements for printing. In the loop we increment J by -1 each time; outside the loop J must be initialized to the value 50 so on the first execution PERSON(50) is printed. The index I of an array goes from 1 to N where N is the size of the array.

Suppose, as a second example, we had a list of 50 integers and we wanted the sum of all the numbers. Here is the program:

```
C       THIS PROGRAM SUMS 50 NUMBERS
        INTEGER NUMBER(50),SUM,I
C       READ IN NUMBERS
        DO 40 I=1,50
           READ,NUMBER(I)
40         CONTINUE
C       SUM THE NUMBERS
        SUM=0
        DO 80 I=1,50
           SUM=SUM+NUMBER(I)
80         CONTINUE
        PRINT,SUM
```

In this example, it is not necessary to read all the numbers and then add them up but we did it that way just to show what is necessary for reading or summing a list. We could have written only one loop, combining the two operations.

```
C       READ AND SUM THE NUMBERS
        SUM=0
        DO 50 I=1,50
           READ,NUMBER(I)
           SUM=SUM+NUMBER(I)
50         CONTINUE
        PRINT,SUM
```

Usually, there is more to be done that requires having the list still present. For instance we could think of dividing each member of a list by the sum and multiplying by 100. This would express each entry as a percentage of the group. To do this we would add these statements:

```
C       COMPUTE PERCENTAGES
        DO 60 I=1,50
           NUMBER(I)=(NUMBER(I)*100.)/SUM+.5
           PRINT,NUMBER(I)
60         CONTINUE
```

In the DO loop the assignment statement with the index I results in each member of the list being operated on and changed to a percentage.

AN EXAMPLE PROGRAM

Arrays can be used in manipulating various kinds of lists. We will now give an example in which the list is the timetable for teachers in a high school. The timetable has been prepared as a deck of cards. Each card has a teacher's name, a period (1 to 6) and a room number.

The cards look like the following:

(teacher)	(period)	(room)
'MS. WEBER'	1	216
'MRS. IRELAND'	6	214
'MRS. REID'	1	103
'MS. WEBER'	4	200
'MRS. CAIN'	2	216
...		
'XXX'	0	0 (dummy card)

A program is needed to print out the timetable in order of periods. First, all teachers with their classrooms for the first period should be printed; then all teachers with their classrooms for period 2 and so on up to period 6. The output from the program should begin this way:

```
PERIOD                   1
MS. WEBER              216
MRS. REID             103
...
```

The following program produces this output:

```
 1    C THIS PROGRAM SHOWS TEACHER ROOM ASSIGNMENTS BY PERIOD
 2            CHARACTER*20 TEACHR(12)
 3            INTEGER PERIOD(50),ROOM(50)
 4            INTEGER I,NOW,NUMBER
 5    C       INITIALIZE FOR READING TIMETABLE
 6            I=1
 7            READ,TEACHR(I),PERIOD(I),ROOM(I)
 8    C       READ THE TIMETABLE
 9            WHILE(TEACHR(I).NE.'XXX')DO
10               I=I+1
11               READ,TEACHR(I),PERIOD(I),ROOM(I)
12               END WHILE
13            NUMBER=I-1
14    C       PRINT THE TIMETABLE BY PERIODS
15            DO 14 NOW=1,6
16               PRINT,'PERIOD       ',NOW
17               DO 8 I=1,NUMBER
18                  IF(PERIOD(I).EQ.NOW)THEN DO
19                     PRINT,TEACHR(I),ROOM(I)
20                     END IF
21    8           CONTINUE
22    14       CONTINUE
23            RETURN
24            END
```

The first loop in this program reads in the cards representing the timetable. In lines 6 and 7, the initialization for this loop sets the count to 1 and reads the first element of the TEACHR, PERIOD, and ROOM arrays.

Our program is able to read in a timetable consisting of <u>at most 50 cards</u>, including the dummy card. If there are more than 50 cards in the timetable, then line 10 will eventually set I to 51; this value of I will be used in line 11 as an index for the TEACHR, PERIOD and ROOM arrays. This would be an error, because the declarations specify that 50 is the largest allowed array index. The problem is that the index is <u>out of bounds</u> in line 11 when I exceeds 50.

You should take care that array indexes in your programs stay within their declared bounds. In our example program, we can prevent bounds errors by changing line 9 to the following.

```
WHILE(I.LT.49.AND.TEACHR(I).NE.'XXX')DO
```

Our change guarantees that no more than 50 cards will be read. Unfortunately, the modified program fails to report the situation

when   there were too many data cards.   We can remedy this problem
by inserting the following between lines 12 and 13:

```
IF(TEACHR(I).NE.'XXX') THEN DO
    PRINT,'**ERROR:ONLY 50 CARDS WERE READ'
END IF
```

The   program   now   supplies a more appropriate error message than
the system might provide, and continues on to give   a   period-by-
period listing of the cards it actually read.

TWO-DIMENSIONAL ARRAYS

It is possible to have arrays that correspond to entries in a
table rather than just a single list.   For instance, a   table   of
distances in miles between 4 cities might be

```
            1     2     3     4
        -------------------
    1 |  0    20    38    56
    2 |20     0    12    30
    3 |38    12     0    15
    4 |56    30    15     0
```

We could call this array MILES and MILES(1,4) is 56 or MILES(3,4)
is 15.   The first number in the parentheses refers to the row   in
the table, the second to the column.   You can see that MILES(3,1)
has the same value as MILES(1,3); the table is symmetric in   this
case   about   the   diagonal   line   running from top left to bottom
right.   All entries on this diagonal are zero; the distance   from
a city to itself is zero.

We   must   learn   how to declare such a two-dimensional array.
All that is necessary is to write

```
INTEGER MILES(4,4)
```

The   first   index   is the number of rows, the second the number of
columns.   As an example, we will read in this table and store   it
in the memory.   On each input data card we will punch one element
of the table; we will go across the rows, then   go   to   the   next
row.   We are entering the data row by row.

```
    INTEGER MILES(4,4),I,J
    DO 10 I=1,4
        DO 5 J=1,4
            READ,MILES(I,J)
 5          CONTINUE
10      CONTINUE
```

In this program there is one DO loop nested inside another. We have used two indexes, I to give the row number, J to give the column number. When I=1 the inner loop has J go from 1 to 4. This means the elements of the array on the first card are stored in these variables:

MILES(1,1) MILES(1,2) MILES(1,3) MILES(1,4)

These are the elements in row 1 of the table. Since our table is symmetric it does not matter if we interchange rows and columns, because we get exactly the same result. For most tables it does matter, and you must be careful.

ANOTHER EXAMPLE PROGRAM

We will illustrate the use of two-dimensional arrays in terms of a set of data collected by a consumers' group. This group has been alarmed about the recent rapid rise in price of processed wallalumps. They sampled grocery store prices of processed wallalumps on a monthly basis throughout 1972, 1973 and 1974 and observed that prices varied from 75 cents to 155 cents as the following table shows:

Month

	1	2	3	4	5	6	7	8	9	10	11	12
1972	87	89	89	89	85	85	85	75	90	100	100	100
1973	95	95	95	95	90	90	85	90	100	110	120	110
1974	110	110	115	115	115	100	100	110	120	140	145	155

These 36 prices were made available on data cards and a program was needed to analyze the price changes.

The following program reads in the data and determines the average price for 1973:

```
C THIS PROGRAM COMPUTES AVERAGE PRICE OVER A YEAR
      INTEGER PRICE(3,12)
      INTEGER MONTH,YEAR,TOTAL
      DO 16 YEAR=1,3
C        READ IN PRICES FOR ONE YEAR
         DO 7 MONTH=1,12
            READ,PRICE(YEAR,MONTH)
7        CONTINUE
16    CONTINUE
C     DETERMINE THE AVERAGE PRICE IN 1973
      TOTAL=0
      DO 19 MONTH=1,12
         TOTAL=TOTAL+PRICE(2,MONTH)
19    CONTINUE
      PRINT,'AVERAGE 1973 PRICE:',TOTAL/12.
C     ADD STATEMENTS HERE TO CALCULATE OTHER AVERAGES
      RETURN
      END
```

In this program, the array PRICE is declared so it can have a
first index which can range from 1 to 3 which corresponds to 1972
to 1974 and a second index which can range from 1 to 12
corresponding to the columns in the table. Effectively, the
PRICE array is a table in which entries can be looked up by month
and year if you subtract 1971 from the year. The first part of
the program uses the data to fill up the PRICE array. The second
part of the program sums up the prices for each month during 1973
and calculates the average 1973 price. The value of the array
index of 2 corresponds to the year 1973.

We could as well calculate the average price for a particular
month. For example, the following calculates the average price
in February:

```
      TOTAL=0
      DO 25 YEAR=1,3
         TOTAL=TOTAL+PRICE(YEAR,2)
25       CONTINUE
      PRINT,'AVERAGE FEB. PRICE:',TOTAL/3.
```

We could calculate the average price for the entire three-year
period as follows.

```
      TOTAL=0
      DO 50 YEAR=1,3
         DO 40 MONTH=1,12
            TOTAL=TOTAL+PRICE(YEAR,MONTH)
40          CONTINUE
50       CONTINUE
      PRINT,'OVERALL AVERAGE:',TOTAL/36.
```

This example has illustrated the use of two-dimensional
arrays. It is also possible to use arrays with three dimensions.
For example, our consumers' group might want to record prices for
five grades of processed wallalumps (that makes one dimension),
each month (that makes two dimensions), for three years (that
makes three dimensions). The array declaration

```
      INTEGER PRICE(5,12,3)
```

would set up a table to hold all this data.

ARRAYS AS DATA STRUCTURES

We have spoken of structured programming and shown how
control flow is structured in a program. Now we can speak of the
structure of data. Giving variables identifiers that are
meaningful has been the only way we could systematize data so
far. But with arrays we find that data can be structured or
organized into one-dimensional forms called lists, or two-
dimensional forms called tables. We could also use three-
dimensional arrays.

When we approach a problem and want to solve it by creating a
computer program we must decide on the data structures we will
use. We must decide in particular whether or not we need to
establish arrays for any of the data, or whether single variables
will serve us well enough.

Arrays will be useful whenever we must store groups of
similar pieces of information. They are not necessary when small
amounts of information come in, are processed, and then go out.

OTHER DATA STRUCTURES

Just so that you do not think that single variables and
arrays are the only kind of data structures we can have, we will
mention a few others.

One common structure is the <u>tree</u> structure. The easiest way
to think of a tree is to imagine a family tree. At the risk of
being called chauvinists we will show only the male members in
the tree and talk of fathers and sons. This keeps it simple.

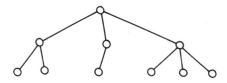

TREE STRUCTURE

The diagram is showing a man with three sons. The first son has
two sons, the second one son, the third three. The grandfather
is the <u>root</u> of the tree. The tree is of course growing upside
down. The lines joining the relatives are called <u>branches</u>; the
people themselves are <u>nodes</u>.

The data we might store could be the names of the people, and
the tree structure would have to be stored also. The way it is
done is to have <u>pointers</u> stored with the data to give the
structure. Each father entry requires a pointer for each of his
sons.

A list can also be arranged with elements and pointers
instead of in an array. This means that some of the information
stored is used to describe the data structure and some to give
the data. With arrays, the structure is given by the fact that

one element follows right next to the preceding element. It does not need a pointer.

Later we will be investigating other data structures in detail. Often we will use the array structures to implement structures like trees or lists with pointers from one element to another.

CHAPTER 8 SUMMARY

This chapter has introduced array variables, which are used for manipulating quantities of similar data. An array is made up of a number of elements, each of which acts as a simple, non-array variable. The following terms are used in describing arrays and their uses.

Array declaration - sets aside memory space for an array. For example, the declaration

   REAL COST(4)

sets aside space for the array elements COST(1), COST(2), COST(3) and COST(4). Each of these elements can be used like a simple, non-array REAL variable.

Array index (sometimes called array subscript) - used to designate a particular element of array. For example, in COST(I), the variable I is an array index. An array index can be any arithmetic expression. It must have an integer value.

Array bounds - the range over which array indexes may vary. For example, given the declaration

   INTEGER PRICE(12,3)

an array element of PRICE can be specified by PRICE(M,Y), where M can range from 1 to 12 and Y can range from 1 to 3. The lower bound of the array is always 1.

Out-of-bounds index - an array index which is outside the bounds specified in the array's declaration. This is an error.

Multiply-dimensioned arrays - arrays requiring more than one index, such as the PRICE array given above.

CHAPTER 8 EXERCISES

1. What does the following program print?

```
C THIS PROGRAM TALKS ABOUT FLOWERS
      CHARACTER*6 POEM(2)
      INTEGER PART,REPEAT
      POEM(1)='A ROSE'
      POEM(2)='IS'
      DO 5 REPEAT=1,3
         DO 3 PART=1,2
            PRINT,POEM(PART)
3           CONTINUE
5        CONTINUE
      PRINT,POEM(1)
      RETURN
      END
```

2. What does the following program print?

```
$JOB     PHILIP LANGTRY
C THIS PROGRAM STARTS RUMORS
      CHARACTER*6 HE(4),SHE(4)
      INTEGER WHO
      PRINT,'HERE THEY ARE'
      DO 8 WHO=1,4
         READ,HE(WHO),SHE(WHO)
         PRINT,'      ',HE(WHO),SHE(WHO)
8        CONTINUE
      PRINT,HE(1),'SAYS',SHE(2),'LOVES',HE(2)
      PRINT,'HOWEVER--'
      DO 12 WHO=2,3
         PRINT,SHE(WHO),'SAYS',HE(WHO+1),'SAYS'
12       CONTINUE
      PRINT,SHE(2),'IS JUST SHOPPING AROUND'
      RETURN
      END
$ENTRY
      'JOHN' 'ANN'
      'FRED' 'JUDY'
      'ED' 'ALICE'
      'BILL' 'JANE'
```

3. What does this program print?

```
$JOB     DIANNE KITCHEN
C THIS PROGRAM LOOKS AT FURNITURE POLISH
         CHARACTER*10 NAME(50)
         INTEGER PRICE(50)
         INTEGER I,P,N
         READ,N
         DO 5 I=1,N
            READ,NAME(I),PRICE(I)
            PRINT,NAME(I),PRICE(I)
5        CONTINUE
         READ,P
         DO 15 I=1,N
            IF(PRICE(I).GT.P)THEN DO
               PRINT,NAME(I)
               END IF
15       CONTINUE
         RETURN
         END
$ENTRY
      3
   'JOHNSONS'   518
   'LEMON OIL'  211
   'DOMINO'     341
      300
```

4. Write a program which reads yesterday's and today's stock-market selling prices and prints lists of rapidly rising and rapidly falling stocks. A typical data card will look like this:

```
   'GENERAL ELECTRIC' 93.50   81.00
```

The card gives you the company's name followed by yesterday's price, followed by today's price. Your program should print a list of companies whose stock declined by more than 10 per cent, and then a list of companies whose stock rose by more than 10 per cent.

5. What will the following program print? What error would occur if the data item 'GERM' is inserted just before 'ALL DONE'? Explain how this error can be avoided by changing one declaration. Add statements so that if more than six objects are read in, the program will print THANK YOU, YOU HAVE BEEN A WONDERFUL AUDIENCE, and quit.

```
$JOB    BRIAN CLARK
C THIS PROGRAM PRINTS THE WORDS OF A SONG
      CHARACTER*10 OBJECT(8)
      INTEGER VERSE,V
      PRINT,'SONG OF THE GREEN GRASS'
      PRINT,' '
      VERSE=1
      OBJECT(VERSE)='TREE'
      WHILE(OBJECT(VERSE).NE.'ALL DONE')DO
          IF (VERSE.EQ.1) THEN DO
              PRINT,'THERE WAS A TREE'
          ELSE DO
              PRINT,'AND ON THAT',OBJECT(VERSE-1)
              PRINT,'THERE WAS A',OBJECT(VERSE)
              PRINT,'THE PRETTIEST',OBJECT(VERSE)
              PRINT,'THAT YOU EVER DID SEE'
              V=VERSE
              WHILE(V.GT.1)DO
                  PRINT,'AND THE',OBJECT(V),'WAS ON THE',OBJECT(V-1)
                  V=V-1
                  END WHILE
              END IF
          PRINT,'AND THE TREE WAS IN THE GROUND'
C         BELT OUT THE CHORUS
          PRINT,'AND THE GREEN GRASS GREW ALL AROUND, ALL AROUND'
          PRINT,'AND THE GREEN GRASS GREW ALL AROUND'
          PRINT,' '
          VERSE=VERSE+1
          READ,OBJECT(VERSE)
          END WHILE
      RETURN
      END
$ENTRY
(the following strings should be on separate cards)

 'BRANCH' 'NEST' 'BIRD' 'WING' 'FEATHER' 'FLEA' 'ALL DONE'
```

6. Do you know the song about the old lady who swallowed a fly? If so, write a program to print its words. Otherwise, if you know the song "Alouette", write a program to print its words. Otherwise, if you know the song "The Twelve Days of Christmas," write a program to print its words. Otherwise learn one of these three songs and repeat this exercise.

7. You work for the Police Department and you are to write a
program to try to determine criminals' identities based on
victims' descriptions of the criminals. The police have cards
describing known criminals. These cards have the form

    name   height   weight   address

Here is an example:

 'JOEY MACLUNK' 67   125   '24 MAIN ST.'

There is another set of cards giving descriptions of criminals
participating in unsolved crimes. Here is such a deck:

    '14 DEC: SHOP LIFTING'   72   190
    ' 9 NOV: PURSE SNATCHING'   66   130
    ' 6 NOV: BICYCLE THIEVERY'   67   135
    'XXX'   0   0

The two numbers give the criminal's estimated height and weight.
Write a program which first reads in the deck describing the
unsolved crimes. Then it reads the file cards giving the known
criminals' names, descriptions and addresses. Each known
criminal's height and weight should be compared with the
corresponding measurements for each unsolved crime. If the
height is within 2 inches and the weight is within 10 pounds,
your program should print a message saying the criminal is a
possible suspect for the crime. (Note: Joey MacLunk is not a
real person!)

CHAPTER 9

STRUCTURING
YOUR ATTACK
ON THE PROBLEM

STEP-BY-STEP REFINEMENT

Most of the examples of programming so far have been short examples. Nevertheless we have emphasized some of the aspects of good programming. These were:

1. choosing meaningful words as identifiers,

2. placing comments in the program to increase the understandability,

3. paragraphing loops and IF...THEN...ELSE statements to reveal the structure of control flow,

4. choosing appropriate data structures,

5. reading programs and tracing execution by hand, to strive for correctness before machine testing.

All of these are important even in small programs, but it is only when we attempt larger programs that our good habits will really start to pay off.

And when we work on larger programs we will find that we have something else to structure, and that is our attack on the problem. To solve a problem we must move from a statement of what the problem to be solved is, to a solution, which is a well-structured program for a computer. The language of our program will be Fortran.

The original statement of a problem will be in English, with perhaps some mathematical statements. The solution will be in Fortran. What we will look at in this chapter is the way we move

from one of these to the other. We will be discussing a method
whereby we go step by step from one to the other. This
systematic method we will refer to as <u>step-by-step refinement</u>.
Sometimes we say that we are starting at the top, the English-
language statement of the problem, and moving down in steps to
the bottom level, which is the Fortran program for the solution.
We speak of the <u>top-down approach</u> to problem solution.

TREE STRUCTURE TO PROBLEM SOLUTION

To illustrate the technique of structuring the solution to a
problem by the step-by-step refinement, or the top-down approach,
we need a problem as an example. We need a problem that is large
or difficult enough to show the technique, but not so large as to
be too long to follow. If a program is too long and involved we
will use another technique that divides the job into modules and
does one module at a time. This is called <u>modular programming</u>.
It is another form of structured programming. But it must wait
until we have learned SF/7.

The example we choose is sorting a list of names
alphabetically. We will now start the solution by trying to form
a tree which represents the structure of our attack. The root of
the tree is the statement of the problem. In the first move we
show how this is divided into three branches:

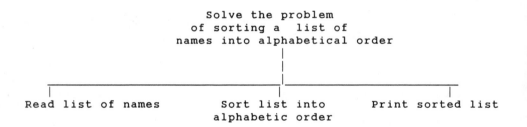

At each of the three nodes that descend from the root we have an
English statement. These statements are still "what-to-do"
statements, not "how-to-do-it." A statement of how to do
something or other is called an <u>algorithm</u> for doing it. A set of
instructions for assembling a hi-fi amplifier is an algorithm for
making a hi-fi amplifier. A cake recipe in a cookbook is an
algorithm for making a cake. The problem of making a cake is
solved by following the recipe.

We will be moving down each branch of the solution tree
replacing a statement of "what to do" by an algorithm for doing
it. The algorithms will not necessarily be in the Fortran
language. We will use a mixture of English and Fortran at each
node until, in the nodes farthest from the tree root, we have a
Fortran program.

CHOOSING DATA STRUCTURES

Before we try to add more branches to the solution tree, we should decide on some data structures for the problem of sorting the list of names. We need not make all the decisions at this stage, but we can make a start.

We will use a one-dimensional array called NAME to hold the list of names to be sorted. The length of this list we will call N and we will allow names up to 30 characters in length. What we are deciding on is really the declarations for the Fortran program, and for now we have decided that we need

```
CHARACTER*30 NAME(50)
INTEGER N,I
```

In these declarations we are allowing a maximum size for the list of 50 names. The actual list will have N names, and we must read this number in as part of the input. For indexing the list we clearly will need an index I. We will assume for the moment that we will keep the sorted list in the same locations as the original list. The names will have to be rearranged, and this means some swapping will be needed. We will need a single variable TEMP with type CHARACTER*30 to do this swapping.

GROWING THE SOLUTION TREE

Having decided on at least some of the data structures, we are prepared to continue the process of structuring the solution tree. We can see how to develop the left and right branches now, even as far as transforming them into Fortran program segments. The middle branch can be refined a little by saying that sorting will be accomplished by element swapping. Here is the tree now:

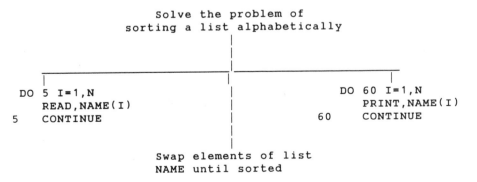

At this stage we must obviously face up to designing an algorithm for producing a sorted list by swapping.

DEVELOPING AN ALGORITHM

We want the names to be in the sorted list so that each name
has a smaller value than the name ahead of it in the list.

In the sorted list

        HOLT
        HORNING
        HULL

we see   ('HORNING'.GT.'HOLT')
          ('HULL'.GT.'HORNING')

are both true conditions.

In our solution tree one branch must be developed further;
this is, "Swap elements of list NAME until sorted." We have seen
from the example that a sorted list has the largest value in the
last position. This is also true of the list if an element is
removed from the end. The new last element is the largest one of
the smaller list. So our next refinement in the solution is to
arrange the list in this way. We write:

    "Do with LAST varying from N to second,
          swap elements so largest is in LAST"

We must still refine the part,

    "Swap elements so largest is in LAST"

but the first part of this can be written in Fortran. If
Fortran permitted counting backwards we might write

        DO 15 LAST=N,2,-1

But this is not possible so we must have an auxiliary index J for
the DO that counts forward as LAST is moved backward. This means
we must write

    "DO with I varying from first to (LAST-1),
          if element(I).GT.element(I+1),
          swap elements"

The first two parts of this can now become Fortran; this produces

        LIMIT=LAST-1
        DO 25 I=1,LIMIT
            IF(NAME(I).GT.NAME(I+1))THEN DO
                swap elements
                END IF
    25   CONTINUE

We are not able to have LAST-1 in the DO itself so we introduce the variable LIMIT. We must now refine the statement "swap elements". It is

```
TEMP=NAME(I)
NAME(I)=NAME(I+1)
NAME(I+1)=TEMP
```

Now we can assemble the complete program.

```
$JOB     RICK BUNT
C SORT LIST OF N NAMES ALPHABETICALLY
      CHARACTER*30 NAME(50),TEMP
      INTEGER I,LAST,N,J,LIMIT,TEST
C     READ NAME LIST
      READ,N
      DO 5 I=1,N
         READ,NAME(I)
5     CONTINUE
C     SWAP ELEMENTS OF LIST UNTIL SORTED
C     DO WITH LAST VARYING FROM N TO SECOND
C         SWAP ELEMENTS SO LARGEST VALUE IS IN LAST ELEMENT
      LAST=N
      TEST=N-1
      DO 30 J=1,TEST
C         DO WITH I VARYING FROM FIRST TO LAST-1
C             IF ELEMENT(I) .GT. ELEMENT(I+1)
C             SWAP THESE ELEMENTS
          LIMIT=LAST-1
          DO 25 I=1,LIMIT
             IF(NAME(I).GT.NAME(I+1))THEN DO
                TEMP=NAME(I)
                NAME(I)=NAME(I+1)
                NAME(I+1)=TEMP
                END IF
25           CONTINUE
          LAST=LAST-1
30        CONTINUE
C     PRINT SORTED LIST
      DO 60 I=1,N
         PRINT,NAME(I)
60       CONTINUE
      RETURN
      END
$ENTRY
 4
 'ANN'
 'ALLEN'
 'AXELBLATT'
 'AYNE'
```

Notice that the English parts of the solution tree remain as comments in the final program. Comments are not added after a

program is written, so that it can be understood at a later date,
but are an integral part of the program construction process.

ASSESSING EFFICIENCY

In this approach to problem solution we have moved step by
step to refine the statement of the problem in English into a
program in a language that is acceptable to a computer, namely
Fortran. In the process, as we constructed the solution tree, we
gradually replaced statements of what is to be done by statements
of how it is to be done; we devised an algorithm for performing
the process. The algorithm was expressed in English, or a
mixture of English and Fortran. Finally we had a Fortran
program.

Nowhere during this process have we spoken about the
efficiency of the method that we have chosen, that is, the
efficiency of our algorithm. This is because the issue of
efficiency complicates the solution. Since in structured
programming we are trying to control complexity, we have in this
first attempt eliminated efficiency from our considerations.

This means that to now add the refinement of a more efficient
algorithm will require us to back up to an earlier point in the
solution tree and redo certain portions. In the step-by-step
refinement method of problem solution we do not always move from
the top down in the solution tree. In practice this would be
impractical, as afterthoughts must be allowed to improve a method
of solution. The only reason to reject afterthoughts is that the
work in incorporating them is not justified, considering the gain
that would result.

In our particular example you can see that it is possible, at
a certain stage, that the list might be sorted and that there is
no need to keep on to the bitter end. What we should incorporate
is a way of recognizing that the list is sorted so that the
mechanical sorting process can stop.

A BETTER ALGORITHM

What we must do is to back up in the solution tree to the
point where we had in the middle branch the words, "Swap elements
of NAME until sorted." We have translated this essentially by
the statement, "Swap elements of NAME in such a way that at the
end of the swapping process the list is sure to be sorted."

We are going to change now to the statement, "Swap elements
of NAME in such a way that at the end of the swapping process the
list would be sorted, and stop either when the list is sorted or
when the normal end of the swapping process is reached." You can
see that we are going to have a DO loop now with two conditions.
The condition of the swapping process's being finished is the

same as what we have now. What we must add is the second condition

        WHILE (list is not sorted)DO

But how do we know when the list is sorted? We must devise an algorithm to test whether or not the list is sorted. You will notice that if in any iteration of the inner DO loop there are no names swapped, the list <u>must</u> be sorted. We should have a flag called SORTED that can be set to 1 to indicate that the list is sorted or 0 to indicate that the list is not sorted. The outer DO loop would then be

        WHILE(SORTED.NE.1.AND.LAST.GE.2)

We would have to initialize this loop by having these instructions precede it.

        SORTED=0
        LAST=N

These set the flag and start the count. Inside the loop we must perform the adjustment in the index LAST by -1; since we are now using a WHILE...DO loop instead of a counted DO loop we can count backward if we want to. This would mean we need as before the instruction

        LAST=LAST-1

just before the end of the loop. We want SORTED to be changed to 1 if no swapping takes place in the inner DO loop. This can be accomplished if we set it to 1 just before we enter the inner loop and return it to zero if any swapping does take place. The altered part of the program is as follows.

```
C       SWAP ELEMENTS OF LIST UNTIL
C          EITHER SWAPPING PROCESS IS COMPLETED
C          OR THE LIST IS SORTED AS INDICATED
C          BY THE FLAG 'SORTED' BEING 1
        SORTED=0
        LAST=N
        WHILE(SORTED.NE.1.AND.LAST.GE.2)DO
           SORTED=1
           LIMIT=LAST-1
           DO 25 I=1, LIMIT
              IF(NAME(I).GT.NAME(I+1))THEN DO
                 SORTED=0
                 TEMP=NAME(I)
                 NAME(I)=NAME(I+1)
                 NAME(I+1)=TEMP
                 END IF
25            CONTINUE
           LAST=LAST-1
           END WHILE
C       PRINT SORTED LIST
        (as before)
```

BETTER ALGORITHMS

In our example we could see that an improvement in the efficiency of the sorting algorithm could be achieved, and we backed up the solution tree and redid a portion to incorporate the improvement. This was an easier job than trying to think about efficiency in the first place. This is why in the step-by-step refinement method we do not consider efficiency at first. In a way we were lucky that our algorithm could be modified so readily. We might have done the swapping in an entirely different way, in which we would not be able to detect a sorted list by the absence of swapping on any iteration of the process.

To see how this might be, suppose that to sort this list each element were compared with the first element. If it were smaller, the two would be swapped. With the smallest in the first position the list would be shortened by one and the process repeated. The difficulty here is that the fact that no swapping occurs in any round only means that the smallest is already in the first position, not that the list is sorted. We have no way of seeing that the list is sorted unless we compare each list member with its next-door neighbor. And this is what we did in our sorting method.

So our method is more suited to this particular improvement than a method that involves swapping by comparison of each element with one particular element. If we had started this way we would have had to revise completely. To say that efficiency considerations are left until after a first algorithm is programmed produces disadvantages. For many standard processes like sorting, various algorithms have been explored, their efficiencies evaluated, and a best algorithm determined. The method we have developed is certainly not the best that has been devised.

This best, or optimal, algorithm often depends on the problem itself. For instance, one algorithm may be best for short lists, another for long lists. Establishing "the" best method is very difficult and depends on circumstances. Always try to pick a "good" algorithm if you are programming a standard process. At least avoid "bad" algorithms. Very often, programs are already written using good algorithms and you can use them directly in your own program. But that is something we will discuss in the subset SF/7. We can create programs from modules that are already made for us. Then one of the branches of your solution tree is filled by a <u>prefabricated</u> <u>module</u>. We need only learn how to hook it up to our own program. We can also create modules of our own. This technique is called <u>modular</u> <u>programming</u> and it is an additional way to conquer problem solving, by dividing the problem into parts.

CHAPTER 9 SUMMARY

In previous chapters we concentrated primarily on <u>learning</u> a programming language; we have covered variables, loops, character strings, arrays and so on. In this chapter, the focus has been on <u>using</u> a programming language to solve problems.

The method of problem solving which we described is based on the idea of dividing the problem into parts - the divide-and-conquer strategy. Each of these parts in turn is divided into smaller parts. This continues until eventually the solution to the problem has been broken into small parts which can be written in a programming language like Fortran. We will review this method of problem solving using the following terms:

Top-down approach to programming. When using a computer to solve a problem, you should start by understanding the problem thoroughly. You start at the "top" by figuring out what your program is supposed to do. Next you split your prospective program into parts, for example, into a reading phase, a computation phase, and a printing phase. These phases represent the next level in the design of your program. You may continue by defining the data which these phases use for passing information among themselves, and then by writing Fortran statements for each of the phases. The Fortran statements are the bottom level of your design; they make up a program which should solve your problem. In larger programs, there may be many intermediate levels between the top - understanding the problem completely - and the bottom - a program which solves the problem. (Beware: top-down program design does <u>not</u> mean writing declarations at the top of the page, followed by statements! The top level in top-down design means gaining an understanding of the problem to be solved, rather than writing the first line of Fortran.)

Step-by-step refinement. When you are writing a program, you should start with an overall understanding of the program's purpose. You should proceed step by step toward the writing of this program. These steps should each refine the proposed program into a more detailed method of solving the problem. The last step refines the method to the level where the computer can carry out the required operations. This means that the final refinement results in a program which can be executed by the computer. As you can see, the idea behind top-down programming is step-by-step refinement leading from the problem statement to the final program.

Tree structures to problem solution. In this chapter we have illustrated top-down programming by drawing pictures of trees. The root, or base, of the tree is labeled by the

statement of the problem. Once the problem has been refined
into subproblems, we have our tree grow a branch for each
subproblem. In turn, each subproblem can be divided,
resulting in sub-branches, and so on. When you are actually
solving problems, you will probably not actually draw such a
tree. However, you may well use the idea behind drawing this
tree, namely, step-by-step refinement leading from problem
statement to problem solution.

Use of comments. One of the purposes of comments in a program is
to remind us of the structure of the program. This means
that comments are used to remind us that a particular
sequence of Fortran statements has been written to solve one
particular part of the problem.

CHAPTER 9 EXERCISES

1. You are to have the computer read a list of names, followed by
the dummy name 'ZZZ', and print the names in reverse order.   In
your top-down approach to writing your program, you first decided
your program should have the overall form:

   (a) Read in all of the names;

   (b) Print the names in reverse order;

Next, you decided that the names will be passed from part (a) to
part (b) via an array declared by

     CHARACTER*10 NAME(50)

The index of the last valid name read into this array will be
passed to part (b) in an integer variable called NUMBER. Making
no changes to this overall form, you must now complete the
program. Include comments at the appropriate places to record
the purpose of the two parts of your program. Answer the
following questions about your completed program.

   - Can you think of another way to write part (a) of your
   program without changing part (b)? How?

   - Can you think of another way to write part (b) of your
   program without changing part (a)? How?

2. The school office wants a list of all A students and a list of
all B students. There is a punched card for each student giving
his grade, for example:

     'DAVID TILBROOK' 'A'

Each grade is A,B,C,D or F. The names and grades are followed by
the dummy card

```
'ZZZ'              'NONE'
```

The school's programmer has designed the following three possible structures for a program to read these cards and print the two required lists.

   First program structure:
   (a) Read names and grades and save all of them in arrays.
   (b) Print names having A grades.
   (c) Print names having B grades.

   Second program structure:
   (a) Read names and grades and save only those with As or Bs
       in arrays.
   (b) Print names having A grades.
   (c) Print names having B grades.

   Third program structure:
   (a) Read names and grades, printing names with As and saving
       only names with Bs.
   (b) Print names having Bs.

Suppose the final program will have room in arrays to save at most 50 students' names. What advantage does the second program structure have over the first one? What advantages does the third program structure have over the second one? You do not need to write a program to answer these questions.

3. A company wants to know the percentage of its sales due to each salesman. Each salesman has a card giving his name and the dollar value of his sales. The last salesman's card is followed by a card giving the dummy name 'NOBODY' and sales of zero dollars. The top-down design of a program to print the desired percentages has resulted in this program structure:

   (a) Read in salesmen and sales and add up total sales.
   (b) Calculate each salesman's percentage of the total sales.
   (c) Print the salesmen's names and percentages.

Parts (a) and (c) have been written in Fortran. You are to write part (b) in Fortran, add declarations and complete the program. Here is part (a) written in Fortran:

```
C     READ IN SALESMEN AND SALES AND ADD UP TOTAL SALES
      TOTAL=0
      I=1
      READ,MAN(I),SALES(I)
      WHILE(MAN(I).NE.'NOBODY')DO
         TOTAL=TOTAL+SALES(I)
         I=I+1
         READ,MAN(I),SALES(I)
         END WHILE
```

Here is part (c) written in Fortran:

```
C     PRINT SALESMEN'S NAMES AND PERCENTAGES
      PRINT,'SALESMAN     ','PERCENT'
      I=1
      WHILE(MAN(I).NE.'NOBODY')DO
         PRINT,MAN(I),PRCENT(I)
         I=I+1
         END WHILE
```

You are to complete the program without changing parts (a) and (c).

CHAPTER 10

SF/6: CONTROLLING INPUT AND OUTPUT

So far we have had one statement for input, the READ statement, and one statement for output, the PRINT statement. These allowed us to read data from cards, or write data on the printer. Often we would like to arrange the format of output in a way that is different from the standard format provided by the PRINT statement. Input has been more flexible; we have been able to accept REAL numbers either in the form without an exponent, such as 25.32, or the form with an exponent, such as 2.532E1. As well, we could arrange the input numbers in any columns of the card that we wanted, as long as each pair of numbers was separated by a at least one blank; there were no standard widths for <u>fields</u> on the card as there were on the printed page.

In this chapter we will introduce new versions of the READ and PRINT statements that use <u>format items</u> to specify exactly how each data item is to be read or printed. The old version of the READ and PRINT statements are format-free and are easier for the beginning programmer. The new formatted versions are more complicated, so that reading and printing can be precisely controlled.

FORMAT DESCRIPTION

Each formatted READ or PRINT statement has associated with it a labeled FORMAT specification. The label must be a number that appears just following the word READ or PRINT and is repeated in columns 1 to 5 of the following card, which contains the FORMAT specification, for example,

```
          PRINT 3,'SHE BOUGHT ',N,' EGGS'
3         FORMAT('1',A11,I2,A5)
```

The label 3 must be different from any other label in columns 1 to 5 in the program. If N has the value 12 then this is printed:

```
     SHE BOUGHT 12 EGGS
```

In the format specification, the '1' is the <u>carriage</u> <u>control</u> <u>character</u> and specifies that the line is to be printed on the top of a new page. Other carriage control characters will be given in this chapter. There are three format items, A11, I2, and A5. A11 specifies that 'SHE BOUGHT ' is to be printed in 11 positions, then I2 specifies that 12 is to be printed in the next 2 positions and finally A5 specifies the ' EGGS' is printed in the next five positions. Besides A format items, for alphabetic information, and I format items, for integers, there are others including E format items for numbers with exponents. Each data item in a formatted READ or PRINT must have a format item in the immediately following FORMAT specification. The data items are expressions in the Fortran language, that is, constants, literals, variables, or arithmetic expressions.

Basically, the format items describe the location of the data item on the card or printed line, the size of the field that is to be allotted to it, and the form that it is to take if alternate forms are possible. Alternate forms are possible for REAL numbers; as you already know, on input we can use either the exponent form, or the form with a decimal point and no exponent.

PRINTING REAL NUMBERS

The F format item lets you avoid printing exponents with REAL numbers. As well, it allows control over the number of digits printed to the right of the decimal point. For example,

```
          PRINT 8, 4/3.0, 2/3.0
8         FORMAT(' ', F10.4, F6.3)
```

will output

```
     bbbb1.3333b0.667
```

We have used b to represent a blank. Notice that the 8 is the label and is not a data value. We have used the ' ' (blank) carriage control character, which simply means that a new line is to be printed, just like what happens with the format-free PRINT statement. The first number after the F in each format item gives the total width of the field in which the data is to appear. The second number, after the period, is the number of digits to be printed to the right of the decimal point. The fractional parts are rounded off. Note that the numbers are right-justified in their fields and that the decimal point takes up one character position. If a minus sign occurs it also takes a position.

Printing REAL numbers in this way requires more thought on your part because you must be sure to leave enough room to the left of the decimal point. In the format-free form with the exponent there is always first a zero to the left of the decimal point and a fixed number of digits to the right.

For example, suppose the dimensions of a box in centimeters are expressed to the nearest hundredth of a centimeter and punched on a card as

    10.31   4.25   6.35

and you want the volume to the nearest hundredth of a cubic centimeter. Here is the program for doing this.

```
$JOB     CATHY TAFLER
         REAL LENGTH,WIDTH,HEIGHT,VOLUME
         READ,LENGTH,WIDTH,HEIGHT
         VOLUME=LENGTH*WIDTH*HEIGHT
         PRINT 1,VOLUME
1        FORMAT(' ',F14.2)
         RETURN
         END
$ENTRY
 10.31  4.25   6.35
```

The output will be

    bbbbbbbb278.24

We have one format item F14.2, as there is only one data item.

The printing of REAL numbers can also be controlled in the exponent form. The format-free PRINT instruction always prints the same number of digits to the right of the decimal point; compilers usually print seven. This represents about the maximum number of digits that are meaningful or <u>significant</u>. Since numbers are stored in memory locations that have a fixed size, only a limited precision is possible in representing them. You might, however, want to print fewer than seven digits to the right of the decimal. Also, you might want to allow fewer total print positions for the entire number. With a format item E12.3 you would be allowing a total of 12 character positions for the printing and 3 digits to the right of the decimal in the fractional part. For example,

```
     PRINT 7, -12.3665E1
7    FORMAT(' ',E13.4)
```

would produce an output

        bb-0.1237E 03

Notice that the number being printed is rounded off. The minimum
field width must be 7 plus the number of digits to the right of
the decimal; this allows for the sign, the zero to the left of
the point, the decimal point itself, and the four spaces for the
exponent. The number is right-justified in its field.

PRINTING CHARACTER STRINGS

    In the example with the volume of the box we did not include
our usual labeling of the results with VOLUME=. This was because
we have not yet said how to describe the format for a character
string. We do this by the format item Aw where w is the width of
the field to be allotted to the string. So for our box volume
program, if we had used the output statement

        PRINT 13,'VOLUME IS',VOLUME,' CUBIC CM'
13   FORMAT(' ',A9,F7.2,A9)

the output would have been

        VOLUME IS 278.24 CUBIC CM

Here we have reduced the size of the field used for printing the
numerical value and allowed character string fields of just the
right size to hold the strings that are printed. This permits
much greater flexibility for making attractive output. The width
w given in Aw should be the same as the number of characters in
the string to be printed.

PRINTING INTEGERS

    Using   the   formatted   PRINT   statement   requires   the
specification of the field width for all numbers, whether INTEGER
or REAL.   The format item for INTEGERs is Iw where w is the
number of character positions allotted to the number.   The
integer will be right-justified in this field. For example,

        PRINT 1,235,26,5261
1   FORMAT(' ',I4,I3,I6)

will produce the output

        b235b26bb5261

CARRIAGE CONTROL CHARACTERS

In SF/k each formatted PRINT statement has a carriage control character in its FORMAT specification. We have seen that ' ' (blank) causes printing to proceed to the next line (just as in the format-free PRINT statement) and that '1' causes a new page to be started. The other allowed carriage control characters are '0' (zero) for double spacing and '+' for overprinting.

```
        PRINT 2,'IS O A GREEK LETTER'
2       FORMAT('0',A21)
        PRINT 3,'    /'
3       FORMAT('+',A4)
```

This causes a blank line to be skipped before 'IS O A GREEK LETTER' is printed. Then, on top of this is printed '   /' which produces:

    IS Ø A GREEK LETTER

The '/' on top of the 'O' makes 'Ø'. Sometimes overprinting using the '+' is used to underline words in a title; first the title is printed and then it is overprinted with underscores (_).

Carriage control characters are used in every formatted PRINT statement to specify where the line is to be printed. They are not used in formatted READ statements, because reading always proceeds to the next input card.

READING NUMBERS

There is considerable flexibility in the input of INTEGER or REAL numbers provided by the format-free READ statement since the numbers need not occupy any specific fields on the card; REAL numbers can be presented in either the exponent form or simply with a decimal point. There are reasons why you might want to use the formatted READ statement for numbers. One of these is to insert a decimal point into an integer. This can be done by using an Fw.d format item. The number of card columns allotted to the integer is w. It is punched right-justified in this card field. It would be read into a REAL variable as if there were a decimal point punched so as to give d of its digits to the right of the point. As an example, suppose that measurements are given in centimeters and we want, on reading, to store the values in meters. We could use

```
        READ 4,WIDTH
4       FORMAT(F5.2)
```

If the integer 416 was right-justified in the first five columns of the card, it would be read as a real number whose value was 4.16, or 4.16E0, into the REAL variable WIDTH.

READING CHARACTER STRINGS

One awkward feature of using the format-free READ statement is that character strings must be surrounded by quotes. We may have available punched cards with data such as names and addresses already punched on them, and there are no quotes punched. Provided they are punched consistently in definite fields of the card they can be read using an Aw format item where w indicates the field width. For instance, if names are left-justified in the first 30 card columns, addresses in the next 42 columns and an integer code number in the next 7 columns, the following input statement would be appropriate:

```
      READ 4,NAME,ADRESS,CODE
4     FORMAT(A30,A42,I7)
```

Since each READ proceeds to a new input card, the last column on the card, after the CODE, will be ignored.

SKIPPING POSITIONS

Some format items do not correspond to any data items but have the effect of either skipping card columns on input or leaving blank positions on output. This is accomplished by writing a format item nX where n is the number of positions to be skipped. For example, the statement

```
      PRINT 3,'COST','VALUE','SALES'
3     FORMAT(' ',5X,A4,6X,A5,5X,A5)
```

would give a printed line suitable for heading columns. It would be

bbbbbCOSTbbbbbbVALUEbbbbbSALES

In this way you can space headings without having to include all the blanks in the literal itself. Notice that the X format items do not cause a data item to be read or printed.

READING AND PRINTING CHARACTER ARRAYS

Sometimes an entire card is to be read as a unit. If CARD is declared as CHARACTER*80 then a punched card can be read by:

```
      READ 1,CARD
1     FORMAT(A80)
```

There is a more convenient way to read the card when the program is to inspect various card columns. This is done by declaring CARD to be an array of 80 CHARACTER*1 elements and using the nAw format item. The card can be read by

```
      READ 6,CARD
6     FORMAT(80A1)
```

Here n is 80 and w is 1 meaning to read 80 single characters into CARD. The first column of the card goes into CARD(1), the second into CARD(2) and so on. Now the program can inspect any column of the card. In this example, column 1 is inspected:

```
      IF(CARD(1).EQ.'C')THEN DO
         PRINT 7,'COMMENT CARD: ',CARD
7        FORMAT(' ',A14,80A1)
      END IF
```

The n in nAw must be the same as the size of the array, in this case 80. The nAw format item will be used in the next chapter to show how the computer can read English text.

CHAPTER 10 SUMMARY

In this chapter we have introduced the formatted READ and PRINT statements. These use format items to give details about how to perform the input-output. The formatted PRINT statement has the form:

```
      PRINT label, variables separated by commas
label FORMAT(control, format items separated by commas)
```

The label is a number, repeated in the PRINT and FORMAT parts, that is different from other labels in the program. In the FORMAT part it must appear in columns 1 to 5. The control is a carriage control character and must be one of the following:

```
    ' ' (blank)    - means start a new line.
    '1' (one)      - means start a new page.
    '0' (zero)     - means double space.
    '+' (plus)     - means overprint the last printed line.
```

Formatted READ statements are similar to formatted PRINT statements but do not include a carriage control character:

```
      READ label, variables separated by commas
label FORMAT(format items separated by commas)
```

Variables listed in READ and PRINT statements cannot be entire arrays, with one exception. If the array has one dimension and is of character type, then the entire array can be read using the nAw format item. The following format items are available in SF/k.

Format Item	Example	Explanation
nX	3X	Skips the next n columns.
Iw	I5	Prints or reads an integer in a field of w columns.
Fw.d	F6.2	Prints or reads a REAL quantity without an exponent, e.g., 216.53, using a field of w columns. The number of digits to the right of the decimal point is given by d.
Ew.d	E12.5	Prints or reads a REAL quantity with an exponent, e.g., 0.21653E+03, using a field of w columns. The number of digits to the right of the decimal point is given by d.
Aw	A5	Prints or reads w characters.
nAw	80A1	Prints (reads) n sets of w characters from (into) an array of n CHARACTER*w elements.

The following restrictions and details should be noted. Each of n, w and d must be unsigned non-zero integer constants, as in 80A1. REAL quantities are rounded off before printing.

Numbers read or printed by the I, F and E format items are right-justified in their fields. The variable or literal that corresponds to Aw must be w characters long.

Each variable in a formatted READ or PRINT must correspond to an I, F, E or A format item. The X format item can precede or be intermixed with I, F, E and A items, but must not be last in a list of format items.

Here are examples illustrating the use of formatted READ and PRINT statements.

```
        PRINT 1, 24, 5
1       FORMAT(' ',I2,3X,I2)    (prints 24bbbb5)
        PRINT 2, 61.248E+00
2       FORMAT(' ',F7.2)        (prints bb61.25)
        READ 3, CARD
3       FORMAT(80A1)            (reads 80 characters)
```

CHAPTER 10 EXERCISES

1. What do the following statements print? Assume J is INTEGER, Y is REAL and C is CHARACTER*15.

```
      J=29
      Y=5.427
      C='TRY FORMATTING'
      PRINT 1,J,Y,C
1     FORMAT(' ',1X,I3,F6.2,2X,A14)
      PRINT 2,C,Y
2     FORMAT('0',A14,F6.1)
      PRINT 3,'___ _____'
3     FORMAT('+',A14)
```

2. What do the following statements print? Assume CREDIT is an INTEGER variable.

```
      CREDIT=2154
      PRINT 1,'OCTOBER CREDIT: ',CREDIT
1     FORMAT(' ',A16,I5)
      CREDIT=CREDIT-10000
      PRINT 2,'AS UPDATED: ',CREDIT
2     FORMAT(' ',A12,5X,I5)
      PRINT 3,'YOU WIN ',100000000
3     FORMAT('0',A8,I10)
      PRINT 4,10000
4     FORMAT('0',6X,I6)
      PRINT 5,CREDIT
5     FORMAT(' ',6X,I6)
      PRINT 6,'_____'
6     FORMAT(' ',6X,A6)
      PRINT 7,'TOTAL',2154
7     FORMAT('0',A5,1X,I6)
```

3. Write a program that reads all the characters on a card and prints them all. Use the A format item so that quotes are not required on the card.

4. The first five columns of a particular card contain five digits. Give a formatted READ statement that reads those five digits into INTEGER variables A, B, C, D and E.

5. The layout of stock ordering cards for P & A Groceries is:

columns	contents
1-5	stock number
6-12	supplier's name
13-14	month first ordered
15-16	year first ordered
17-27	item name

Give a READ statement that reads the stock number and the product name into variables declared by

```
INTEGER STOCK
CHARACTER*11 ITEM
```

The READ statement should skip over columns 6-16.

6. Write a program that prints out a calendar. The program should read the day of the week for January 1 and the year. The program can determine whether it is a leap year via the IF statement:

```
IF(MOD(YEAR,4).EQ.0)THEN DO
    FEB=29
ELSE DO
    FEB=28
    END IF
```

As used here the built-in function MOD will return a value of zero for years that can be exactly divided by 4. If your program prints the calendar for the entire year, it will produce 12 pages of output, if it uses one page for each month. You should use less paper by making your program read the number of a month and print the calendar only for that one month or by putting several months on one page. Can you get the entire year's calendar on one page?

7. You are to write a program for the First Gibraltar Bank to print monthly statements for checking accounts. Here is a sample monthly statement:

FIRST GIBRALTAR BANK

MS. MARIE BEYER
2116 OAK BLVD.
CLINTONVILLE

FOR PERIOD ENDED	ACCOUNT NO.	DATE FWD.	BALANCE FWD.
DEC 14,1975	8881-605223	NOV 16	114142

CHECKS	DEPOSITS	DATE	BALANCE
2000		NOV 21	112142
1500		NOV 22	110642
1685		NOV 25	108957
	84146	NOV 28	193103
15449		DEC 08	177654
6012		DEC 14	171642
			(FINAL BALANCE)

DEPOSITS	1	84146	
CHECKS	5	26646	

This statement was printed as a result of reading the following cards:

```
DEC  14,1975
MS.  MARIE  BEYER
2116  OAK  BLVD.
CLINTONVILLE
8881-605223
NOV  16  114142
NOV  21    2000
NOV  22    1500
NOV  25    1685
NOV  28   84146CR
DEC  08   15449
DEC  14    6012
XXX  00        0
```

Your program should read a set of cards, such as the above, and print a monthly statement.

CHAPTER 11

THE COMPUTER
CAN READ ENGLISH

In the subset SF/4 you learned how to handle character strings. You learned how to compare strings, either for the purpose of recognizing particular strings or for putting various strings in order. Now that you have been introduced to arrays in SF/5 and formatted input and output in SF/6 you can do many more things with character strings. In this chapter we will show how these capabilities can be used to create the illusion that the computer does things that we normally associate with people, and we might say that it is "intelligent". We say it has an artificial intelligence, since it is of course <u>not</u> human, and thinking is what humans do. The field of artificial intelligence in computer science concerns itself with getting the computer to perform acts that we think of as the province of humans. Of course, when we see how it is done, we realize it is just a mechanical process. It has to be mechanical or a machine could not do it. But if you do not know how the "trick" is performed, it does seem as if the machine can "think".

The field of artificial intelligence is involved with many different activities of man as imitated by machine, but one of the most interesting is the way that a machine is made to deal with statements made in <u>natural language</u>. We call a language, like English, a natural language because it evolved over a period of time through use. A language like Fortran is a <u>formal language</u>. It has been defined, it is unambiguous and it is really very limited. Trying to get computers to deal with natural language is a major task. We would like to be able to write questions in natural language and have the computer provide answers to our questions from a bank of information. This is a goal in information retrieval systems.

We have not yet got very far along the way towards question-answering systems in natural language, but it is clear there are basic "skills" the computer must have to ever cope with this at all. One of these skills is the ability to read.

WORD RECOGNITION

When you first learn how to read you must learn to recognize words. To do this you must recognize what a word is. You learn the basic characters, the letters, then you learn that a word is a string of characters with a blank in front and a blank after it and no blanks in between. We are now going to write a program that will input a line of text and split it up into words. To simplify the job, we will begin our problem without any punctuation marks in the text. The method of dealing with problem solving by simplification is very helpful. Solve a simpler problem before you try a harder one. We will learn to cope with punctuation marks later. Our solution tree for this problem is:

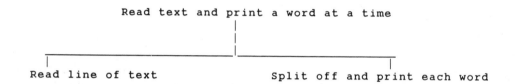

All the parts are straightforward except "Split off and print each word." We will refine it further:

```
DO for each character of text
    IF(character is not a blank) THEN DO
        add character to word
    ELSE DO
        IF(there is a word)THEN DO
            Print word and prepare for next word
        END IF
    END IF
End of DO loop
```


We must choose a way of storing our character strings that will allow us to have access to one character at a time. The way that this is done in Fortran is to store each string in an array of locations each of which has the space to hold one character. For instance, for holding TEXT we choose an array of 80 elements, each to hold one character. It would be declared as

CHARACTER*1 TEXT(80)

To read the contents of a data card into this array we can use the formatted input statement

```
          READ 5,TEXT
5         FORMAT(80A1)
```

This will cause column 1 of the card to be read into TEXT(1), column 2 to go to TEXT(2), and so on. If we use a second array to hold a word of maximum length 20 characters declared by CHARACTER*1 WORD(20) we can move characters one at a time from the TEXT array to the WORD array by an assignment statement such as WORD(LETTER) = TEXT(COLUMN). The index LETTER will keep track of the proper character position in WORD, the index COLUMN the proper character position in TEXT.

```
$JOB     JULIE SANDORFI
C READ TEXT AND PRINT A WORD AT A TIME
         CHARACTER*1 TEXT(80),WORD(20)
         INTEGER COLUMN,LETTER,FILL
C        READ A LINE OF TEXT
         READ 5,TEXT
5        FORMAT(80A1)
C        INITIALIZE LOOP, SET WORD TO RECEIVE FIRST LETTER
         LETTER=1
C        SPLIT OFF AND PRINT EACH WORD
         DO 10 COLUMN=1,80
            IF(TEXT(COLUMN).NE.' ')THEN DO
C              ADD CHARACTER TO WORD
               WORD(LETTER)=TEXT(COLUMN)
               LETTER=LETTER+1
            ELSE DO
C              SEE IF THERE IS A WORD
               IF(LETTER.NE.1)THEN DO
C                 PRINT WORD AND PREPARE FOR NEXT WORD
C                 FILL OUT WORD WITH BLANKS
                  DO 7 FILL=LETTER,20
                     WORD(FILL)=' '
7                 CONTINUE
                  PRINT 8,WORD
8                 FORMAT(' ',20A1)
                  LETTER=1
               END IF
            END IF
10          CONTINUE
         RETURN
         END
$ENTRY
 SEE THE COMPUTER READ
```

The output from this program will be

```
SEE
THE
COMPUTER
READ
```

Again, we see how the English entries in the solution tree become comments in the program. We have added two more comments concerning loop initialization and filling out WORD with blanks. Since the array WORD is used over and over again, it either must all be set to blanks after each use or the remaining parts set to blank when the correct characters are in place.

WORDS WITH PUNCTUATION

We want now to modify the previous program to do the same thing when there are punctuation marks present, that is, find the words in a text and print them out one by one. We usually try to build on the previous work so that we do not need to do everything from scratch. If we could reduce the text with the punctuation marks to one without such marks, we could then use the old program. The solution tree would be:

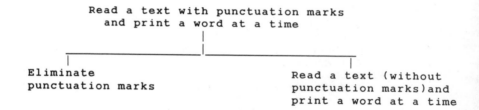

Our problem is to eliminate punctuation marks from the text. This is accomplished in this program segment:

```
DO for each character of punctuated text
   IF(character is not punctuation mark)THEN DO
      Move character to new text
   END IF
End of DO loop
```

The program for this will be:

```
C ELIMINATE PUNCTUATION MARKS FROM TEXT
        CHARACTER*1 TEXT1(80),TEXT2(80)
        INTEGER I1,I2,FILL
        I2=1
        READ 1,TEXT1
1       FORMAT(80A1)
        DO 10 I1=1,80
C           IF CHARACTER OF TEXT1 NOT A PUNCTUATION MARK,
C           MOVE IT TO TEXT2
            IF(TEXT1(I1).NE.',',AND.TEXT1(I1).NE.'.'.AND.
     +          TEXT1(I1).NE.'?'.AND.TEXT1(I1).NE.':'.AND.
     +          TEXT1(I1).NE.';'.AND.TEXT1(I1).NE.')'.AND.
     +          TEXT1(I1).NE.'(')THEN DO
            TEXT2(I2)=TEXT1(I1)
            I2=I2+1
            END IF
10          CONTINUE
C       FILL TEXT2 WITH BLANKS
        DO 20 FILL=I2,80
            TEXT2(FILL)=' '
20          CONTINUE
        PRINT 30,TEXT2
30      FORMAT(' ',80A1)
        RETURN
        END
$ENTRY
THIS TEXT HAS COMMAS, PARENTHESES (TWO OF THEM), AND A PERIOD.
```

The output for this program is

THIS TEXT HAS COMMAS PARENTHESES TWO OF THEM AND A PERIOD

This program for eliminating punctuation marks could now be combined with the program for reading text without punctuation marks word by word to produce a program for reading a text with punctuation marks word by word.

NAME RECOGNITION

You often want to sort names alphabetically, and this is a problem if the names are written out in full with the surname last. For a name like FRANCES CORLEY PHILLIPS the sorting must be on PHILLIPS. We are not certain in general how many names precede the surname. Some people have one, some two, some even three or four. We would like to write a program that takes a full name and rewrites it with the surname first then initials like

        PHILLIPS, F. C.

Since in a sorting process blanks have a lower value than any character, it is important that the position and number of the blanks be consistent from one person's name to another, so we will have one blank after the comma and one after each period.

This book is set by a computer so that the words in any line are both left and right justified; there is one non-blank character in the leftmost and one in the rightmost position of each line of text. This is accomplished by inserting extra blanks between words so that some have two or three blanks instead of one. It is a job that used to require a skilled linotype operator. You will notice that the computer never hyphenates words, and this may mean that some lines have rather a lot of blanks. This happens when the first word of the next line is a long one. We will speak more of text editors a little later, but now we are working on reading a person's name and bringing it to a standard form. We want the standard form so that a list of names can be sequenced alphabetically. As we read the full name initially we should not count on there being only one blank between names.

The full name is a string of characters which is a series of words separated by one or more blanks. The last of the series is the surname. We now have two different ways of handling this problem. One is to start at the end of the string and read the surname backwards until a blank is reached; after finding the surname, the process of extracting the initials from the first names can proceed using a loop. Another method would be to read the character position of the beginning of each name into an array location, keeping count of the number of names in the full name. Then the name in the form of surname followed by initials can be assembled. We will use this method.

We will use the one-dimensional array variable TEXT for the name as input, the one-dimensional array NAME to store the name in form with initials following surname. We will assume that TEXT contains a surname and one to seven first names. The character position in TEXT of the start of each word will be recorded in an integer array START. The words are counted in the integer variable WORDNO. The last name must be followed by blanks.

Here is the program:

```
$JOB     GLEN MACEWEN
C CHANGE FORM OF NAME TO SURNAME FOLLOWED BY INITIALS
         CHARACTER*1 TEXT(80),NAME(80),LASTCH
         INTEGER START(8),WORDNO,COLUMN,I,INIT,FILL
C        FULL NAME IS READ INTO 'TEXT' AND THEN PUT IN STANDARD
C           FORM IN 'NAME'.
C        BEGINNING OF EACH WORD IS RECORDED IN 'START'
C        LAST INSPECTED CHARACTER OF TEXT IS 'LASTCH'
         READ 10,TEXT
10       FORMAT(80A1)
         LASTCH=' '
         WORDNO=0
         COLUMN=1
         WHILE(COLUMN.LE.80)DO
            IF(TEXT(COLUMN).NE.' '.AND.LASTCH.EQ.' ')THEN DO
C              RECORD POSITION OF START OF THIS WORD
               WORDNO=WORDNO+1
               START(WORDNO)=COLUMN
               END IF
            LASTCH=TEXT(COLUMN)
            COLUMN=COLUMN+1
            END WHILE
C        MOVE SURNAME INTO BEGINNING OF NAME
         COLUMN=START(WORDNO)
         I=1
         WHILE(TEXT(COLUMN).NE.' ')DO
            NAME(I)=TEXT(COLUMN)
            I=I+1
            COLUMN=COLUMN+1
            END WHILE
         NAME(I)=','
         I=I+1
C        ADD INITIALS TO SURNAME
         INIT=1
         WHILE(INIT.LT.WORDNO)DO
            NAME(I)=' '
            NAME(I+1)=TEXT(START(INIT))
            NAME(I+2)='.'
            I=I+3
            INIT=INIT+1
            END WHILE
C        FILL OUT NAME WITH BLANKS
         DO 30 FILL=I,80
            NAME(FILL)=' '
30          CONTINUE
         PRINT 40,NAME
40       FORMAT(' ',80A1)
         RETURN
         END
$ENTRY
 JAMES NAIRN PATTERSON HUME
```

The output for this program is

    HUME, J. N. P.

WORD STATISTICS

We have learned to read words of a text, eliminate punctuation marks and rearrange words and parts of words as we did with the surname and initials. Another important use of a computer in dealing with words involves keeping statistics about the lengths of words. Different authors have different patterns of use of words and this shows up in the frequency with which they use words of different lengths. Some authors use a lot of long words; others rarely do.

In this section we will read a text and from it prepare a frequency distribution of word lengths. To add a little extra interest to this problem, we will display the results in graphic form. For instance, we will have a display like this for output:

        LENGTH OF WORD   FREQUENCY
              1   ***
              2   ******
              3   ********
              4   *****

This display, called a histogram, represents the result of analyzing the frequency of different word lengths in a text. It shows that there were 3 one-letter words, 6 two-letter words, 8 three-letter words, and 5 four-letter words.

We will use what we have learned so far about reading words, but instead of forming the words we will just count the number of letters, then after each word add 1 to the value stored in an array location corresponding to the letter count. We will use the array FREQ to store the letter counts; FREQ(4) will store the number of four-letter words. We will assume a maximum of 20 letters in a word and that there are no punctuation marks. We will assume that the total number of words is small enough that there are no more than 30 words of any given length. Here is our program:

```
$JOB      PHYLLIS GOTLIEB
C DETERMINE FREQUENCIES OF WORD LENGTHS
          CHARACTER*1 TEXT(80),STARS(30)
          INTEGER FREQ(20),I,COUNT,J,COLUMN
C         INITIALIZE FREQUENCY ARRAY
          DO 2 I=1,20
              FREQ(I)=0
2         CONTINUE
          READ 5,TEXT
5         FORMAT(80A1)
          WHILE(TEXT(1).NE.'+')DO
            COUNT=0
            DO 10 COLUMN=1,80
               IF(TEXT(COLUMN).NE.' ')THEN DO
C                 COUNT LETTERS IN WORD
                  COUNT=COUNT+1
               ELSE DO
                  IF(COUNT.NE.0)THEN DO
C                    ADD WORD LENGTH TO FREQUENCY
                     FREQ(COUNT)=FREQ(COUNT)+1
                     COUNT=0
                  END IF
               END IF
10          CONTINUE
            READ 12,TEXT
12          FORMAT(80A1)
          END WHILE
C         PRINT LABELS ON OUTPUT
          PRINT 15,'LENGTH OF WORD','FREQUENCY'
15        FORMAT(' ',A14,6X,A9)
C         PRINT DISPLAY OF ASTERISKS
          DO 40 I=1,20
C            PUT STARS INTO ARRAY, PADDED WITH BLANKS
             DO 20 J=1,30
                IF(J.LE.FREQ(I))THEN DO
                   STARS(J)='*'
                ELSE DO
                   STARS(J)=' '
                END IF
20           CONTINUE
             PRINT 30,I,STARS
30           FORMAT(' ',I7,13X,30A1)
40        CONTINUE
       RETURN
       END
$ENTRY
 ROSES ARE RED
 VIOLETS ARE BLUE
 HONEY IS SWEET
 AND SO ARE YOU
+
```

The output for this is


```
    LENGTH OF WORD        FREQUENCY
          1
          2             **
          3             ******
          4             *
          5             ***
          6
          7             *
               . . .
         20
```

You can see how similar the program is to the one for reading
names. In the chapter on SF/7 we will see how to make standard
parts of programs available as modules for use in other programs.

READING FORTRAN

We have been reading English text and performing operations
on it, or as the result of it. All these operations, we see, are
absolutely mechanical but give the impression that the computer
is capable of doing things we think of as "intelligent work".
One of the fields of artificial intelligence that has been
explored is the translation from one language to another. The
translation of one natural language into another, such as English
to French, has had only qualified success. It works, but not
well when the text is ambiguous or difficult. The translations
are not good literature, to say the least.

But computers are being used for language translation every
day, for the translation of programming languages into machine
languages. The reason this is possible is that programming
languages are well defined and quite limited.

Your Fortran programs are translated by the compiler program
into machine language programs before execution. We want to look
a little at how this can be done. The different parts of the
program are placed on separate cards for input. Right after
column 6 of the card there is a keyword with one exception, and
that is if the statement is an assignment statement. These
keywords are limited to a very small list; they include READ,
PRINT, RETURN, WHILE, CONTINUE, DO, IF, END. We can thus decide
whether or not a statement is an assignment statement by reading
the first word after column 6. If it is not one of the keywords
it is an assignment statement.

We will look later at the problem of actually preparing a
translation for the various types of statements, but at this
stage you can at least see how the keywords can be used in the
translation process.

CHAPTER 11 SUMMARY

In this chapter we have shown how the computer can, in a sense, understand English. The computer can recognize words by scanning for their beginnings and endings. Typically, words in English are surrounded by blanks or special characters; programs can be written which separate out words by searching for these characters. Due to the great speed of computers, they sometimes have the appearance of being intelligent, in spite of the fact that their basic mode of operation is very simplistic, such as seeing if a given character is a blank. Fortran compilers, such as the Watfiv-S compiler, have been developed to read text which looks somewhat like English; the text which it has been designed to read is Fortran programs.

CHAPTER 11 EXERCISES

1. A palindrome is a word or phrase which is spelled the same backwards and forwards. The following are examples of word palindromes: "I", "mom", "deed" and "level". Blanks and punctuation are ignored in phrase palindromes, for example, "Madam, in Eden I'm Adam" and "A man, a plan, a canal, Panama". Write a program which reads a string and determines if it is a palindrome.

2. You are to write a program which will help in reviewing a script to determine its suitability for television screening. Your program is to give a list of the frequency of use of the following unacceptable words:

    'PHOOEY' 'SHUCKS' 'JEEPERS' 'GOLLY'

Make up a few lines of script to test out your program.

3. You are employed by an English teacher who insists that "and" should not be preceded by a comma. Hence, "Crosby, Stills, Nash and Young" is acceptable, but "Merril, Fynch, and Lynn" is not. Write a program which reads lines of text, searches for unacceptable commas, removes them, and makes stern remarks such as the English teacher would make about errors.

4. Write a program which reads text and then prints it so that its left and right margins are vertical. First the program is to read the number of characters to print per line. Whenever enough words for one line have been collected, blanks are inserted between words to expand the line to the desired width. Then the expanded line is printed.

5. Write a program that reads a Fortran program and prints the first word on each card appearing after column 6. Note that there may be blanks in front of the word. Assume that a blank

follows the first word. In a Fortran program it is not necessary
to have a blank after a keyword or variable identifier.

CHAPTER 12

SF/7: SUBPROGRAMS

In this subset we will be introducing the idea of subprograms. The purpose of having subsidiary programs or subprograms is so that a larger program can be divided into parts. In this way we "divide and conquer" a complicated problem. Sometimes a part of the solution of one problem can be used in many different problems, and making it into a subprogram creates a module or building block which can be used in many programs.

DEFINITION OF A SUBPROGRAM

The process of sorting a list alphabetically is a very common one; if we had a subprogram for doing this we might use it frequently. The subprogram must take in certain information, in particular the name of the list of items say LIST and the number of items N in the list. It must then give out information, namely the sorted list. We say that the subprogram has two input parameters, LIST and N, and one output parameter LIST, the list sorted in alphabetic order. To define a subprogram that will do this we must give it a name, say SORT, and begin the subprogram definition in this way:

SUBROUTINE SORT(LIST,N)

This gives the keyword SUBROUTINE followed by the name of the subroutine. In parentheses is a list of the subprogram parameters. Some of these are input to the subprogram; some are output from the subprogram. In this case LIST is both an input and an output parameter. Each subprogram must contain declarations for all its parameters. The declarations must give the parameter types.

The declaration for the variable LIST must show the length of each element, we choose 30 characters as before, and the number of elements in the array LIST must be the same as declared in the main program. We will let it have 50 elements. We thus have declarations

```
INTEGER N
CHARACTER*30 LIST(50)
```

As well as these declarations for the parameters of the subprogram we will also declare some variables that are used in the subprogram but are neither input nor output. Following our sorting program of Chapter 9 we will declare integer variables I, LAST, LIMIT, SORTED and character variable TEMP.

Here is the complete definition for the SORT subprogram:

```
C THIS SUBPROGRAM SORTS A LIST OF NAMES
      SUBROUTINE SORT(LIST,N)
C     DECLARATIONS FOR PARAMETERS
      INTEGER N
      CHARACTER*30 LIST(50)
C     DECLARATION FOR LOCAL VARIABLES
      INTEGER I,LAST,LIMIT,SORTED
      CHARACTER*30 TEMP
C     SWAP ELEMENTS OF LIST UNTIL SORTED
      SORTED=0
      LAST=N
      WHILE(SORTED.NE.1.AND.LAST.GE.2)DO
        SORTED=1
        LIMIT=LAST-1
        DO 25 I=1,LIMIT
          IF(LIST(I).GT.LIST(I+1))THEN DO
            SORTED=0
            TEMP=LIST(I)
            LIST(I)=LIST(I+1)
            LIST(I+1)=TEMP
          END IF
25        CONTINUE
        LAST=LAST-1
      END WHILE
      RETURN
      END
```

In SF/k, subprograms are placed after the main program's END just before the $ENTRY

USING SUBPROGRAMS

We have just constructed a subprogram for sorting a list alphabetically. Now we must learn how to use this subprogram. You will notice that the reading of the list to be sorted and the printing of it after it is sorted is not included in the subprogram. We could now write a main program that will use the SORT subprogram and handle the input and output. We will read, sort, and print a list of names as we did in Chapter 9.

```
$JOB    DON IVEY
C THIS PROGRAM USES THE SUBPROGRAM SORT
        CHARACTER*30 NAME(50)
        INTEGER NUMBER,I
C       READ NUMBER THEN LIST OF NAMES
        READ,NUMBER
        DO 5 I=1,NUMBER
          READ 3, NAME(I)
3         FORMAT(A20)
5         CONTINUE
        CALL SORT(NAME,NUMBER)
C       PRINT SORTED LIST OF NAMES
        DO 10 I=1,NUMBER
          PRINT 8,NAME(I)
8         FORMAT(' ',A20)
10        CONTINUE
        RETURN
        END
(include complete SORT subprogram here)
$ENTRY
 3
SCOTT, G.D.
COLLINS, A.
NEWMAN, C.
```

You can see how convenient it is to have a subprogram. The single statement

        CALL SORT(NAME,NUMBER)

causes the list to be sorted.

SUBROUTINE SORT (LIST, N)
parameters

argument

ARGUMENTS AND PARAMETERS

We have introduced two words in connection with subprograms, the words "arguments" and "parameters". The parameters are the identifiers used in the definition of a subprogram for information that is to be fed into a subprogram or to be given out. Arguments are the expressions (often variables) in the calling subprogram that are to be put into correspondence with the subprogram parameters. And there must be a one-to-one correspondence between the number and type of the arguments and the parameters.

You may have guessed that there is something different about parameters. The fact is that no space reservations are made for the parameters because the space needed is already reserved in the calling program for the arguments. All references to

parameters in a subprogram actually refer to the corresponding
argument. This is done by means of pointers to the locations
that hold the arguments.

These pointers are set automatically at the time the
subprogram is called. When the subprogram is executing, changes
to the value of a parameter cause the the corresponding argument
to be altered. In our example, the argument NAME is in
correspondence with the parameter LIST and the argument NUMBER
with the parameter N. When the statement

     LIST(I)=LIST(I+1)

of the subprogram is executed, it is equivalent to the statement

     NAME(I)=NAME(I+1)

being executed.

Here is a diagram to show the association between parameters
and arguments, and the variables local to the subroutine SORT.

```
     NAME     <------LIST
     NUMBER   <------N
                 I
                 LAST
                 LIMIT
                 SORTED
                 TEMP
```

Because the parameters of a subprogram are associated with
arguments at the time the subprogram is called, it means that a
subprogram may be used in the same program with a different set
of arguments in another CALL statement. Notice that I, LAST,
LIMIT, SORTED, TEMP, the local variables, are ordinary variables
in the subprogram and do not refer to any variables in the
calling program. These local variables cannot be referenced
outside the subprogram. Each time the subprogram is called,
these variables must be given values before being used, because
their values from any previous calls may be discarded.

CONSTANTS AS ARGUMENTS

We will do another simple example to show how constants can
be used as arguments. Suppose we write a subprogram that will
add the elements of an integer array, ARRAY, of N elements and
call the total SUM. Let us call the subprogram TOTAL.

```
C ADD THE N ELEMENTS OF ARRAY
      SUBROUTINE TOTAL(ARRAY,N,SUM)
      INTEGER N,SUM
      INTEGER ARRAY(N)
      INTEGER I
      SUM=0
      DO 5 I=1,N
         SUM=SUM+ARRAY(I)
5        CONTINUE
      RETURN
      END
```

Here the number of elements of ARRAY is given as N. This kind of declaration is possible only in subprograms. Notice that the N must be declared as integer before ARRAY can be declared as having a dimension N. Now let us write a calling program for this. This program finds the gross total for a number of outstanding bills.

```
$JOB     LARRY LAFAVE
C THIS IS A MAIN PROGRAM THAT USES SUBPROGRAM TOTAL
      INTEGER BILL(5),I,GROSS
      DO 10 I=1,5
         READ,BILL(I)
10       CONTINUE
      CALL TOTAL(BILL,5,GROSS)
      PRINT,'GROSS=',GROSS
      RETURN
      END
(include definition of TOTAL subprogram here)
$ENTRY
(data items are placed one to a card)
 25  36  21  7  2
```

The output will be

```
    GROSS=        91
```

In this example, notice that the argument BILL is in correspondence with the parameter ARRAY. References in the subroutine to ARRAY(1) will point at BILL(1). It is essential that the number of elements of the array BILL be the same as the number of elements of ARRAY. Since the parameter N is given the value 5 the array BILL must have 5 elements.

Sometimes subroutines involving arrays have two parameters, one giving the maximum size of array ever used, the other the actual number of elements being used.

Notice that the same variable identifier I is used in the main program and also as a variable in the subprogram TOTAL.

These are treated as absolutely separate variables. These is no
need to worry about accidental coincidences between names of
variables.   Inside the subprogram, the local one is used
exclusively. Outside the subprogram, the one local to the
subprogram is not visible. We will show later how it is possible
for programs and subprograms to share variables in common.

FUNCTIONS

     There are really two kinds of subprograms. The ones we have
described so far are called <u>subroutine</u> <u>subprograms</u> or subroutines
for short.   We will now describe a quite different kind of
subprogram called a <u>function</u> <u>subprogram</u> or function for short.

     Function subprograms may have many arguments but give as a
result a single value. To understand this we will look at a
function that we have already been using, the square root
function SQRT. To use the function we write:

     SQRT (number whose square root is wanted)

There is one argument provided to this function and the function
itself provides the result, namely the required square root.

     To program a function subprogram ourselves we do exactly what
we did for a subroutine subprogram, but we add two things.
Ahead of the name of the function we write FUNCTION preceded by
the type (INTEGER or REAL) of the value of the function that is
returned as a result.   Then before the RETURN and END that
terminates the body of the subprogram, we write an assignment
statement whose left-hand side is the name of the function and
whose right-hand side is an expression whose value is what is to
be returned as a result. For example, if we were preparing a
function subprogram for the function SQRT, it would be of the
form

          REAL FUNCTION SQRT(NUMBER)
          REAL NUMBER
          (declarations of variables other than parameter)
          (statements of function subprogram)
          SQRT=value to be returned
          RETURN
          END

This would be the function subprogram definition and would be
included after the END of the main program. SQRT is a built-in
function; it is already stored in the computer with the
particular Fortran compiler that you are using. So there is no
need to include its definition.

     A function that is not built into the Fortran compiler is one
to determine the length of a string of characters.   When it is

used in the form LENGTH(string) it returns a value whose type is INTEGER. It has just one argument. We would have the function subprogram defined as:

```
INTEGER FUNCTION LENGTH(STRING)
(declarations)
(statements of function subprogram)
LENGTH=expression giving value to be returned
RETURN
END
```

We can program a function to find the length of a string provided one character, such as a blank, is not allowed in the string, we cannot do it for any string in general. The string for this particular subprogram must be stored as an array of 20 elements each holding one character. Here is a complete definition for the function subprogram called LENGTH.

```
C THIS FUNCTION FINDS LENGTH OF STRING ENDING WITH A BLANK
      INTEGER FUNCTION LENGTH(STRING)
      CHARACTER*1 STRING(20)
      INTEGER I
      I=1
C     SCAN STRING UNTIL BLANK REACHED
      WHILE(STRING(I).NE.' ')DO
         I=I+1
         END WHILE
      LENGTH=I-1
      RETURN
      END
```

Here is a program that uses the function LENGTH, so it must include a declaration specifying LENGTH to have an INTEGER value.

```
C READ WORDS AND DETERMINE THEIR LENGTHS
      INTEGER LENGTH
      CHARACTER*30 WORD
      READ 10,WORD
10    FORMAT(A30)
      WHILE(WORD.NE.'ZZZ')DO
         PRINT 20,LENGTH(WORD)
20       FORMAT(' ',I2)
         READ 30,WORD
30       FORMAT(A30)
         END WHILE
      RETURN
      END
(include LENGTH subprogram here)
$ENTRY
ELEPHANT
DIAGRAM
VECTOR
ZZZ
```

The output for this program is
```
8
7
6
```

EXAMPLES OF SUBROUTINES AND FUNCTIONS

There are two kinds of subprograms in Fortran: subroutines and functions. Essentially, subroutines allow you to invent new Fortran statements, while functions allow you to invent new operations. We will give examples of these two possibilities.

Suppose we wish to determine the larger of two integer numbers. We could write a subroutine to find the larger one; this is done in the following program:

```
$JOB    STEWART LEE
C THIS IS THE MAIN PROGRAM USING A SUBROUTINE
      INTEGER DATA1,DATA2,MAXI
      READ,DATA1,DATA2
      CALL LARGER(DATA1,DATA2,MAXI)
      PRINT,'THE LARGER IS',MAXI
      RETURN
      END
C THIS SUBROUTINE FINDS THE LARGER OF 2 NUMBERS
      SUBROUTINE LARGER(FIRST,SECOND,RESULT)
      INTEGER FIRST,SECOND,RESULT
      IF(FIRST.GT.SECOND)THEN DO
         RESULT=FIRST
      ELSE DO
         RESULT=SECOND
         END IF
      RETURN
      END
$ENTRY
  5  31
```

When the LARGER subroutine is called, via the statement

```
      CALL LARGER(DATA1,DATA2,MAXI)
```

the parameter FIRST is in correspondence with DATA1, SECOND with DATA2 and RESULT with MAXI. The LARGER subroutine is entered and RESULT, which is really MAXI, is set to the larger of FIRST and SECOND, which are really DATA1 and DATA2. When the LARGER subroutine reaches its RETURN statement, execution returns to the statement just beyond the CALL statement, which is the PRINT statement. Given the data values 5 and 31, the program will print

```
THE LARGER IS          31
```

Conceptually, our subroutine provides us with a new Fortran statement which we can use whenever we want to find the larger of two numbers.

This has been a very simple example; if you were writing such a simple program as this one you would not bother to use a subprogram.

We could have found the larger number by writing a function rather than a subroutine. A function named BIGGER is used in the following version of the program.

```
$JOB    RON BAECKER
C THIS IS A MAIN PROGRAM USING A FUNCTION
      INTEGER BIGGER
      INTEGER DATA1,DATA2,MAXI
      READ,DATA1,DATA2
      MAXI=BIGGER(DATA1,DATA2)
      PRINT,'THE LARGER IS',MAXI
      RETURN
      END
C THIS FUNCTION RETURNS THE BIGGER OF 2 NUMBERS
      INTEGER FUNCTION BIGGER(FIRST,SECOND)
      INTEGER FIRST,SECOND
      IF(FIRST.GT.SECOND)THEN DO
         BIGGER=FIRST
      ELSE DO
         BIGGER=SECOND
         END IF
      RETURN
      END
$ENTRY
 5   31
```

This job will print the same as the previous job, namely:

THE LARGER IS   31

The BIGGER subprogram is a function because it has a type, namely INTEGER, in its definition. This type must also be declared in the main program. The name BIGGER appears in the first INTEGER declaration. Since BIGGER is a function, it must explicitly return a value. This is done by giving BIGGER a value as is done in either

      BIGGER=FIRST or BIGGER=SECOND

The BIGGER function is entered as a result of the fact that its name appears in the assignment statement:

      MAXI=BIGGER(DATA1,DATA2)

When the BIGGER function is entered, the parameter FIRST is in correspondence with DATA1 and SECOND with DATA2. BIGGER is given the value of the larger of FIRST and SECOND. The statement,

      RETURN

both terminates the BIGGER function and returns the value of BIGGER so it can be assigned to MAXI. Conceptually, our function provides us with a new arithmetic operation which we can use in arithmetic expressions. We could without changing the printed

answer have replaced the assignment to MAXI and the immediately
following PRINT statement by the statement

        PRINT,'THE LARGER IS',BIGGER(DATA1,DATA2)

    Our example subprograms LARGER and BIGGER illustrate the
following differences between subroutines and functions. The
definition of a function must include the type of the function
both in the main program and in the first line of the function
definition, a subroutine does not have any type.

The "returned value" for a function must match the type of the
function. A subroutine is entered when it is invoked via the
CALL statement. A function is entered when its name appears in
an expression, such as the right-hand side of an assignment
statement.

SUBPROGRAMS AND NESTING

    Once a subroutine has been defined, it can be used, via the
CALL statement, just like any other Fortran statement. It is
even possible to use CALL statements inside subprograms. We will
give simple examples to illustrate this. The following job
prints the largest of its three data values.

```
$JOB    SCOTT GRAHAM
C THIS PRINTS THE LARGEST OF ITS 3 DATA ITEMS
      INTEGER DATA1,DATA2,DATA3,MAXI
      READ,DATA1,DATA2,DATA3
      CALL LARGST(DATA1,DATA2,DATA3,MAXI)
      PRINT,'THE LARGEST IS',MAXI
      RETURN
      END
C THIS SUBROUTINE FINDS THE LARGER OF 2 NUMBERS
      SUBROUTINE LARGER(FIRST,SECOND,RESULT)
      (exactly as previous version of LARGER subroutine)
      RETURN
      END
C THIS SUBROUTINE FINDS THE LARGEST OF 3 NUMBERS
      SUBROUTINE LARGST(FIRST,SECOND,THIRD,RESULT)
      INTEGER FIRST,SECOND,THIRD,RESULT
      INTEGER GREATR
      CALL LARGER(FIRST,SECOND,GREATR)
      CALL LARGER(GREATR,THIRD,RESULT)
      RETURN
      END
$ENTRY
 5  31  27
```

This job will print:

THE LARGEST IS   31

The subroutine named LARGST determines which of its first three parameters is largest and assigns the largest value to its fourth parameter, named RESULT. It accomplishes this by first using LARGER to assign the larger of the first two parameters to the variable GREATR, and by using LARGER again to assign the larger of GREATR and the third parameter to RESULT.

The subroutines LARGER and LARGST both have parameters named FIRST and SECOND. This causes no trouble because the parameters of LARGER are hidden from LARGST and vice versa. As a rule it is good programming practice to avoid duplicate names, as they may confuse people reading a program. However, in some cases, such as this example, it seems natural to repeat names in separate subprograms. Since duplicate names in separate subprograms are kept separate in Fortran, this causes no difficulty.

We will now show an example of nesting calls to our BIGGER function. We will use it in the following job to print the largest of three numbers.

```
$JOB      HUGH DEMPSTER
C THIS PROGRAM PRINTS THE LARGEST OF 3 DATA ITEMS
      INTEGER BIGGER
      INTEGER DATA1,DATA2,DATA3
      READ,DATA1,DATA2,DATA3
      PRINT,'LARGEST IS',BIGGER(BIGGER(DATA1,DATA2),DATA3)
      RETURN
      END
C THIS FUNCTION RETURNS THE BIGGER OF 2 NUMBERS
      INTEGER FUNCTION BIGGER(FIRST,SECOND)
      (definition as before)
      RETURN
      END
$ENTRY
  5   31   27
```

This job finds the larger of the first two data items using the BIGGER function, and uses the BIGGER function again to compare that value to the third data value. In the PRINT statement, the first argument to the BIGGER function is actually another call to the BIGGER function. This causes no trouble, because the inner call to BIGGER first returns 31, which is the larger of 5 and 31. Then the outer call to BIGGER compares 31 to 27 and returns the value. Using a call to BIGGER inside a call to BIGGER is actually no more complicated than, say,

```
((5+31)+27)
```

This expression means add 5 and 31 and add 27 to the result. By comparison,

```
BIGGER(BIGGER(5,31),27)
```

means find the larger of 5 and 31 and then find the larger of this and 27.

In Fortran it is illegal for a subprogram to contain a call to itself. A program that does this is said to be a <u>recursive</u> program. Recursive programs are not legal in Fortran. Note that the BIGGER subprogram does not call itself.

VARIABLES IN COMMON

So far we have indicated that with subprograms there is a one-to-one correspondence between the arguments given in the calling statement and the parameters given in the definition of the subprogram. Arguments and parameters in correspondence must be of the same type. Arrays that are in correspondence must have the same type and dimensions. Corresponding strings must be of the same length. Variables in the calling program other than the arguments are not accessible to the subprogram. Variables in the subprogram other than the parameters are not accessible to the calling program. Communication between program and subprogram is only through the argument-parameter list.

There is another way for programs to communicate; it is done through special areas of storage called COMMON. When variables are placed in the COMMON storage they may be made accessible to two, or more, programs. To accomplish this we must include, as well as the type declarations, a definition of variables to be held in COMMON. We will give the area in COMMON a name; we say that it is labeled. The form of the COMMON definition that must appear in each program that shares the variables is

COMMON/name/list of variables

When two subprograms share variables in COMMON the definition of them must appear in the main program as well as in each subprogram that uses the variables. Corresponding lists must be identical lists of variables. You can have as many different labeled blocks of COMMON as needed.

We will now show an example in which a program calls two different subprograms. One block of COMMON named GRADES is shared by all three; a second block called WIDTH is shared by the main program and the subroutine called RANGE. The subroutines have no parameters because all communication is through the COMMON blocks. Each subroutine has a single local integer variable with the identifier I. In giving the declarations for a subprogram the sequence to be followed is

        declaration of parameters
        declaration of function names called by the subprogram
        declaration of blocks in COMMON
        declaration of local variables

The purpose of the example program with its subprograms is to read a list of students' names and marks and print out those which fall within a certain letter grade. In the example we are printing all students that got a D grade mark.

```
$JOB     CHARLES CAPSTICK
C LIST STUDENTS WITH PARTICULAR MARKS
      COMMON/GRADES/PUPIL,MARK,SIZE
      CHARACTER*25 PUPIL(40)
      INTEGER MARK(40),SIZE
      COMMON/WIDTH/MAXI,MINI
      INTEGER MAXI,MINI
      CHARACTER*1 LETTER
C     READ LETTER GRADE AND ITS NUMERIC RANGE
      READ,LETTER,MINI,MAXI
C     READ NAMES,MARKS AND DETERMINE CLASS SIZE
      CALL INPUT
      PRINT,'STUDENTS WITH LETTER GRADE',LETTER
C     PRINT NAMES OF STUDENTS WITH THE GRADE
      CALL RANGE
      RETURN
      END
C INPUT STUDENTS' NAMES AND MARKS
      SUBROUTINE INPUT
      COMMON/GRADES/PUPIL,MARK,SIZE
      CHARACTER*25 PUPIL(40)
      INTEGER MARK(40),SIZE
      INTEGER I
      I=1
      READ,PUPIL(I),MARK(I)
      WHILE(PUPIL(I).NE.'ZZZ')DO
         I=I+1
         READ,PUPIL(I),MARK(I)
         END WHILE
      SIZE=I-1
      RETURN
      END
C PRINT NAMES HAVING MARKS IN GIVEN RANGE
      SUBROUTINE RANGE
      COMMON/GRADES/PUPIL,MARK,SIZE
      CHARACTER*25 PUPIL(40)
      INTEGER MARK(40),SIZE
      COMMON/WIDTH/MAXI,MINI
      INTEGER MAXI,MINI
      INTEGER I
      DO 10 I=1,SIZE
         IF(MARK(I).GE.MINI.AND.MARK(I).LE.MAXI)THEN DO
            PRINT,PUPIL(I),MARK(I)
            END IF
10       CONTINUE
      RETURN
      END
```

```
$ENTRY
 'D' 50 59
 'BRODIE,MICHAEL' 84
 'SPARKS,MICHAEL' 52
 ...
 'ZZZ'              0
```

In this example the division of the program into subprograms
seems somewhat artificial but in the chapter on Modular
Programming we will show how dividing larger programs into parts
can simplify the work. Communication through COMMON blocks is
used frequently in modular programming.

CHAPTER 12 SUMMARY

    In this chapter we have introduced subprograms. Subprograms
allow us to build up programs out of modules. The reasons for
using subprograms in programs include the following:

1. Dividing the program into parts which can be written by
    different people.

2. Dividing a program into parts which can be written over a
    period of time.

3. Making a large program easier to understand by building it up
    out of conceptually simple parts.

4. Factoring out common parts of a program so they need not be
    written many times within a program.

5. Factoring out commonly-used logic so that it can be used in a
    number of different programs.

6. Separating parts of a program so they can be individually
    tested.

There are two kinds of subprograms in Fortran: subroutines and
functions. Essentially, a subroutine provides a new kind of
Fortran statement and a function provides a new kind of
operation. The following important terms were discussed in this
chapter.

Subprogram definition - means giving the meaning of a subprogram
    to the computer. Subprogram definitions in SF/k must come
    just after the END of the main program. Subroutine
    subprograms can be defined using the following form:

```
SUBROUTINE name(parameters)
declarations for parameters
declarations for variables for this subprogram
...
RETURN
END
```

Function subprograms can be defined using the following form:

```
type FUNCTION name(parameters)
declarations for parameters
declarations for variables for this subprogram
...
name=expression
RETURN
END
```

If a subroutine has no parameters, the parameters and their enclosing parentheses are omitted. Often there are no parameters when the subroutine shares variables in COMMON with other subprograms or the main program. Functions must have at least one parameter and must be declared as INTEGER or REAL in each calling program.

Subprogram name - follows the rules for variable identifiers. Names for subprograms are limited to 6 characters.

Calling a subprogram (invoking a subprogram) - causing a subprogram to be executed. A subroutine subprogram is called by a statement of the form

```
CALL subroutine name(arguments)
```

If the subroutine has no parameters, then the arguments with their enclosing parentheses are omitted. A function subprogram is called by using its name, followed by a parenthesized list of arguments, in an expression. It must have at least one argument. The types of corresponding arguments and parameters must agree.

Returning from a subprogram - terminating the execution of a subprogram and passing control back to the calling place. When the end of a subroutine is reached, there is a return to the statement just beyond the calling statement. A function subprogram must return a value by assigning a value to its name. This assignment statement followed by RETURN terminates the function and causes the returned value assigned to the name to be used in the expression containing the function call.

Arguments - A call to a subprogram can pass it arguments. For
example, in the statement

```
        CALL SORT(NAME,NUMBER)
```

the arguments are NAME and NUMBER.

Parameters - Inside a subprogram, the arguments for each call are
referred to via parameters. All parameters must be declared
in a subprogram. There must be a one-to-one correspondence
between the arguments and the parameters.

COMMON   -   blocks of variables may be shared between two
subprograms or between the main program and a subprogram by
putting a definition of the form

```
        COMMON/name/list of variables
```

in each of the sharing programs and the main program. The
name is the same and the list of variables is the same.

CHAPTER 12 EXERCISES

1. What does the following program print?

```
$JOB    JOHN MYLOPOULOS
        INTEGER MAG
        INTEGER I
        DO 10 I=1,10
            PRINT,MAG(I-6)
10          CONTINUE
        RETURN
        END
        INTEGER FUNCTION MAG(VALUE)
        INTEGER VALUE
        IF(VALUE.GE.0)THEN DO
            MAG=VALUE
        ELSE DO
            MAG=-VALUE
            END IF
        RETURN
        END
$ENTRY
```

2. What does the following program print?

```
$JOB    TOM HULL
        REAL TEMP(31),RAIN(31)
        INTEGER DAY,TIME
        READ,TIME
        DO 5 DAY=1,TIME
            READ,TEMP(DAY),RAIN(DAY)
5           CONTINUE
        PRINT,'AVERAGE TEMPERATURE:'
        CALL AVRAGE(TEMP,TIME)
        PRINT,'AVERAGE RAINFALL:'
        CALL AVRAGE(RAIN,TIME)
        RETURN
        END
        SUBROUTINE AVRAGE(ARRAY,COUNT)
        INTEGER COUNT
        REAL ARRAY(31)
        INTEGER I
        REAL SUM
        SUM=0.
        DO 8 I=1,COUNT
            SUM=SUM+ARRAY(I)
8           CONTINUE
        PRINT,SUM/COUNT
        RETURN
        END
$ENTRY
 4
 45.0  0.
 47.2  0.
 48.0  .3
 47.5  2.1
```

3. Design a function like LENGTH given in this chapter to find the length of the first word on a card assuming that it may or may not have blanks in front of it.

4. Read words placed one to a card and join them into lines of not more than 80 characters for printing. Arrange that there is one blank between each word. You may use the function LENGTH if you like.

5. Eliminate the first word from a text and print the remaining text.

6. Write a subroutine that sorts an array of names into alphabetical order by a different method than the ones shown in this book. For example, your subroutine could be used in the following program.

```
$JOB    BILL MCKEEMAN
        CHARACTER*20 WORKER(50)
        INTEGER I
        DO 5 I=1,50
            READ,WORKER(I)
5           CONTINUE
        CALL SORT(WORKER,50)
        DO 10 I=1,50
            PRINT,WORKER(I)
10          CONTINUE
        RETURN
        END
        SUBROUTINE SORT(NAME,COUNT)
        INTEGER COUNT
        CHARACTER*20 NAME(50)
        (you write this part)
        RETURN
        END
$ENTRY
 (list of 50 employees' names, each in quotes, one to a card)
```

7. Design a subroutine for determining the roots of a quadratic equation of the form $AX^2+BX+C=0$.

8. Without having any arguments or parameters, but by making use of a COMMON block, design a subroutine to eliminate punctuation marks from a text of length 80 characters.

CHAPTER 13

PROGRAMMING
IN STANDARD FORTRAN

In this book we have been using a language called SF/k, which is part of the extended Fortran language implemented by the Watfiv-S compiler. The Watfiv-S compiler allows a number of features, such as format-free reading and printing, that are not a part of Standard Fortran.

SF/k uses some of these extra features. As a result, if a Fortran processor does not support the required language extensions then SF/k programs cannot be compiled. Most Fortran processors do not support them, so this chapter tells you how to get along without the extensions.

WHAT IS STANDARD FORTRAN?

The Fortran language has been in use since 1956. It was the first high-level programming language, designed for the convenience of people wishing to use a computer. It was a huge success and is one of the reasons that computers are now so widely used. The name Fortran comes from FORmula TRANslation, which emphasizes the original purpose of the language, for solving numerical problems.

Much has happened in programming since 1956. Many other programming languages have been developed, such as, Algol, Cobol, PL/1, Basic and APL. Some of these languages are more convenient to use than Fortran, especially in applications other than strictly numeric calculations. The language called Cobol, standing for COmmon Business Oriented Language, is used more than any other language for business data processing. But Fortran is still the most used language in scientific work. The PL/1 language incorporates essentially all the programming features of Fortran and Cobol and is designed to be suitable for both scientific and data processing applications. PL/1 is a more

modern and convenient language than Fortran or Cobol, but it is
not clear that it will ever completely take over from these older
languages.

It is hardly surprising that many improvements have been made
in programming languages since 1956. Although Fortran has
occasionally been extended to incorporate these improvements, in
many ways it is out-of-date. This book has presented programming
in terms of SF/k rather than Standard Fortran, because Standard
Fortran is very clumsy in some of its features. For example,
format-free reading and printing, character variables,
IF...THEN...ELSE and WHILE...DO are not in Standard Fortran, but
are in SF/k and can be used with the Watfiv-S processor.

In 1966 the American National Standards Institute (ANSI)
published specifications for what is known as Standard Fortran.
Before that time, each Fortran compiler supported a slightly
different version of the language and so it was necessary to
learn Fortran for each particular computer. And it was
impossible to run Fortran programs written for one computer on
another computer because the language had incompatible dialects.
Fortunately, this problem has been largely solved because most
Fortran processors now support the Standard version of Fortran.
Except for a few minor omissions, the Watfiv compiler supports
Standard Fortran. Since Standard Fortran is quite limited, and
has some awkward restrictions, most Fortran compilers provide
extensions, but there is no standard for these extensions. If
you want to write Fortran programs that will work on many
different computers, your only hope is to stay inside Standard
Fortran and avoid any extensions. A program is called portable
if it can be run on many different computers; this chapter tells
you how to make your Fortran programs portable.

LOGICAL IF AND GO TO STATEMENTS

The advantage of the IF...THEN...ELSE and WHILE...DO
constructs is that they provide a simple but convenient way of
specifying flow of control in a program. They are nicely
structured in that they allow statements to be nested inside
statements while guaranteeing that the flow of control among all
the statements is orderly. Standard Fortran lets us specify flow
of control, but in a way that easily leads to confusing, poorly
structured programs. We have to work harder to write
understandable programs in Standard Fortran.

Standard Fortran allows the counted DO loop, just as in SF/k.

```
      DO label identifier=start,limit,step
          statements
label     CONTINUE
```

The "step" is optional as in SF/k. But IF...THEN...ELSE and
WHILE...DO must be built up out of two statement types that we

have not included in the SF/k subsets. These are <u>GO TO</u>
<u>statements</u> and <u>logical</u> <u>IF</u> <u>statements</u>. The first of these is used
as follows:

```
      GO TO label
      statements
label CONTINUE
```

This causes execution to jump from the GO TO statement to the
labeled CONTINUE and thus on to the statement following CONTINUE.
The label is an unsigned non-zero integer constant that is
different from other labels in the particular main program or
subprogram. Any number of statements can appear between the GO
TO and the CONTINUE and the CONTINUE can occur before the GO TO.

The logical IF statement can be used in the following way.

```
      IF(condition)GO TO label
      statements
label CONTINUE
```

If the condition is found to be true then a jump is made to the
CONTINUE and execution proceeds from there. Otherwise, execution
proceeds to the statement immediately following the logical IF.
The CONTINUE can precede rather than follow the logical IF.

TRANSLATING IF...THEN...ELSE AND WHILE...DO

We can make the logical IF statement act like an IF...THEN
statement as shown in this example, where the SF/k version is on
the left and the Standard Fortran version is on the right.

```
      IF(N.GT.0)THEN DO           IF(.NOT.(N.GT.0))GO TO 5
          SUM=SUM+N                   SUM=SUM+N
      END IF                5     CONTINUE
```

We used the NOT in the logical IF because its GO TO is used when
the condition is true. We could have accomplished the same thing
by writing:

```
                                  IF(N.LE.0)GO TO 5
                                     SUM=SUM+N
                            5     CONTINUE
```

The next example shows a translation from IF...THEN with an ELSE
to logical IF and GO TO statements.

```
      IF(N.GT.0)THEN DO           IF(.NOT.(N.GT.0))GO TO 5
          SUM=SUM+N                   SUM=SUM+N
      ELSE DO                         GO TO 6
          ERRORS=ERRORS+1     5     CONTINUE
      END IF                         ERRORS=ERRORS+1
                            6     CONTINUE
```

In a similar way, the WHILE...DO can be translated into Standard Fortran, as the next example shows.

```
   J=1                                    J=1
   WHILE(LIST(J).NE.KEY)DO        7       CONTINUE
      J=J+1                                IF(.NOT.(LIST(J).NE.KEY))GO TO 8
      END WHILE                              J=J+1
                                             GO TO 7
                                     8       CONTINUE
```

The NOT can be avoided by changing the logical IF to the following

```
                              IF(LIST(J).EQ.KEY)GO TO 8
```

Even when the NOT is gone, the translation into Standard Fortran loses much of the readability of the more structured SF/k version.

One of the difficulties is that when we read a logical IF, we cannot immediately tell if it is being used to construct a loop. We always know that WHILE is the start of a loop, but when we see a logical IF it may be used for a loop, for an IF...THEN...ELSE, or for some new unstructured method of flow of control.

There is another kind of loop that is available in some high-level languages and is convenient to construct in Standard Fortran. This loop is like WHILE...DO except it is always executed at least once. The condition that causes the loop to terminate is at the end rather than the beginning. We call such a loop a REPEAT...UNTIL statement and on the left we show how such a statement might look if added to Fortran.

```
   J=0                                    J=0
   REPEAT                         4       CONTINUE
      J=J+1                                J=J+1
      UNTIL(LIST(J).EQ.KEY)                IF(LIST(J).NE.KEY)GO TO 4
```

For the translation on the right we have avoided using NOT by changing EQ to NE.

The translation of IF...THEN...ELSE and WHILE...DO into Standard Fortran is quite mechanical. It can be done automatically by a program called a <u>preprocessor</u> that reads an SF/k program and punches out a modified version of the program with the appropriate translations of IF...THEN...ELSE and WHILE...DO. The punched program can then be submitted to a compiler that does not support the extensions. For example, the SF/k program as modified could be handled by Watfiv, which is the precursor of Watfiv-S, even though Watfiv does not recognize IF...THEN...ELSE and WHILE...DO.

READING AND PRINTING

The simplest way to read and print in SF/k is by using format-free statements such as:

```
      PRINT,KEY
```

For more detailed control of the output we use a formatted statement such as:

```
      PRINT 10,KEY
10    FORMAT(' ',I6)
```

Standard Fortran does not include convenient format-free statements, as used in the first example. Instead lines are printed and cards are read using format specifications. In Standard Fortran the example becomes:

```
      WRITE(6,10)KEY
10    FORMAT(' ',I6)
```

In the WRITE statement, the 6 means that the output is to be sent to the printer. Other numbers could be used for other output devices such as magnetic tape drives and disk drives. Some computer centers may require a number other than 6 for the printer.

In SF/k an integer can be read using this statement:

```
      READ 20,KEY
20    FORMAT(I6)
```

In Standard Fortran this becomes

```
      READ(5,20)KEY
20    FORMAT(I6)
```

The 5 means the input is to come from the card reader. Other numbers could be used for other input devices. Some computer centers may require a number other then 5 for the card reader.

All the carriage control items and format items, such as Ew.d, that have been introduced in SF/6 are included in Standard Fortran. So, standard reading is easy; essentially all that is new is the device number (5). Printing requires a device number (6) and the word PRINT is replaced by WRITE.

In SF/k the value of an arithmetic expression can be printed as in:

```
      PRINT 30,LENGTH*WIDTH
30    FORMAT(' ',F10.3)
```

Standard Fortran does not allow such expressions or constants to be used in output statements. But we can avoid the expression by re-writing the example as shown here:

```
        AREA=LENGTH*WIDTH
        WRITE(6,30)AREA
30      FORMAT(' ',F10.3)
```

In Standard Fortran the expression or constant must be assigned to a variable and then the variable can be printed.

WHERE HAVE ALL THE CHARACTERS GONE?

Electronic computers were originally developed to do numerical calculations, and Fortran was designed with similar objectives. It is interesting that today more computers do business data processing than scientific calculations. These business applications make extensive use of character strings, such as customers' names and addresses. Although Fortran is poorly suited for handling character strings, it is sometimes used for data processing. Although characters are not used directly in numerical calculations they are necessary in scientific programs, for example, when labeling results and plotting graphs.

Standard Fortran has methods of handling character strings, but these are tedious and confusing. In SF/k we can print and label the value of KEY in the following way.

```
        PRINT 10,'KEY IS',KEY
10      FORMAT(' ',A6,I12)
```

Standard Fortran does not allow literals, such as 'KEY IS', in the list of items to be printed. Many Fortran compilers will accept the following:

```
        WRITE(6,10)KEY
10      FORMAT(' ','KEY IS',I12)
```

However, this is still not quite Standard Fortran, because the quote character(') is not standard and literals must be written as an integer followed by H followed by the characters in the literal. For example, 'KEY IS' must be written as 6HKEY IS. The 6 gives the length of the literal. In a similar way a literal containing a single blank, written in SF/k as 'b', must be written as 1Hb, where we are using b to mean blank. In Standard Fortran, the example becomes

```
        WRITE(6,10)KEY
10      FORMAT(1H ,6HKEY IS,I12)
```

Literals like 6HKEY IS are called <u>H-type</u> <u>literals</u>. For historical reasons, these are sometimes called <u>Hollerith</u> <u>constants</u>.

Besides being unattractive, these H-type literals are error-prone because the programmer easily forgets to change the length, given before the H, when he changes a message to be printed.

There are no character variables in Standard Fortran, but it is possible to hide character values in numeric variables. In SF/k, the characters on a card can be read and printed as follows:

```
      CHARACTER*1 CARD(80)
      READ 10,CARD
10    FORMAT(80A1)
      PRINT 20,CARD
20    FORMAT(' ',80A1)
```

We already explained how to change READ and PRINT statements to make them Standard Fortran. Curiously enough, by changing the first line to:

```
      INTEGER CARD(80)
```

we can complete the conversion to Standard Fortran and still have a program that reads and prints the characters on a card. Each character is converted to its internal computer representation, which is actually an integer, and this is stored in an element of the CARD array. (In pure SF/k we do not allow characters to be read into or assigned to numeric variables.)

In general, CHARACTER*1 variables can be replaced by INTEGER variables. These can be read and printed using A1 format items. However, Standard Fortran does not allow literals in assignment statements or in comparisons, so it is inconvenient to do character manipulation except by reading and printing a character at a time.

Several characters can be held in a single integer variable. For example, on the IBM 360, a Fortran integer can hold up to four characters. This means that CHARACTER*1, CHARACTER*2, CHARACTER*3 and CHARACTER*4 variables can be replaced by INTEGER variables. There is no easy way to manipulate strings of length greater than 4, except as arrays of integers.

Two INTEGER variables that hold character values can be safely compared using EQ and NE with the expected results. The other comparisons, such as LE, can also be used, but Standard Fortran does not guarantee that, for example, A is less than B, as we would expect. Luckily, for many computers, these other comparisons actually work as we would like, and we can use them for purposes such as alphabetizing.

(Standard Fortran provides a construct other than reading for initializing INTEGER variables to have character values, but this is not covered in this book).

VARIOUS RESTRICTIONS

There are several additional minor restrictions that must be followed to make SF/k programs become standard. Here is the list.

The STOP statement. Standard Fortran does not allow RETURN statements in the main program. Any such RETURN must be replaced by STOP, which has the same meaning. Do not put a STOP in a subprogram, as this will cause the entire program to terminate.

Mixed mode arithmetic. Integers and real numbers should not be compared or combined using arithmetic, but real values can be assigned to integer variables and vice versa as in SF/k. If there is any such mixed mode comparison or arithmetic, assign the integer value to a real variable first and then use the real variable in place of the integer value.

Expressions as array indexes. Standard Fortran has peculiar restrictions on array indexes, that go back to the early Fortran compilers that were not very clever at handling expressions. Fortunately, typical index expressions, such as I+1 in A(I+1), are legal. The exact rule is that the index expression must be one of the following: k, v, v-k, v+k, c*k, c*v-k or c*v+k, where k and c are unsigned integer constants and v is an integer variable.

Limits on precision. Different computers have differing amounts of precision in REAL values. For example, the IBM 360 has about 7 decimal digits of precision, but other computers may have more or less. Similarly, the maximum exponents and integers vary from computer to computer. Programs that depend on these precisions or sizes may work on one computer but not on another.

AN EXAMPLE IN SF/k AND STANDARD FORTRAN

We will now give a complete program that illustrates many of the differences between SF/k and Standard Fortran, and how these differences can be resolved.

```
C THIS SF/K PROGRAM SUMS          C THIS STANDARD FORTRAN PROGRAM
C     POSITIVE NUMBERS UNTIL      C     SUMS POSITIVE NUMBERS UNTIL
C     IT FINDS A ZERO             C     IT FINDS A ZERO
      INTEGER N,SUM                     INTEGER N,SUM
      SUM=0                             SUM=0
      READ,N                            READ(5,10)N
      WHILE(N.NE.0)DO             10     FORMAT(I10)
         IF(N.GT.0)THEN DO        20     CONTINUE
            SUM=SUM+N                    IF(N.EQ.0)GO TO 70
         ELSE DO                           IF(N.LE.0)GO TO 30
            PRINT,'ERROR'                     SUM=SUM+N
         END IF                             GO TO 50
         READ,N                  30     CONTINUE
      END WHILE                            WRITE(6,40)
      PRINT,'SUM IS',SUM         40     FORMAT(1H ,5HERROR)
      RETURN                     50     CONTINUE
      END                               READ(5,60)N
                                 60     FORMAT(I10)
                                        GO TO 20
                                 70     CONTINUE
                                        WRITE(6,80)SUM
                                 80     FORMAT(1H ,6HSUM IS,I13)
                                        STOP
                                        END
```

Although format-free input-output is sufficient for this example, we had to use format specifications for Standard Fortran. The format-free READ accepts the input numbers in any card columns, but the formatted READ requires that the numbers be right-justified in the first 10 card columns. The structured flow of control of SF/k was replaced by GO TO and logical IF statements and RETURN was replaced by STOP. Both versions of the program use indentation to show the structure of the flow of control, but the Standard Fortran version is not as clear to read without convenient constructs like WHILE...DO.

                    OTHER STANDARD FORTRAN CONSTRUCTS

     The SF/k language was purposely kept small so that it would be easy to learn and use. There are some Standard Fortran programming constructs that we have not covered, because they do not correspond to SF/k constructs. We will list the most important of these other constructs.

     Double precision numbers. It is possible to define variables that have more precision than REAL variables. For example, in the IBM 360, variables declared as REAL have about 7 decimal digits of precision, but variables declared as DOUBLE PRECISION have about 16 decimal digits of precision. The difference is that a REAL variable uses only one word in the computer's memory, but a DOUBLE PRECISION variable uses two.

Complex numbers. Certain scientific calculations use numbers which have an "imaginary" part, as well as the usual "real" part. Variables that are declared as COMPLEX have these two parts and can be used in much the same way as REAL variables.

Functions as parameters. Sometimes it is useful for a subprogram to call a function to produce some desired result. For example, a subprogram can be written to find the area under a curve that is defined by a function. Standard Fortran allows the name of the function to be passed as a parameter to such a subprogram, and the subprogram can then call the function with various arguments. This allows the subprogram to be used with various different functions without making any changes to it.

Initialization of variables. There is a way of setting the initial values of variables including arrays, other than by assignment or READ statements. This facility is especially useful when there are numeric arrays full of information that is known at the time the program is being written, or when the information is character strings.

Selective GO TO statements. There are special kinds of GO TO statements, called computed and assigned GO TOs that cause jumps to various labels, depending on the values of integer variables. For example, a jump could be made to label 21, 21, 22, ..., or 27 depending on whether the value of J is 1, 2, 3, ..., or 7. This kind of GO TO statement can be used to replace a whole set of logical IF statements.

Overlaying variables. Sometimes there is a shortage of memory space, and it may be that one array has been used but will not be used again and another array has not yet been used. Standard Fortran provides a construct, called EQUIVALENCE, that allows variables, including arrays, to re-use the same memory space. Of course, disaster can result if two arrays represented by the same memory locations are used at the same time.

CHAPTER 13 SUMMARY

This chapter has shown how SF/k programs can be re-written in Standard Fortran. This is a simple matter and consists of the following steps.

- Replace IF...THEN...ELSE and DO...WHILE by logical IF, GO TO and CONTINUE.
- Do all card reading and printing by formatted READ and WRITE statements. These use device numbers; typically 5 specifies the card reader and 6 specifies the printer.
- Move literals, such as 'SUM IS', from the output list into the format specification and change them into H-type literals, for example, 6HSUM IS.

- Replace character variables by integer variables. You are safe if you put only one character in each integer variable or array element. Remember that literals such as 'JONES' and 5HJONES cannot be used in comparisons and assignments.
- If a constant or any arithmetic expression appears as an item to be printed, assign the value to a variable and print the variable.
- Replace RETURN in the main program by STOP.
- Do not compare or directly combine integer and real numbers. Instead, use assignment to convert between real and integer values.
- Keep array indexes simple.

The following important terms were introduced in this chapter.

Incompatible – dialects of the same programming language are incompatible if programs that are correct in one dialect are incorrect in another. Fortran was standardized to minimize incompatibilities among the various Fortran compilers.

Extensions – constructs that are added to a language. The IF...THEN...ELSE and WHILE...DO statements are extensions to Standard Fortran. The various extensions to Standard Fortran may be incompatible from compiler to compiler.

Portable – a program is portable if it can be run on different computers. One way of making programs portable is to write them in Standard Fortran.

Preprocessor – a program that reads programs and makes certain modifications to them. A preprocessor can be used to translate Fortran extensions into Standard Fortran.

CHAPTER 13 EXERCISES

1. Translate the following to Standard Fortran

(a)   IF(A.GE.B)THEN DO
            A=5
            PRINT,B
            END IF

(b)   IF(A.GE.LOWER.AND.A.LE.UPPER)THEN DO
            PRINT,'A IN BOUNDS:',A
        ELSE DO
            PRINT,'ERROR: A SET TO 20'
            A=20
            END IF

```
(c)    I=1
       SUM=0
       WHILE(SUM.LE.100)DO
          SUM=SUM+COST(I)
          I=I+1
          END WHILE
       PRINT,'THE FIRST',I-1,'EXCEED 100'
```

2. Translate the following to Standard Fortran.

```
       IF(OPTION.EQ.1)THEN DO
          PRINT,'TAKE STANDARD DEDUCTION:',1500
          DEDUCT=1500
       ELSE DO
          PRINT,'ITEMIZE DEDUCTIONS:'
          DEDUCT=0
          I=1
          WHILE(ITEM(I).GT.0)DO
             PRINT,ITEM(I)
             DEDUCT=DEDUCT+ITEM(I)
             I=I+1
             END WHILE
          END IF
```

3. Write a program that reads and prints cards and then prints the number of each card that started with the word WHILE or IF. Blanks may precede WHILE and IF. Your program must be in Standard Fortran and so integer variables or array elements each can hold a single character. You should precede the cards you are to read by a special card having the words WHILE and IF on it. This special card should be used to initialize integer arrays to hold the letters W, H, I, L, E, I, and F so that these arrays can be used to detect WHILE and IF.

4. Take the complete Standard Fortran program given in this chapter, as translated from SF/k, and run it on different computers, or under different Fortran compilers on the same computer. You will see differences in what is printed on each run. What is the nature of these differences? You should purposely make an error in the program, such as mispunching CONTINUE as CONTNNUE and see what happens in each case.

5. Answer the following questions.

   (a)Why was this book written using extensions to Standard Fortran?
   (b)Logical IF and GO TO statements in Standard Fortran can completely replace WHILE...DO statements. Since this is true why would anyone go to the trouble of extending Standard Fortran with WHILE...DO?
   (c)Some programs need to be portable and some do not. Explain and give examples.

6. Find any three complete programs or subprograms in other chapters of this book, each at least 15 lines long, and translate them to Standard Fortran.

CHAPTER 14

MODULAR
PROGRAMMING

In a previous chapter we learned how to use subprograms in the Fortran language. One of the important purposes of subprograms in programming languages is to divide programs into parts - parts that are convenient to use and easy to understand. This idea of dividing a program into parts is called modular programming. In this chapter we will show how a program can be divided into convenient modules; each of these modules will be a subprogram.

A PROBLEM IN BUSINESS DATA PROCESSING

We will illustrate modular programming by solving a problem which might arise in a small business. Suppose that Acme Automotive Supplies uses a computer to help keep track of its customers' accounts. For each customer, there is an account card, giving the customer's name, account number, credit limit and balance owing to Acme.

For example, Cooks Garage has account number 14 and presently owes $28.32 to Acme. Cooks Garage is allowed a credit limit of $200.00; this means that if Cooks Garage is less than $200.00 behind in paying its bills to Acme, Acme will not press for payment. This information is recorded on a punched card as follows:

    'COOKS GARAGE'   14   20000   2832

To avoid the use of decimal points, a dollar amount such as $200.00 is given in cents as 20000.

The payments to Acme from its customers are recorded on transaction cards. Each transaction card gives a customer's

account number and the amount of a payment by the customer. For
example, the card

        14   2832

records the fact that $28.32 was received from the customer with
account number 14. Since Cooks Garage corresponds to the account
number 14, this means that Cooks Garage has paid $28.32 to Acme.

     The account manager for Acme needs a program to read the
account cards and the month's transaction cards and print the
accounts as they stand after the payments. For example, suppose
that corresponding to the account card

        'COOKS GARAGE'   14   20000   2832

there is only the one transaction card

        14   2832

The account manager would like the program to print the fact that
account number 14, for Cooks Garage, has a credit limit of 20000
and a current balance owing of 0. The program is supposed to
read data such as:

        'COOKS GARAGE'   14   20000   2832
        'JONES REPAIR'   6   5000   8240
        . . .   (more account cards)
        'XXX'   -1   0   0   (dummy account card)
         6   1000
        14   2832
         6   1000
        . . .   (more transaction cards)
        -1   0   (dummy transaction card)

The program is to print the updated accounts; a report such as
the following should be printed.

             ACME AUTOMOTIVE SUPPLIES ACCOUNTING REPORT

      CUSTOMER   ACCOUNT NO.   CREDIT LIMIT   BALANCE

      COOKS GARAGE   14   20000   0
      JONES REPAIR   6   5000   6240
      . . .

The account manager says that Acme has accounts for 16 customers.
He has told us that each customer has one account card and that
an account number can be any number from 1 to 999. The
transaction records are not in any particular order, and the
number of payments by a particular customer each month varies
widely - from no payment to quite a number of payments.

DIVIDING THE PROGRAM INTO PARTS

We need a program which reads the accounts, updates them using the month's transactions and prints the updated accounts. We start designing our program by dividing it into the three parts:

```
Input accounts
Update accounts
Output accounts
```

Since Fortran does not provide a statement, "Input accounts," we will write a Fortran subroutine called INPUT. Our subroutine will have the following form:

```
SUBROUTINE INPUT
(common definition for accounts)
(declarations local to this subroutine)
(statements)
END
```

Similarly, we will write Fortran subroutines called UPDATE and OUTPUT. Assuming these three subroutines are available, then we can write:

```
CALL INPUT
CALL UPDATE
CALL OUTPUT
```

The subroutines will have no parameters and instead will communicate by means of COMMON variables. If our three subroutines are written correctly, then this sequence of three CALL statements will solve our business data processing problem.

We have divided our program into three parts, or modules. Now we need to define common data so the parts can communicate.

COMMUNICATION AMONG MODULES

The INPUT subroutine must have a place to store the information from the account cards, so this information can be used by the UPDATE subroutine. Similarly, the UPDATE subroutine must store the updated account information, so it can be printed by the OUTPUT subroutine.

To meet these communication needs, we can declare arrays for the customer names, account numbers, credit limits and balances. The following declaration creates the desired arrays:

```
COMMON/LEDGER/CUSTMR,ACCT,LIMIT,BALNCE
CHARACTER*13 CUSTMR(20)
INTEGER ACCT(20),LIMIT(20),BALNCE(20)
```

For possible future growth, we have allowed for more accounts than Acme's present 16 accounts. The upper limit of 20 for the arrays provides room for 19 accounts plus a dummy account. We checked with the account manager to verify that 13 characters are enough to record each customer's name.

We will place this common definition with declarations in each of the three subroutines. The overall program organization is:


```
C INPUT, UPDATE AND OUTPUT ACCOUNTS FOR ACME
C      AUTOMOTIVE SUPPLIES
(definition of COMMON variables)
      CALL INPUT
      CALL UPDATE
      CALL OUTPUT
      RETURN
      END
(definition of the INPUT subroutine)
(definition of the UPDATE subroutine)
(definition of the OUTPUT subroutine)
```


The subroutine INPUT will finish by reading the dummy account card into the arrays. The subroutines UPDATE and OUTPUT will recognize the end of the list of accounts when they encounter the dummy account number -1.

The three subroutines communicate by changing and inspecting the arrays. First, the INPUT subroutine reads the information on the account cards into the four arrays. Next, the UPDATE subroutine reads the transaction cards and updates the account information accordingly. This updating will modify the BALNCE array, but does not change the other three arrays. Finally, the OUTPUT subroutine prints the updated accounts. Note that this subroutine does not change any of the four arrays.

WRITING THE MODULES

We are now ready to write the subroutines because we have designed the overall program structure and the data to be used for communication among the three subroutines.

We will start the INPUT subroutine by writing a comment to
explain its purpose:

```
C INPUT ACCOUNT CARDS INTO THE ARRAYS CUSTMR,
C     ACCT, LIMIT AND BALNCE.
```

Immediately following this comment will come the line:

```
    SUBROUTINE INPUT
```

Next will come the definition of COMMON variables and then the
declarations for variables that are local to the INPUT
subroutine.   We are not ready to write these local declarations,
because we have not yet designed the body of the subroutine.

The subroutine requires a loop such as the following, which
repeatedly reads account cards.

```
    Loop initialization
    WHILE(There are more account cards)DO
        Read another card
        END WHILE
```

We can fill up the arrays starting with item 1, then item 2 and
so on. We will declare a variable called ITEM to keep track of
the number of the item.   The body of the loop, "Read another
card," will use a READ statement to read account cards. But the
loop body must also get ready for the reading of the next card,
and it must provide information to be tested to see if "There are
more account cards."   This can be accomplished by writing the
loop body this way:

```
    READ,CUSTMR(ITEM),ACCT(ITEM),LIMIT(ITEM),BALNCE(ITEM)
    ACCTNO=ACCT(ITEM)
    ITEM=ITEM+1
```

We will declare ACCTNO to be an integer variable; the loop is
terminated when ACCTNO becomes -1.   We now write "Loop
initialization" so that the loop is started correctly, and we
have:

```
    ITEM=1
C       SET ACCTNO SO LOOP WILL START PROPERLY
    ACCTNO=0
    WHILE(ACCTNO.NE.-1)DO
        READ,CUSTMR(ITEM),ACCT(ITEM),LIMIT(ITEM),BALNCE(ITEM)
        ACCTNO=ACCT(ITEM)
        ITEM=ITEM+1
        END WHILE
```

This sequence of statements has the meaning:

> Read in the account cards together with the dummy
>   account card

The variable ITEM is left having as its value one more than the number of accounts.

This completes the writing of the INPUT subroutine. Putting the pieces together, it looks like this:

```
C INPUT ACCOUNT CARDS INTO THE ARRAYS CUSTMR,
C     ACCT, LIMIT AND BALNCE
      SUBROUTINE INPUT
      COMMON/LEDGER/CUSTMR,ACCT,LIMIT,BALNCE
      CHARACTER*13 CUSTMR(20)
      INTEGER ACCT(20),LIMIT(20),BALNCE(20)
      INTEGER ITEM, ACCTNO
      ITEM=1
C     SET ACCTNO SO LOOP WILL START PROPERLY
      ACCTNO=0
      WHILE(ACCTNO.NE.-1)DO
          READ,CUSTMR(ITEM),ACCT(ITEM),LIMIT(ITEM),BALNCE(ITEM)
          ACCTNO=ACCT(ITEM)
          ITEM=ITEM+1
          END WHILE
      RETURN
      END
```

We have written the INPUT subroutine using step-by-step refinement. We started by deciding the purpose of the subroutine. Then we divided the subroutine into pieces. Finally, we wrote the pieces in SF/k.

We will not give detailed descriptions of the writing of the UPDATE and OUTPUT subroutines. Similar methods can be used in writing those two subroutines.

THE COMPLETE PROGRAM

Assuming the other two subroutines have been written, we can put the pieces together to make the program given on the next page.

```
C INPUT,UPDATE AND OUTPUT ACCOUNTS FOR ACME
C     AUTOMOTIVE SUPPLIES
      COMMON/LEDGER/CUSTMR,ACCT,LIMIT,BALNCE
      CHARACTER*13 CUSTMR(20)
      INTEGER ACCT(20),LIMIT(20),BALNCE(20)
      CALL INPUT
      CALL UPDATE
      CALL OUTPUT
      RETURN
      END
C
C INPUT ACCOUNT CARDS INTO THE ARRAYS CUSTMR,
C     ACCT,LIMIT AND BALNCE
      SUBROUTINE INPUT
      (exactly as given previously)
      END
C
C INPUT TRANSACTION CARDS AND UPDATE THE ACCOUNTS
      SUBROUTINE UPDATE
      COMMON/LEDGER/CUSTMR,ACCT,LIMIT,BALNCE
      CHARACTER*13 CUSTMR(20)
      INTEGER ACCT(20),LIMIT(20),BALNCE(20)
      INTEGER ITEM,ACCTNO,PAYMNT
      READ,ACCTNO,PAYMNT
      WHILE(ACCTNO .NE. -1)DO
         ITEM=1
         WHILE(ACCT(ITEM) .NE. ACCTNO .AND.
     +         ACCT(ITEM) .NE. -1)DO
           ITEM=ITEM+1
           END WHILE
         IF(ACCT(ITEM).EQ.ACCTNO)THEN DO
           BALNCE(ITEM)=BALNCE(ITEM)-PAYMNT
         ELSE DO
           PRINT,'ERRONEOUS TRANSACTION:',ACCTNO
           END IF
         READ,ACCTNO,PAYMNT
         END WHILE
      RETURN
      END
C
C OUTPUT THE ACCOUNTS
      SUBROUTINE OUTPUT
      COMMON/LEDGER/CUSTMR,ACCT,LIMIT,BALNCE
      CHARACTER*13 CUSTMR(20)
      INTEGER ACCT(20),LIMIT(20),BALNCE(20)
      PRINT,'    ACME AUTOMOTIVE SUPPLIES ACCOUNTING REPORT'
      PRINT,' '
      PRINT,'CUSTOMER    ACCOUNT NO.  CREDIT LIMIT  BALANCE'
      ITEM=1
      WHILE(ACCT(ITEM).NE.-1)DO
         PRINT,CUSTMR(ITEM),ACCT(ITEM),LIMIT(ITEM),BALNCE(ITEM)
         ITEM=ITEM+1
         END WHILE
      RETURN
      END
```

In this program we used local and COMMON variables to our advantage. The arrays are defined to be COMMON to the INPUT, UPDATE and OUTPUT subroutines. We made some variables, such as PAYMNT, local to the subroutines using them. Although we declared three variables named ITEM, they are kept separate by Fortran because they were declared in different subroutines.

USING MODULES

In our example, we divided our program into three modules, namely, the INPUT, UPDATE and OUTPUT subroutines.

```
CALL INPUT
CALL UPDATE
CALL OUTPUT
```

This main program is very easy to understand because it specifies the order of using the modules, without giving internal details about the modules. These details are important, but are best understood separately, in the definitions of the modules. Many of these details can be changed inside a particular module without changing either the main program or our understanding of the program's overall structure.

Programs that process business data typically have an organization similar to that of our example. In particular, they are often based on a set of modules which are called by a main program. For larger and more complex programs, individual modules may be composed of sub-modules, the sub-modules may be composed of sub-sub-modules, and so on.

Our example is not a large program. Even though it is relatively small, we have been able to make it simple by dividing it into distinct parts. It is almost impossible for programmers to write, understand or modify a large, complex program unless the program is divided into distinct parts, each having a relatively simple purpose.

MODIFYING A PROGRAM

It is common for programs to be changed during their lifetime. Sometimes a change is required to fix errors in the program. Sometimes a change is required because the purpose of the program is changed. For example, the account manager for Acme Automotive Supplies may discover that in addition to the printing of all updated accounts, he needs a separate list of customers whose credit limits have been exceeded. This is an example of <u>exception reporting</u>; such reporting helps managers by listing only those items that require action.

When a useful program is modified, we call this <u>program maintenance</u>. We do not <u>maintain</u> a program because it wears out!

Instead, we maintain a program when there are new requirements
for the program or there are errors in the program.

As an example of a program modification, we will take the
situation in which a <u>credit exception report</u> is required by the
Acme account manager.   The program must list those customers
whose balance owing is greater than their credit limit.   We
already have modules which read accounts, update them and print
them.   Given the updated accounts, we need a module which prints
the names of customers with exceeded credit.   The main program is
changed to make the calls:

```
CALL INPUT
CALL UPDATE
CALL OUTPUT
CALL CREDIT
```

Using our old program, we add a new subroutine named CREDIT and a
call to this subroutine.

We are able to produce a program to print credit exceptions
very easily.   This is because our old program is easy to
understand and thus easy to modify.

Since our program is modular, we can use the pieces - the
modules - to build new programs.   Suppose the Acme account
manager decides he needs a list of accounts both before and after
the update.   We can easily modify our program to meet this
requirement by changing the calls to:

```
CALL INPUT
CALL OUTPUT
CALL UPDATE
CALL OUTPUT
(more calls to subroutines)
```

We simply call the OUTPUT subroutine twice - before and after
calling UPDATE.   No modules need to be added or changed.

CHAPTER 14 SUMMARY

In this chapter we showed how modular programming can be used
in solving a simple problem in data processing.   We developed a
program containing three modules to solve the problem.   Each of
these modules was a subroutine.

The overall structure of our program was designed using step-
by-step refinement.   Once we had stated the data processing
problem to be solved, we refined the idea "solve the problem"
into the three steps:

```
Input accounts
Update accounts
Output accounts
```

We wrote three modules to carry out these steps.

Modules should be designed to perform conceptually simple activities, and they should use their parameters and any shared variables in a straightforward manner. When a program has been carefully divided into good modules, it can be easily understood and maintained.

CHAPTER 14 EXERCISES

All the exercises for this chapter are based on the program which reads, updates and prints accounts for Acme Automotive Supplies. Each exercise asks you to modify the program; you may need to add new modules, change or improve old modules or change the main program. When making these changes, be sure that old comments are appropriately modified and new comments are added as needed.

1. Add a new subroutine named CREDIT that prints each account having a balance greater than its credit limit. Write the main program so that the accounts are read and updated, then the credit exceptions are printed and then all of the accounts are printed. Test the modified program.

2. Make modifications so that the number of accounts and the number of transactions are printed before the listing of accounts. Test the modified program.

3. Make the program less vulnerable to data errors by having it check for and report the following problems:

   (a) More accounts than can be stored in the arrays.

   (b) Negative credit limits.

   (c) Unlikely payments - negative or more than $999.99.

Test the modified program.

4. Modify the program so that it prints the total of the balances of the accounts. Test the modified program.

CHAPTER 15

SEARCHING
AND SORTING

When a large amount of information is stored in a computer, it must be organized so that you are able to get at the information to make use of it. This problem of data retrieval is at the heart of all business operations. Records are kept of employees, customers, suppliers, inventory, in-process goods, and so on. These records are usually grouped in some way into what are called files. We might have, for example, a file of employee records, a file of customer records, an inventory file, and so on. Each file must be kept up to date.

A file that we all have access to is printed in the telephone book. It consists of a series of records of names, addresses, and telephone numbers. We say that there are three fields in each of these records: the name field, the address field, and the phone-number field. The file is in the alphabetic order of one of the three fields, the name field. We say that the name field is the key to the ordering of the file. The file is in alphabetic order on this field because that is how it can be most useful to us for data retrieval. We know someone's name and we want his phone number. We might also want his address and that too is available. The telephone company also has the same set of records, ordered using the phone-number field as the key.

In this chapter we will be investigating how a computer can search for information in a file and how records can be sorted.

LINEAR SEARCH

One way to look for data in a file is to start at the beginning and examine each record until you find the one you are looking for. This is the method people use who do not have large files. But for more than about 12 records it is not a good filing system. It will serve as an example to introduce us to the idea of searching mechanically and give us a bad method to compare our better methods to. We will create a file which consists of names

and telephone numbers but the file will not be ordered by either
name or number.

We will keep the file in two one-dimensional arrays, one
called NAME and one called PHONE. PHONE(I) will be the correct
telephone number for NAME(I). We will read this file, then read
a list of names of people whose phone numbers are wanted. We are
assuming that our file of names and phone numbers is punched
without quotes around the names,

```
$JOB   DON MCQUARRIE
C THIS PROGRAM LOOKS UP PHONE NUMBERS
       CHARACTER*20 NAME(25),FRIEND
       CHARACTER*8 PHONE(25)
       INTEGER I,SIZE
C      READ FILE OF NAMES AND NUMBERS
       I=1
       READ 10,NAME(I),PHONE(I)
10     FORMAT(A20,A8)
       WHILE(NAME(I).NE.'ZZZ')DO
          I=I+1
          READ 20,NAME(I),PHONE(I)
20        FORMAT(A20,A8)
          END WHILE
       SIZE=I-1
       READ 30,FRIEND
30     FORMAT(A20)
       WHILE(FRIEND.NE.'ZZZ')DO
C         LOOK UP FRIEND'S NUMBER
          I=1
          WHILE(FRIEND.NE.NAME(I).AND.I.LE.SIZE)DO
             I=I+1
             END WHILE
          IF(FRIEND.EQ.NAME(I))THEN DO
             PRINT 40,FRIEND,PHONE(I)
40           FORMAT(' ',A20,A8)
          ELSE DO
             PRINT 50,FRIEND,'UNLISTED'
50           FORMAT(' ',A20,A8)
             END IF
          READ 60,FRIEND
60        FORMAT(A20)
          END WHILE
       RETURN
       END
$ENTRY
PERRAULT,R.          483-4865
SCHUSTER,S.          769-5662
BORODIN,A.           782-8928
COOK,S.A.            763-3900
ENRIGHT,W.H.         266-1234
ZZZ
BORODIN,A.
BERNSTEIN,P.
ZZZ
```

The output will be

```
BORODIN,A.        782-8928
BERNSTEIN,P.      UNLISTED
```

We have stored the phone number as a character string because of the dash between the first three and the last four digits.

TIME TAKEN FOR SEARCH

In the last section we developed a program for a linear search. The searching process consists of comparing the friend's name, FRIEND, with each name in the file of names NAME(1), NAME(2), NAME(3), and so on until either the name is found or the end of the file is reached. For a small file, a linear search like this one may be fast enough, but it can be time-consuming if there is a lengthy file.

If there are N records in the file and the name is actually in the file, then on the average there will be $N/2$ comparisons. The largest number of comparisons would be N if the name were last in the file, the least number would be 1 if the name were first. A file of 1000 names would require 500 comparisons on the average. This gets to look rather formidable. It is for this reason that we do something to cut down on the effort. What we do is to sort the file into alphabetic order and then use a method of searching called binary searching. We will look at sorting later, but first we will see how much faster binary searching can be.

BINARY SEARCH

The telephone book is sorted alphabetically and the technique most of us use for looking up numbers is similar to the technique known as binary searching. We start by opening the book near where we think we will find the name we are looking for. We look at the page that is open and compare any name on it with the name being sought. If the listed name is alphabetically greater we know we must look only between the page we are at and the beginning of the book. We have eliminated the second part of the book from the search. This process is repeated in the part that might contain the name until we narrow the search down to one page.

In binary searching, instead of looking where we think we might find the name, we begin by looking at the name in the middle of the file and discard the half in which it cannot lie. This process cuts the possible number of names to be searched in half at each comparison.

A file of 16 names would require a maximum of 4 comparisons: one to cut the list to 8, another to 4, another to 2, and another

to 1. Of course, we might find it earlier, but this is the <u>most</u>
work we have to do. It is the maximum number of comparisons.
With a linear search of 16 records we might have to make 16
comparisons, although 8 is the average. If we have a file of
1024 records, the binary search takes a maximum of 10
comparisons. This can be calculated by seeing how many times you
must divide by 2 to get down to 1 record . Put mathematically,
1024 is equal to

            2*2*2*2*2*2*2*2*2*2

Just one more comparison, making 11 altogether, will let you
search a list of 2048 entries. Then 4096 can be done with 12
comparisons. You can see how much more efficient binary
searching can be when the file is a long one.

                    A SUBROUTINE FOR BINARY SEARCH

    We will now design a program for doing a binary search and
write it so that it can be called as a subroutine. When we write

        CALL SEARCH(FILE,KEY,SIZE,WHERE)

we are asking for the value of WHERE for which FILE(WHERE)=KEY.
FILE is an array of SIZE items declared as CHARACTER. If the KEY
is not in the file, WHERE will be set to zero.

    We will develop the algorithm for the binary search in two
stages as an illustration of step-by-step refinement. We will
write out our proposed solution in a mixture of English and SF/k.

        Set WHERE to zero in case KEY is not in FILE
        WHILE(there is more of the file to search)DO
            Find middle of file
            IF(middle value matches KEY)THEN DO
                Set WHERE to middle
                Discard remainder of file
            ELSE DO
                IF(middle value comes after KEY)THEN DO
                    Discard last half of remainder of file
                ELSE DO
                    Discard first half of remainder of file
                    END IF
                END IF
            END WHILE

    It will be important to know the FIRST and LAST of the
remainder of the file at any time in order to establish the
MIDDLE and to discard the appropriate half. We initially set
FIRST to 1 and LAST to SIZE. Then to find the middle we use

        MIDDLE=(LAST+FIRST)/2.0

It will not matter that this division is truncated as the process
of finding the middle is approximate when the number of entries
in the file is an even number. Refining the expression, "Discard
last half of remainder of file," becomes

        LAST=MIDDLE-1

and, "Discard first half of remainder of file," becomes

        FIRST=MIDDLE+1

Notice that we are discarding FILE(MIDDLE) as well in each case.
The subroutine can now be written:

```
C LOCATE KEY USING BINARY SEARCH
        SUBROUTINE SEARCH(FILE,KEY,SIZE,WHERE)
        INTEGER SIZE,WHERE
        CHARACTER*20 FILE(SIZE),KEY
        INTEGER FIRST,LAST,MIDDLE
C       SET WHERE TO ZERO FOR CASE OF KEY NOT IN FILE
        WHERE=0
        WHILE(FIRST.LE.LAST)DO
           MIDDLE=(FIRST+LAST)/2.0
           IF(FILE(MIDDLE).EQ.KEY)THEN DO
              WHERE=MIDDLE
C             DISCARD ALL OF FILE
              FIRST=LAST+1
           ELSE DO
              IF(FILE(MIDDLE).GT.KEY)THEN DO
C                DISCARD LAST HALF
                 LAST=MIDDLE-1
              ELSE DO
C                DISCARD FIRST HALF
                 FIRST=MIDDLE+1
                 END IF
              END IF
           END WHILE
        RETURN
        END
```

A program that uses this subroutine can now be written.

    We will use it to find the telephone numbers, and so replace
the four lines of our phone-number look-up program following the
comment LOOK UP FRIEND'S NUMBER by this single statement:

    CALL SEARCH(NAME,FRIEND,SIZE,I)

We   are   assuming   now   that   the   file   of names is sorted
alphabetically. The subroutine SEARCH would be included right
after the main program.

    You will notice that the binary search program has more
instructions than the linear search that it is replacing.   Each
step is more complicated, but the whole process is much faster
for a large file because fewer steps are executed.

SEARCHING BY ADDRESS CALCULATION

We have seen that the efficiency of the searching process is very much improved by having a file sorted. The next method of searching uses data organized in a way so there is "a place for everything, and everything in its place".

Suppose you had a file of N records numbered from 1 to N. If you knew the number of the record, you would immediately know the location. The number would be the index of the array that holds the file entries. Each entry would have a location where it belonged. The trouble usually is to find the location of a record when what you know is some other piece of information such as a person's name.

Files are sometimes arranged so that they are organized on serial numbers that can be calculated from some other information in the record. For example, we could take a person's name and, by transforming it in a certain definite way, change it into a serial number. This transformation often seems bizarre and meaningless, and we say the name is hash-coded into a number. When the number has been determined the location is then definite and you can go to it without any problem.

Usually with hash coding it happens that several records have the same hash code. This means that, instead of the code providing the address of the exact record you want, what you get is the address of a location capable of containing several different records. We call such a location a bucket or bin. We then must look at the records in the bin to find the exact one we are interested in. Since the number is small they need not be sorted. A linear search is reasonable when the file is small.

If fixed-size bins are used to store the file, it is important to get a hash coding algorithm that will divide the original file so that roughly the same number of records is in each bin.

As an example of a hash-coding algorithm, suppose that we had 1000 bins and wanted to divide a file of 10,000 records into the bins. The file might already have associated with each record an identifying number. For example, it might be a Social Insurance number or a student number. These numbers might range from 1 to 1,000,000. One way to divide the records into bins would be to choose the last three digits of the identifying number as the hash code. Another hash code might be formed by choosing the third, fifth, and seventh digit. The purpose is to try to get a technique that gives about the same number of records in each bin. More complicated hashing algorithms may be necessary.

SORTING

We have already developed a sorting program as an example of step-by-step refinement in Chapter 9. The method we used is called a _bubble_ _sort_. Each pair of neighboring elements in a file is compared and exchanged, to put the element with the larger key in the array location with the higher index. On each exchange pass, the element with the largest key gets moved into the last position. The next pass can then exclude the last position because it is already in order.

We have shown that the binary search technique is much more efficient for a large file than a linear search. In the same way, although a bubble sort is a reasonable method for a small file, it is not efficient for a large file. What we usually do to sort a large file is to divide it into a number of smaller files. Each small file is sorted by a technique such as the bubble sort, then the sorted smaller files are merged together into larger files.

We will look at an example in which two sorted files are merged into a single larger sorted file.

SORTING BY MERGING

We will develop a subroutine called MERGE to merge FILE1, which has SIZE1 records, with FILE2, which has SIZE2 records. The records in FILE1 and FILE2 are already in order. We will invoke this subroutine with the statement

    CALL MERGE(FILE1,SIZE1,FILE2,SIZE2,FILE3)

Here is the MERGE subroutine:

```
C MERGE TWO SORTED FILES
      SUBROUTINE MERGE(FILE1,SIZE1,FILE2,SIZE2,FILE3)
      CHARACTER*20 FILE1(25),FILE2(25),FILE3(50)
      INTEGER SIZE1,SIZE2
      INTEGER I1,I2,I3
      I1=1
      I2=1
      I3=1
c     MERGE UNTIL ALL OF ONE FILE IS USED
      WHILE(I1.LE.SIZE1.AND.I2.LE.SIZE2)DO
         IF(FILE1(I1).LT.FILE2(I2))THEN DO
            FILE3(I3)=FILE1(I1)
            I1=I1+1
         ELSE DO
            FILE3(I3)=FILE2(I2)
            I2=I2+1
            END IF
         I3=I3+1
         END WHILE
C     ADD REMAINING ITEMS TO END OF NEW FILE
      WHILE(I1.LE.SIZE1)DO
         FILE3(I3)=FILE1(I1)
         I1=I1+1
         I3=I3+1
         END WHILE
      WHILE(I2.LE.SIZE2)DO
         FILE3(I3)=FILE2(I2)
         I2=I2+1
         I3=I3+1
         END WHILE
      RETURN
      END
```

EFFICIENCY OF SORTING METHODS

The number of comparisons required to merge the two previously sorted files in our example is SIZE1+SIZE2. To sort a file of length N by the bubble sort we can count the maximum number of comparisons that are needed. It is

$$(N-1)+(N-2)+(N-3)+...+1$$

This series can be summed and the result is

$$N(N-1)/2 \quad \text{which is}$$

$$N^2/2 - N/2$$

When N is large, the number of comparisons is about $N^2/2$, since this is very large compared to N/2. We say the execution time of the algorithm varies as N^2; sorting 100 items takes 100 times the

number of comparisons that sorting 10 items does. We will now
make calculations to see why sorting by merging is useful for
long files. To sort a file of N items, by first using a bubble
sort on two files N/2 in length then merging, requires $N^2/4-N/2$
for the bubble sort and N for the merge. This makes a
combination total of

$$N^2/4 + N/2 \quad \text{comparisons.}$$

Using a bubble sort on the whole file gives a result of

$$N^2/2 - N/2 \quad \text{comparisons.}$$

When N=100, the bubble sort merge method requires 2,550
comparisons, the straight bubble sort requires 4,950 comparisons.
Other methods that are more efficient than the bubble sort may be
used.

CHAPTER 15 SUMMARY

    This chapter has presented methods of searching and sorting
that are used in computer programs.   These methods manipulate
files of records. Each record consists of one or more fields.

    A search is based on a key, such as a person's name, that
appears as one field in a record of a file.   A linear search
locates the desired record by starting at the first record and
inspecting one record after another until the given key is found.
A linear search is slow and should not be used for large files; a
faster search method, such as binary search, should be used for
large files.

    A binary search requires that the file be ordered according
to the key field of the records.   An unordered file can be
ordered using one of the sorting methods given in this chapter.
The binary search inspects the middle record to determine which
half of the file contains the desired record. Then the middle
record of the correct half is inspected, to determine which
quarter of the file contains the desired record, and so on, until
the record is located.

    If the key is a number that is identical to the index of the
desired record then no searching is required, because the key
gives the location of the record.   Sometimes the key can be
manipulated to create a hash code that locates a small set of
records, called a bucket, that includes the desired record.

    A file of records can be ordered using the bubble sort. This
method repeatedly passes through the file, interchanging adjacent
out-of-order records until all records are in order. The bubble
sort is slow and should not be used for large files; a faster
sorting method, such as sorting by merging, should be used for
large files.

A file can be sorted by merging in the following manner. First the file is divided into two sub-files and each of the sub-files is sorted by some method, such as the bubble sort. Then, starting with the first records of the two sub-files, the ordered file is created by passing through the sub-files and successively picking the appropriate (smaller key or alphabetically first key) record. If the sub-files are large, they should be sorted by a fast method, such as a merge, instead of by a bubble sort.

CHAPTER 15 EXERCISES

1. The students for a particular high-school class have their names recorded on cards, for example:

    'ABBOT, HAROLD'

These cards are arranged alphabetically. Another deck of cards contains the names of newly-entered students for the same class; these cards are also alphabetically arranged. Write a program that reads the two sets of cards and prints out all the names alphabetically. Your program should read the smaller deck first and store its names in an array. Then the alphabetized list should be printed at the same time the larger deck is read. Explain why it is better to read the smaller deck first. What is the advantage of printing the list while the second deck is being read, rather than waiting till both decks are read?

2. Do exercise 1 assuming that the large deck is alphabetized, but the small deck is not.

3. Write a program that maintains a "lost and found" service. First the program reads cards giving found objects and the finders' names and phone numbers. For example, this card

    'SIAMESE CAT'   'MISS MABEL DAVIS'   '714-3261'

means Miss Mabel Davis, having phone number 714-3261, found a Siamese cat. These cards are to be read and ordered alphabetically and then a similar set of cards for losers of objects is to be processed. If a lost object matches a found object, then the program should print the name of the object as well as the finder, the loser and their telephone numbers. Assume the loser cards are not alphabetized. Process each loser card as it is read, using a binary search.

CHAPTER 16

MAKING SURE
THE PROGRAM WORKS

Throughout this book, we have emphasized structured programming techniques; these include step-by-step refinement, programming without the GO TO statement, choosing good variable names and so on. These techniques make it easier to write correct programs. We have also given techniques for testing and debugging programs. In this chapter we will collect and expand upon these techniques for making sure a program works.

SOLVING THE RIGHT PROBLEM

The specifications for a program tell what the program must do to solve a problem. Before starting to write a program, the programmer needs the detailed specifications for the program. Suppose the problem is to print pay checks for the employees of a company; there is a card giving each employee's name and amount of payment. The programmer needs to know the format of the data on the cards as well as the format for the pay checks. These formats are part of the specifications for the program to print pay checks.

Sometimes the program specifications are not completely agreed upon and written down. If an employee's card indicates an amount of $0.00, this may mean that the employee is on leave and is to receive no pay check. If the programmer does not know the special significance of $0.00 - because the specifications are not complete - he may write a program that prints hundreds of worthless pay checks. All too often programs fail to handle special situations such as $0.00 correctly. If the programmer is in doubt about such a situation, he should check the specifications and make sure they are complete.

DEFENSIVE PROGRAMMING

Errors are sometimes made in the preparation of data for a program. Amounts may be mispunched on cards; more data may be supplied than anticipated. The method of handling data errors may be given in the program specifications, or it may be left to the discretion of the programmer. Sometimes a programmer can write his program so that it detects and reports bad data. This is called defensive programming. Some programs are written to accept absolutely any data; after reporting a bad data item, the program ignores the item or attempts to give it a reasonable interpretation. If a program is written assuming no data errors, bad data items may prevent the program from doing its job. It is the programmer's responsibility to make his program sufficiently defensive to solve the problem at hand.

ATTITUDE AND WORK HABITS

The quality of a computer program is determined largely by the attitudes and work habits of the programmer. Some programmers underestimate the programming task. They write programs too quickly, they do not test their programs sufficiently, and they are too willing to believe that their programs are correct.

Most programs, when first written, contain some errors. This is not surprising when you consider the vast number of possible programming errors and the fallibility of every programmer. The programmer should take the attitude that a program is not correct until it is shown to be correct.

One good method of preparing computer programs is to write them using a soft lead pencil. This allows easy corrections and improvements by erasing and replacing lines. If a major change is required, an entire page should be recopied. The program should be submitted to the computer only when the programmer feels confident that no more changes are required. This method of program preparation can save the programmer a lot of time. The savings come because it is easy to change a program when it is still on paper and fresh in the programmer's mind. Each later change requires the programmer to relearn the program before he can confidently make modifications. A few minutes of desk-checking a program can save hours of debugging time. The programmer who tries to "do it right the first time" comes out ahead, saving his own time and writing programs with fewer errors.

PROVING PROGRAM CORRECTNESS

The most effective way to make sure a program works correctly is to study the program thoroughly. It should be read again and again until the programmer is thoroughly convinced that it is right.

It helps if a second programmer reads and approves the program. Ideally, the second programmer should read the program after its author feels that it is correct, but before it is submitted to the computer. The second reader provides a new point of view and may be able to find typical errors such as incorrect loop initialization.

This process of studying programs to make sure they are correct can be called "proving program correctness". Sometimes programs are proven correct using a mathematical approach; proving that a program is correct is then similar to proving that a theorem in geometry is true. More often, programs are proven correct by a non-mathematical, common-sense approach. The program is considered to have errors until proven correct. When one or more programmers study a program until they understand it and are convinced it is correct, we say that they have proven it to be correct.

PROGRAMMING STYLE

A program should be easy to read and understand; otherwise the job of studying it to verify its correctness will be hopeless. The programmer should strive for a good programming style, remembering that other readers will be in a hurry and will be critical of sloppiness or unnecessary confusion in the program. It commonly happens that as a programmer makes a program clearer and easier to understand, he discovers ways to improve or correct the program.

It takes work to write programs that are easy to read - just as it takes work to write clear English. Good writing requires care and practice. One way of making programs readable and understandable is to give them a simple organization - so the reader can easily learn the relationship among program parts. We have previously presented step-by-step refinement and modular programming as techniques for designing programs. As well as aiding in the writing of programs, these techniques help make programs easier to read.

USE OF COMMENTS AND IDENTIFIERS

One of the rules of good programming style is this: comments and identifiers should be chosen to help make a program understandable. Comments should record the programmer's intentions for the parts of the program. It is a good idea to write comments as the program is being written.

Good programs do not require many comments, because the program text closely reflects the intentions of the programmer.

Programs become more difficult to read if they are cluttered with obvious comments such as

```
C       INCREASE N BY 1
        N=N+1
```

Comments are usually needed to record:

- Overall purpose of a program. What problem the program is to solve. As well, comments may be used to record the program's author and its date of writing.

- Purpose of each module. Similar to the comments for an overall program.

- Purpose of a collection of statements. Such a comment might give the purpose of a loop.

- Assumptions and restrictions. At certain points in a program, certain assumptions and restrictions may apply to variables and the data. For example, one program part may assume that another program part has set SIZE to a positive number less than 20 to indicate the number of customer accounts.

- Obscure or unusual statements. As a rule, such statements should be avoided. If they are required they should be explained. Here is an example:

```
C       ROUND CENTS TO NEAREST DOLLAR
        DOLLRS=(CENTS+50)/100.0
        CENTS=100*DOLLRS
```

Well-chosen identifiers make a program easier to read. Each identifier should record the function of the named object. For example, an array used to save credit limits should be named LIMIT and not ARRAY. A subprogram used to input accounts should be named INPUT and not P1 or FRED.

If a variable has a very simple purpose, such as indexing through an array, a one-letter name such as I, J or N may be appropriate. This is because these letters are commonly used for indexing in mathematics. But if the index variable has some additional meaning, such as counting input data cards, a longer name may help the reader.

Avoid obscure abbreviations, such as TBNTR for table entry. Avoid acronyms, such as SAX for sales tax. Unless abbreviations or acronyms are well known to the reader before seeing the program, they impose an extra memorization task that interferes with understanding the program. Unfortunately, Fortran variables can be at most six characters long, so some abbreviations are inevitable; choose these to have maximum readability.

Avoid meaningless identifiers such as A, B, C, D and TEMP1. A single-letter identifier such as D is sometimes appropriate for a simply-used variable when the name D is relevant, for example, it stands for diameter. Adding a digit such as 1 or 2 to the end of an identifier, as in TEMP1, can be confusing unless it explains the purpose of the named object.

TESTING

After the program has been written and studied to verify its correctness, it should be tested. The purpose of testing is to run the program to demonstrate that the program is correct.

The tests must be chosen with care because only a limited number of them can be run. Consider a program designed to sort any list of 100 names into alphabetic order. Certainly we could not test it exhaustively by trying every possible list of 100 names. We would be testing for years! Rather than exhaustive testing we need to design tests which try every type of situation the program is to handle.

Well-designed tests should point out any errors in the program. Ultimately, testing demonstrates errors better than it demonstrates program correctness.

When testing reveals an error, that is, a <u>bug</u>, in the program, the programmer is faced with a <u>debugging</u> task. We shall present debugging techniques later. Right now, we will give techniques for testing.

The programmer will need to study the program in order to design good tests. The tests should make each statement execute at least once - but this is not enough. Suppose the statement

AVRAGE=TOTAL/COUNT

is tested and computes the desired average. This does not demonstrate that all is well; it may be that in some situations COUNT can become zero. If this statement is executed with COUNT set to zero, the statement does not make sense. So, not only should every statement be executed, but it should be executed for the type of situation it is expected to handle. Care should be taken to:

- <u>Test</u> <u>end</u> <u>conditions</u>. See that each loop is executed correctly the first time and last time through. Test situations in which indexes to arrays reach their smallest and largest possible values. Pay particular attention to counters which may take on the value zero.

- <u>Test</u> <u>special</u> <u>conditions</u>. See that data which rarely occurs is handled properly. If the program prints error messages, see that each situation requiring such a message is tested.

Designing tests to exercise all end conditions and special conditions is not easy - but it is worthwhile in terms of program reliability.

The programmer should be able to tell from test results if the program is executing correctly. Sometimes this is easy because the program prints intermediate results as it progresses. Sometimes the programmer will need to add special printing statements so he can verify that the program is running correctly. These statements can:

Print data as it is read. If there is not too much data, it may be good to have the program print the data as it is read.

Print messages to record the statements being executed. For example, a message might say INPUT SUBROUTINE ENTERED.

Print values of variables. This allows the programmer to verify by hand that the values are correct. The best time to print variables is when modules start and when they finish, so the programmer can verify that variables were modified correctly.

Print warnings of violated assumptions. Suppose a subroutine is used to set WHERE to the index of the smallest number in a list of 12 numbers. The assumption that WHERE receives a value from 1 to 12 can be tested by

```
IF(WHERE.LT.1.OR.WHERE.GT.12)THEN DO
    PRINT,'ERROR:WHERE=',WHERE
    END IF
```

Care must be taken to design appropriate printing statements for testing. Too much printing will not be read by the programmer; too little printing will not give the programmer sufficient information about the execution of the program.

Ideally, tests should be designed before the program is submitted to the computer. With the program still fresh in his mind, the programmer can more easily invent tests that try out every statement. Sometimes a programmer discovers that parts of a program are difficult to test; a slight change in the program may overcome this difficulty. It is best to make these changes when the program is still on paper, before time has been invested in punching the program and submitting it to the computer. Designing tests requires the programmer to read his program with a new point of view. It sometimes happens that this point of view uncovers errors in the program. The best time to fix these errors is when the program is still on paper.

As programs become larger, it becomes increasingly difficult to test them thoroughly. Large programs can be tested by first testing the modules individually. Then the modules are combined into larger modules and these are tested and so on. The process is called bottom-up testing. This method of testing uses specially-written test programs that call the modules with various values of parameters, shared variables and input data.

Whenever a program is modified, it should be retested. All the changed parts should be tested. In addition, it is a good idea to test the entire module containing changes, or even the entire program. The reason is that modifications often require a precise understanding of the surrounding program, and this understanding is sometimes not attained. Very commonly, program modifications introduce errors.

DEBUGGING

A program has bugs (errors) when it fails to solve the problem it is supposed to solve. When a program misbehaves we are faced with the problem of debugging - correcting the error. The program's misbehavior is a symptom of a disease and we must find a cure. Sometimes the symptom is far removed from the source of the problem; erroneous statements in one part of a program may set variables' values incorrectly and trigger a series of unpredicted actions by the program. When the symptoms appear via incorrect program output, the program may be executing in a different module. The programmer is left with a few clues: the incorrect output. He has to solve the mystery and cure the disease. Solving these debugging mysteries can take more time than writing the program.

When a program contains a bug, this means that the programmer made at least one mistake. We can categorize programmer errors as follows:

Errors in making the program machine-readable. If the program is prepared on punch cards, RETURN might be mis-punched as RETRUN. These are keypunching errors.

Errors in using the programming language. The programmer did not understand a language construct. For example, his program may be wrong because he assumed that 'JONES' comes alphabetically before 'JONES '. (When SF/k compares the two it concludes they are alphabetically equal.)

Errors in writing program parts. Although a particular program part was properly designed, it was not correctly written in SF/k. For example, a loop designed to read in account cards might always execute zero times because of writing the loop's terminating condition incorrectly.

Errors in program design. The program parts and their interactions might be improperly designed. The program designer might forget to provide for the initialization of variables used by some modules. He might overlook the fact that one module, say, the UPDATE subroutine, should be called only after calling another module, say, the INPUT subroutine.

<u>Solving the wrong problem</u>. The programmer did not understand the nature of the problem to be solved. He may have misunderstood the program specifications. Perhaps the specifications were not correct or complete.

This list of possible errors has proceeded from the least serious to the most disastrous. The first type of errors, such as keypunching errors, can be corrected easily once detected. The last type of error, misunderstanding the purpose of the program, may require scrapping the entire program and starting over again.

Some programmers are overly optimistic and immediately conclude that any bugs in their programs are not very serious. Such a programmer is quick to make little changes in his program to try to make the symptoms of the problem disappear.   The wise programmer knows that program misbehavior is an indication of sloppiness and that sloppiness leads easily to disastrous errors. He takes program misbehavior as a sign that the program is sick - he gives it a checkup by studying it.

The overly optimistic programmer is forever saying, "I just found the last bug." When the wise programmer finds a bug, he looks for five more.

Many of the least serious errors, such as misspelled keywords, are automatically pointed out by error messages, because the error results in an illegal SF/k program. These errors are usually easy to fix. Some errors are particularly treacherous; they seem to defy attempts to correct them. Here is some advice - some of it repeated from earlier parts of this book - to help you track down treacherous bugs.

<u>Read all error messages</u>. In their hurry to read their program's output, some programmers fail to notice error messages. These messages may pinpoint a bug.

<u>Beware of automatic error repair</u>. Some compilers try to make it easier to get programs working by "repairing" errors. For example, the programmer might carelessly write X=2Y. The compiler might repair this to X=2. Such repairs can save time by allowing more of the program to be compiled and executed on one run. However, these repairs should not be taken as intelligent advice; remember, the compiler has no idea what problem you are trying to solve.

<u>The first error messages may help more than later ones</u>. This is because the first messages are closer to the source of the problem. Later messages may simply indicate that a previous error is still causing trouble.

<u>Beware of confusion between I and 1</u>. Some people can consistently read X=X+I to mean increase X by one. Errors like this can be found by reading the program character by character - as a computer does! In general, the human

tendency to read what we want to be there, rather what is actually there makes debugging difficult.

Beware of misspellings. Some words are easily misspelled. A person who is concentrating on understanding a program may overlook WEIGHT occasionally spelled as WIEGHT. In Watfiv - but not in SF/k - new identifiers are automatically declared to be variables. Hence, Watfiv would not warn us that WIEGHT suspiciously did not appear in a declaration.

If everything else fails in the debugging effort, the programmer is forced to rerun his program to gain more information about the errors. The programmer may add statements to print variables or to trace the program's execution. These statements are designed using the same techniques used in testing to show programs work properly. If the original tests had been carefully enough designed, there is a good chance they would have pinpointed the error and eliminated later time-consuming debugging.

CHAPTER 16 SUMMARY

In this chapter we have listed techniques for making sure a program works. There are a vast number of ways a program can be wrong, so the programmer should learn to be careful at all the stages of program preparation. When a programmer is too hasty to submit his program to the computer, this results in persistent bugs and excessive time spent in debugging. The following important techniques and terminology were presented in this chapter.

Program specifications - explanation of what a program is to do. This should include the forms of the input and output data and the type of calculation or data manipulation to be performed. Essentially, program specifications explain how the computer is to be used to solve a particular problem.

Programming habits - the way a programmer goes about his work. Ideally, he should take the slow but sure approach, completing his program in pencil and thoroughly studying it before submitting it to the computer.

Proving program correctness - studying a program to verify that it satisfies its specifications.

Programming style - if the style is good, then the program can be easily read and understood.

Use of comments and identifiers - good programming style requires that comments and identifiers be chosen to make a program understandable. Comments should record the programmer's intentions; identifiers should record the function or use of the named object.

Testing - running a program to demonstrate that it is correct. Tests should be designed to try every type of situation the program is to handle. Ultimately, testing is better at demonstrating bugs than demonstrating program correctness.

Debugging - correcting errors in a program. Debugging can be the most difficult and time-consuming part of trying to make a program work. These difficulties can be minimized by using the techniques listed in this chapter.

CHAPTER 16 EXERCISES

1. In this exercise you are to use defensive programming. Modify the following program so that it will handle errors in the data gracefully. The program reads a list of names and prints the list in reverse order. You have no control over the data, but if you wish, you can add a redundant dummy data card to the end of the data.

```
C PRINT NAMES IN REVERSE ORDER
      CHARACTER*15 NAME(10)
      INTEGER SIZE,I
      READ 10,SIZE
10    FORMAT(I3)
      DO 20 I=1,SIZE
         READ,NAME(I)
20       CONTINUE
      I=SIZE
      WHILE(I.GE.1)DO
         PRINT,NAME(I)
         I=I-1
         END WHILE
      RETURN
      END
```

2. You are to debug the following program. It is supposed to read strings and determine if they are palindromes. A string is a palindrome if reversing it yields the same string again; for example, each of the following are palindromes: 'MOM', 'OH HO', and 'DEED'. Do <u>not</u> submit the corrected program to be run by the computer.

```
$JOB   ID='SUE DENIM'
C THIS PROGRAM IS FULL OF BUGS
       CHARACTER*1 STRING(10),REVRSE(10)
       CHARACTER*20 REPLY
       INTEGER COUNT,I,J,HALF,R
       READ,COUNT
       PRINT,'TEST',COUNT,'STRINGS'
       READ 10,STRING
10     FORMAT(10A1)
       DO 40 I=1,COUNT
          I=10
          WHILE(STRING(I).NE.' ')DO
             I=I-1
             END WHILE
          HALF=I/2.0
          R=1
          WHILE(I.LE.HALF)DO
            REVRSE(R)=STRING(I)
             R=R+1
             I=I-1
             END WHILE
          DO 20 J=1,HALF
             IF(STRING(J).EQ.REVRSE(J))THEN DO
                REPLY='IS A PALINDROME'
             ELSE DO
                REPLY='IS NOT A PALINDROME'
                END IF
20           CONTINUE
          PRINT 30,STRING,REPLY
30        FORMAT(' ',10A1,A20)
40        CONTINUE
       RETURN
       END
$ENTRY
 4
 'DEED'
 'OH HO'
 'AHAH MADAM HAHA'
 'ROTOR'
```

3. Try to write a program that is completely correct before you submit it to the computer. Have a friend help you by studying your program for errors after you are convinced that it is free of errors. Record the time you spend preparing the program and record any programming errors you make. Your program should perform one of the following tasks:

(a) The program should read a series of integers followed by the dummy value 99999. Print the sum of the positive integers and the number of negative integers.

(b) The program should read and print a list of alphabetically ordered names. If a name is repeated in the data, it should be printed only once.

4. The following program reads employees' names, hours worked in a week and hourly rates of pay. It computes each employee's pay based on his rate and number of hours, with one and a half times the rate for overtime hours (hours beyond the first 40 hours). Make the program readable by adding appropriate comments and by choosing meaningful variable names. No other changes to the program are required.

```
$JOB    JEANNE DAIGLE
C THIS PROGRAM HAS POOR IDENTIFIERS AND NEEDS COMMENTS
        CHARACTER*11 B1
        INTEGER B,A,C,B2
        PRINT,'EMPLOYEE   ','REGULAR HRS','OVERTIME   ','PAYMENT'
        READ,B1,A,B
        WHILE(B1.NE.'ZZZ')DO
           C=0
           IF(A.GT.40)THEN DO
              C=A-40
              A=40
              END IF
           B2=B*(A+1.5*C)+0.5
           PRINT,B1,A,C,B2
           READ,B1,A,B
           END WHILE
        RETURN
        END
$ENTRY
 'LEXI KOLT'   5  3
 'JOHN EVANS' 59  5
 ...
 'ZZZ'           0  0
```

CHAPTER 17

SF/8:
FILES AND RECORDS

So far we have spoken about files of records and discussed the process of searching for particular records. This process was made more efficient by having the files sorted. We then looked at ways of sorting files of records. All sorting methods involve moving records around in the computer memory. In our sorting examples, we did not really deal with the situation of sorting records that consisted of more than the one field, namely the key field of the ordering. In our examples, then, moving the record meant only moving this one field. In most data processing applications, records contain a number of fields, so in this chapter we will show how such records are handled in Fortran.

When large quantities of data have to be processed, it is impossible to store files of records completely within the main memory of the computer. It is usual to keep large files in secondary storage such as magnetic tape or magnetic disk storage. We must then be able to read records from such a file and write records into it. We will be looking at the statements in Fortran that permit us to manipulate files in secondary storage.

RECORDS IN FORTRAN

Some programming languages like Cobol and PL/1 provide special constructs for handling records. These allow the programmer to collect several variables into a record and use a name for the entire the record. For example, a CLIENT record could have name, address and phone number fields as this diagram shows.

CLIENT

NAME	ADRESS	PHONE

This is the kind of record that might be found in a telephone book. You have noticed that arrays, which can also be thought of as collections of variables, are different from records because all elements in an array are of the same type. But in records each field can be of a different type.

Since Fortran does not provide a special way of designating records, we must declare each field of the record as an ordinary variable. Our CLIENT record can be created this way:

```
C      SET UP A CLIENT'S RECORD
       CHARACTER*20 NAME
       CHARACTER*30 ADRESS
       CHARACTER*8 PHONE
```

In other languages the record could be assigned as a unit to another record that has the same types of fields. But in Fortran, the record must be assigned field by field. Similarly, if the record is to be read from cards or printed this must be done a field at a time.

ARRAYS OF RECORDS

There can be arrays of records, just like there can be arrays of simple types such as integers. To set up an array of records using Fortran we declare each field to be an array and then consider record number I to be the collection of fields with index I. An array of 100 records such as those used in a telephone book could be declared by:

```
       CHARACTER*20 NAME(100)
       CHARACTER*30 ADRESS(100)
       CHARACTER*8 PHONE(100)
```

Now the collection NAME(I), ADRESS(I), PHONE(I) makes up record number I.

We can use our array of records to group records for sorting purposes. A subroutine for sorting these records will be given. The records are to be sorted on the key PHONE. The array of records will be in COMMON with the main program. The only parameter is SIZE which gives the actual number of records in the array. The sorting will be done by swapping records, so a temporary record is set up to hold a record during a swap.

```
C SORT RECORDS BY PHONE NUMBER
      SUBROUTINE SORT(SIZE)
      INTEGER SIZE
      COMMON/TABLE/NAME,ADRESS,PHONE
      CHARACTER*20 NAME(100)
      CHARACTER*30 ADRESS(100)
      CHARACTER*8 PHONE(100)
C     SET UP A TEMPORARY RECORD
      CHARACTER*20 TNAME
      CHARACTER*30 TADRES
      CHARACTER*8 TPHONE
      INTEGER I,J,BIG,LAST
      I=1
      WHILE(I.LT.SIZE)DO
         LAST=SIZE-I+1
C        PUT BIGGEST PHONE OF 1 TO LAST INTO LAST
         BIG=LAST
         J=1
         WHILE(J.LT.LAST)DO
            IF(PHONE(J).GT.PHONE(BIG))THEN DO
               BIG=J
               END IF
            J=J+1
            END WHILE
C        SWAP RECORD(LAST) AND RECORD WITH BIGGEST
C           PHONE(IN 1 TO LAST)
         TNAME=NAME(LAST)
         TADRES=ADRESS(LAST)
         TPHONE=PHONE(LAST)
         NAME(LAST)=NAME(BIG)
         ADRESS(LAST)=ADRESS(BIG)
         PHONE(LAST)=PHONE(BIG)
         NAME(BIG)=TNAME
         ADRESS(BIG)=TADRES
         PHONE(BIG)=TPHONE
         I=I+1
         END WHILE
      RETURN
      END
```

In many applications the natural way to think of the data is in terms of records. Sometimes each record corresponds to a card or to a print line, but it can also correspond to a larger or smaller collection of information. We will give a program that reads each record of a small telephone directory from cards, uses our SORT subroutine to put the records in order by phone number, and then prints the result. As you can see, each record is read and printed a field at a time in this case by formatted READ and PRINT statements.

```
$JOB     STEPHEN ALEXANDER
C READ A SMALL PHONE DIRECTORY AND PRINT IT IN
C     ORDER BY PHONE NUMBER
      COMMON/TABLE/NAME,ADRESS,PHONE
      CHACATER*20 NAME(100)
      CHARACTER*30 ADRESS(100)
      CHARACTER*8 PHONE(100)
      INTEGER I,SIZE
      READ,SIZE
C     READ ENTRIES INTO ARRAY OF RECORDS
      DO 20 I=1,SIZE
         READ 10,NAME(I),ADRESS(I),PHONE(I)
10       FORMAT(A20,A30,A8)
20       CONTINUE
C     SORT RECORDS BY PHONE NUMBER
      CALL SORT(SIZE)
C     PRINT SORTED ARRAY OF RECORDS
      DO 40 I=1,SIZE
         PRINT 30,PHONE(I),NAME(I),ADRESS(I)
30       FORMAT(' ',A8,2X,A20,A30)
40       CONTINUE
      RETURN
      END
(include here the SORT subroutine)
$ENTRY
 5
JOHNSTON,R.L.          53 JONSTON CRES.              491-6405
KEAST,P.              77 KREDLE HAVEN DR.           439-7216
LIPSON,J.D.           15 WEEDWOOD ROAD             787-8515
MATHON,R.A.          666 REGINA AVE.              962-8885
CRAWFORD,C.R.         39 TREATHERSON AVE.          922-7999
```

The output for this program will be

```
439-7216   KEAST,P.           77 KREDLE HAVEN DR.
491-6405   JOHNSTON,R.L.      53 JONSTON CRES.
787-8515   LIPSON,J.D.        15 WEEDWOOD ROAD
922-7999   CRAWFORD,C.R.      39 TREATHERSON AVE.
962-8885   MATHON,R.A.       666 REGINA AVE.
```


FILES IN SECONDARY MEMORY

    In our discussion of files so far, we have had the files
stored in the main memory. In most real file applications, the
files are too large to be contained in main memory. The part of
the file being processed must be brought into main memory, but
the complete file is stored in secondary memory. The secondary
memory may be magnetic tape or magnetic disk.

    A file in secondary storage is called a data set. One record
at a time may be transferred from the data set to the main

memory, or from the main memory to the data set. The record that
is transferred must be the next record in the sequence of records
in the data set. We say that the file can be read sequentially
from the secondary memory to the main memory or written
sequentially from the main memory to secondary memory. This type
of file is called a sequential file. It is not possible at any
moment to get access to an arbitrary record in the file; the next
record in sequence is the only one that is available.

     Since files in secondary storage are to be accessed
sequentially, there must be a statement in the program that will
position the file reader at the first record of the data set.
Before a file in secondary storage can be accessed, we must write
a statement of the form

        REWIND file number

The file number is an unsigned non-zero integer constant. The
available file numbers are determined by the particular computer
center. Usually the numbers 5 and 6 cannot be used because they
refer to the card reader and printer. If the file is on a
magnetic tape then the word REWIND means wind the tape to the
beginning of the file. The file can as well be on a magnetic
disk that cannot really be "rewound", but we still use the REWIND
statement to initialize the file to its starting position.

     To write the next, or first, record onto a file in secondary
storage, we use a statement of the form

        WRITE(file number)list of variables separated by commas

The list of variables makes up the record to be written. Each of
these must be an array element or a simple, non-array variable.

     The types of the fields of a record are called its template.
For example, in the telephone book example the template consists
of CHARACTER*20, CHARACTER*30 and CHARACTER*8. All the records
written on a file should have the same template.

     After the final record of a file is written the file should
be closed off, or ended, by the statement

        ENDFILE file number

If it is desired, in the same program the file can then be
rewound and read. Otherwise the file can be left to be read by a
different program, possibly days or months later.

     When we want to read a file from secondary storage we must
first rewind it and then use a statement of the form

        READ(file number)list of variables separated by commas

The next, or first, record on the file is read into the list of
variables. The types of the variables must be the same as the
template of the records on the file. Care must be taken not to

try to read beyond the end of the file. This can be avoided by
checking for a special dummy record that is typically the last
record written before the file is ended by the ENDFILE statement.

Once a file has been rewound it can be written or read but
not both. But the file can be rewound again to start reading or
writing from the beginning. Once writing of a file is started,
any previous contents of the file are lost and the file must be
ended by an ENDFILE statement after the final record is written.

FILE MAINTENANCE

As an example of reading and writing files we will program a
simple file-maintenance operation. We will assume that there
exists a file of customer records with file number 3, and we want
to update this file by adding new customers. The information
about the new customers is punched on cards. Each card
corresponds to a transaction that must be posted in the file to
produce an up-to-date customer file, which will have file number
4. This is an example of file maintenance. The original file is
ordered alphabetically by customer name and the transactions are
arranged alphabetically. The last record of each file has a NAME
with a value ZZZ. This program will be very similar to the
merge-sort program of Chapter 15, except that the records of the
two files being merged are not in an array.

```
$JOB     HARRIET LOGAN
C ADD NEW CUSTOMERS TO CUSTOMER FILE
         CHARACTER*20 NAME,TNAME
         CHARACTER*30 ADRESS,TADRES
         CHARACTER*8 PHONE,TPHONE
         REWIND 3
         REWIND 4
C        READ FIRST CUSTOMER RECORD FROM FILE
         READ(3)NAME,ADRESS,PHONE
C        READ FIRST TRANSACTION FROM CARD
         READ 10,TNAME,TADRES,TPHONE
10       FORMAT(A20,A30,A8)
C        POST TRANSACTIONS TO CUSTOMER FILE
         WHILE(NAME.NE.'ZZZ'.OR.TNAME.NE.'ZZZ')DO
             IF(NAME.LT.TNAME)THEN DO
                WRITE(4)NAME,ADRESS,PHONE
                READ(3)NAME,ADRESS,PHONE
             ELSE DO
                WRITE(4)TNAME,TADRES,TPHONE
                READ 20,TNAME,TADRES,TPHONE
20              FORMAT(A20,A30,A8)
             END IF
          END WHILE
C        ADD DUMMY RECORD TO END OF FILE
         WRITE(4)NAME,ADRESS,PHONE
         ENDFILE 4
         RETURN
         END
$ENTRY
(transactions one per card)
ZZZ                    NULL                        NULL
```

The Watfiv compiler requires that each record on secondary storage be at least 16 bytes long. Each integer, real or logical value takes up 4 bytes and each CHARACTER*n string takes up n bytes. Since our example uses character strings of lengths 20, 30 and 8, this record is 58 bytes long and is acceptable to Watfiv.

CHAPTER 17 SUMMARY

In this chapter we showed how records are used in Fortran and how they can be written to or read from files in secondary memory. The following important terms were discussed in this chapter.

Record - a collection of fields of information. For example a record might be composed of a name field, an address field and telephone number field.

Template - the list of types of variables in a record.

Data set - a file of information residing on secondary storage, typically on a disk or tape.

Sequential files - files that are always accessed (read or written) in order, from first record to second record to third record and so on.

REWIND - the REWIND statement of Fortran initializes a file so it can be written or read. The file is started at its first record.

Read from a file - the next or first record is read from a file using the statement

            READ(file number)variables separated by commas

The record is read into the variables. The record's template must match the types of the variables. The file number is a constant integer, such as 3, that refers to a file.

Write to a file - the next or first record is written to a file using the statement

            WRITE(file number)variables separated by commas

ENDFILE - the ENDFILE statement of Fortran must be used to close off a file after the final record is written.

File maintenance - means to keep a file up-to-date. This involves reading transactions and adding, deleting or modifying file records. An existing file can be modified or extended by creating a new file.

CHAPTER 17 EXERCISES

The exercises for this chapter are based on a data processing system to be used by Apex Plumbing Supplies. For each of its customers, Apex has a card with the fields:

    Name   (card column 1-20)
    Address   (card column 21-40)
    Balance   (card column 41-50)
    Credit limit (card column 51-60)

These records are presently on punch cards. However, they are to be transferred to a disk file by the following job:

```
$JOB    M.V. YOUNG
C CREATE MASTER FILE FROM PUNCHED CARDS
        CHARACTER*20 NAME
        CHARACTER*20 ADRESS
        INTEGER BALNCE
        INTEGER CREDIT
        CHARACTER*20 PREV
        REWIND 4
        NAME='AAA'
        WHILE(NAME.NE.'ZZZ')DO
           PREV=NAME
           READ 10,NAME,ADRESS,BALNCE,CREDIT
10         FORMAT(A20,A20,I10,I10)
C          MAKE SURE THAT RECORDS ARE IN ORDER
           IF(NAME.GT.PREV)THEN DO
              WRITE(4)NAME,ADRESS,BALNCE,CREDIT
           ELSE DO
              PRINT,'RECORD OUT OF ORDER:',NAME
           END IF
        END WHILE
        PRINT,'MASTER FILE CREATED'
        ENDFILE 4
        RETURN
        END
$ENTRY
ABBOT PLUMBING        94 N.ELM                    3116      50000
DURABLE FIXIT         247 FOREST HILL                0      10000
ERICO PLUMBING        54 GORMLEY                  9614       5000
   ...
ZZZ                                                  0          0
```

The exercises for this chapter require you to write programs for various parts of the data processing system for Apex.

1. The program given above creates a master file for Apex Plumbing Supplies. Unfortunately, the account cards have been dropped on the floor and are no longer in order. Modify the program so that it sorts the cards before creating the file. You can assume that there are at most 20 accounts.

2. Write a program that takes an existing master file for Apex and creates a new master file by deleting or adding new customer records. For example, the data cards for your program might be

```
DAVIS REPAIR          4361 MAIN                   2511      10000
ERICO PLUMBING        DELETE                          0          0
   ...
ZZZ                                                  0          0
```

You can assume that these cards are in alphabetic order. If the address field on the account card specifies DELETE, the account is to be deleted from the file.

3. Write a program that reads the Apex master file and prints the list of customers whose balances exceed their credit limits.

4. Write a program that reads the Apex master file and prints a bill for each customer whose balance is greater than zero. For example, for the file record

DAVIS REPAIR   4361 MAIN   2511   10000

your program should print

```
     TO: DAVIS REPAIR
         4361 MAIN

     DEAR SIR OR MADAM:
         PLEASE REMIT $   25.11 FOR PLUMBING SUPPLIES.
                          THANK YOU,

                          JOHN APEX, PRES.
                          APEX PLUMBING SUPPLIES
                          416 COLLEGE ST.
```

You can print the decimal point in this bill by dividing by 100.0 and using the F8.2 format item.

5. Write a program that updates the master file using billing and payment transactions. A billing transaction is a card of the form

```
     name        (columns 1-20)
     amount      (columns 41-50)
                 (columns 51-80 are blank)
```

For each billing transaction, the balance of the account is to be increased by the specified amount. A payment transaction is a card of the form

```
     name        (columns 1-20)
     amount      (columns 41-50)
     CR          (columns 51-52)
```

For each payment transaction, the balance of the account is to be decreased by the specified amount. The billing and payment cards are not in order, so they should be sorted before creating the new master file.

CHAPTER 18

DATA STRUCTURES

In previous chapters we have shown that arrays provide a method of organizing data and that records can be used to structure data within a file.

All of the classifications, variables, arrays of variables, records, and files, are examples of what we generally call data structures. Just as we systematize our programs by attempting to write well-structured programs, we systematize the way in which data is stored. We structure data.

In this chapter we will describe other structural forms for data and give examples of how these structures are useful to us. We will describe data structures called linked lists and tree structures. There are many kinds of lists, for example stacks, queues, doubly-linked lists, and so on. Tree structures can be limited to binary trees, or may be more general.

These new data structures are not a part of the Fortran language as arrays are, so that when we want to store data in a linked list or a tree we use an array to implement them. We must program the structure.

LINKED LISTS

Suppose that we had a file of records stored in an array called DATA. The records are arranged in sequence on some key. For simplicity, we will consider that each record consists only of a single field which is the key to the ordering. We know that if the order is ascending and no two keys are identical, then

DATA(I+1).GT.DATA(I)

The difficulty with this kind of data structure for a file comes
when a new item is to be added to the file; it must be inserted
between two items.   This means we would have to move all the
items with a key higher than the one to be inserted, one location
on in the array. For example, you can see what happens when we
insert the word DOG in this list:

	before	after inserting DOG
DATA(1)	CAT	CAT
DATA(2)	DUCK	DOG
DATA(3)	FOX	DUCK
DATA(4)	GOOSE	FOX
DATA(5)	PIG	GOOSE
DATA(6)	–	PIG

Any list that is changing with time will have additions and
deletions made to it. A deletion will create a hole unless
entries are moved to fill the hole.

    When the list changes with time we can use the data structure
called the <u>linked</u> <u>list</u>. In the linked list each item has two
components, the data component and the linking component or <u>link</u>.
We associate with each entry in the DATA array an entry in a
second array called LINK. The number stored in LINK(I) is the
index of the next entry in the sequence of the DATA array.   This
means that the actual or <u>physical</u> <u>sequence</u> in the DATA array is
different from the <u>logical</u> <u>sequence</u> in the list. Here is an
example showing our previous list as a linked list. The start of
the list is stored in the INTEGER variable FIRST.

                        FIRST   3

DATA(1)	PIG	LINK(1)	0
DATA(2)	FOX	LINK(2)	4
DATA(3)	CAT	LINK(3)	5
DATA(4)	GOOSE	LINK(4)	1
DATA(5)	DUCK	LINK(5)	2
DATA(6)	–	LINK(6)	–

Here is a diagram of this:

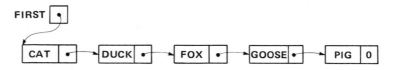

You can follow the list by beginning with the value of FIRST,
which is 3. The first entry will be in DATA(3); it is CAT.   By
looking then at LINK(3) you find a 5 which is the index of the
next list item, DATA(5), which is DUCK. You follow the list down
until you reach a LINK whose value is 0; this is the signal that
you have reached the end of the list. Other signals can be used,
such as having a negative number.

INSERTING INTO A LINKED LIST

To see the merit of a linked list we must see how to insert new entries. We will add DOG in its proper list position. We will do this first by hand; afterwards we will have to program it for the computer. We will place the entry DOG in DATA(6) since it is an available or free location. We must now change the values of certain of the links so that the new entry will be inserted. We must put a value into LINK(6) and change the value of the LINK of the entry before DOG, which is CAT, to point to DATA(6). This means that LINK(3) must be changed to 6 and LINK(6) must be set to 5 so that the entry after DOG is DUCK, which is DATA(5).

The linked list then becomes

	FIRST		3
DATA(1)	PIG	LINK(1)	0
DATA(2)	FOX	LINK(2)	4
DATA(3)	CAT	LINK(3)	6
DATA(4)	GOOSE	LINK(4)	1
DATA(5)	DUCK	LINK(5)	2
DATA(6)	DOG	LINK(6)	5

Here is a diagram:

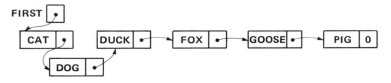

To add DOG, one LINK must be changed and one set. No movement of the existing items in DATA is necessary. This is surely an improvement over moving half the list, on the average, to insert a new entry. The cost of this improved efficiency of operation comes in having to reserve memory space for the LINK array. This array gives the structure of the list and is stored explicitly for a linked list. In an array, the sequence or structure is implicit; each entry follows its neighbor. We will see several other kinds of structures that require us to store the structure information explicitly.

MEMORY MANAGEMENT WITH LISTS

With linked lists, some of the memory is used for structure information and some for data. For any list, as the list grows, we use more memory; as it shrinks, we use less. This means we must reserve enough memory to hold the longest list that we ever expect to have. But we should not waste memory. As we stop using certain elements of the array by deleting entries, we must

keep track of where they are, so when additions occur we can
reuse these same elements. To keep track of the available array
elements we keep them together in a second linked list. The list
of available array elements does not have any useful information
in the DATA part, but it is structured as a list using values in
the LINK part. We must keep track of the beginning of this list
so we keep the index of its beginning in an integer variable
AVAIL.

    Here is an array of 10 elements that stores our previous data
items in a different set of locations and has the available space
linked up:

	FIRST	10	AVAIL	7
DATA(1)	GOOSE		LINK(1)	9
DATA(2)	FOX		LINK(2)	1
DATA(3)	–		LINK(3)	6
DATA(4)	DUCK		LINK(4)	2
DATA(5)	–		LINK(5)	0
DATA(6)	–		LINK(6)	5
DATA(7)	–		LINK(7)	3
DATA(8)	DOG		LINK(8)	4
DATA(9)	PIG		LINK(9)	0
DATA(10)	CAT		LINK(10)	8

In these arrays there are two linked lists, one containing the
actual data, the other containing elements available for use.
Each list has a pointer to its start; each has a last element
with a link of 0. Every element of the array is in one list or
the other.

    The next problem is to write a subroutine for adding a new
item to the list. We will develop the algorithm for this by
step-by-step refinement.

SUBROUTINE FOR INSERTING INTO A LINKED LIST

    The first step is to construct a solution tree. We will
presume the value to be added is in the variable VALUE:

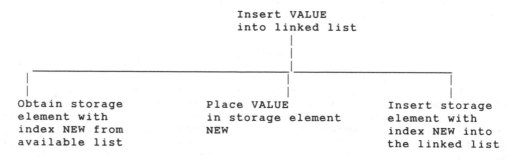

                         Insert VALUE
                         into linked list

Obtain storage	Place VALUE	Insert storage
element with	in storage element	element with
index NEW from	NEW	index NEW into
available list		the linked list

The expansion of the left branch of the solution tree requires us to find the index NEW of the first element of the list of available elements and remove the element from the list. Here is the program segment that does this:

```
NEW=AVAIL
AVAIL=LINK(AVAIL)
```

The middle branch is also simple. It is

```
DATA(NEW)=VALUE
```

We must expand the right branch still further:

```
                          Insert storage
                          element with
                          index NEW into
                          the linked list
                                |
                                |
        IF list is empty THEN DO
            Place element at beginning of list
        ELSE DO
            IF VALUE goes first in list THEN DO
                Place element at beginning of list
            ELSE DO
                Find place to insert VALUE
                    and adjust links to make insertion
                END IF
            END IF
```

VALUE will go first in the list if either the list is empty or VALUE is less than the first element of the list. So we can write, "IF list is empty," in this way:

```
IF(FIRST.EQ.NULL)THEN DO
```

We have assumed that the variable NULL will be initialized to zero. We can write, "Place element at beginning of list," in this way:

```
LINK(NEW)=FIRST
FIRST=NEW
```

For the part of the program after the second ELSE we need to examine the entries in the list and compare them with VALUE. The index of the element being compared we will call NEXT. The index of the element just compared previously we will call PREV. We need to keep track of this previous element, because if

```
VALUE.LT.DATA(NEXT)
```

we must insert our element with index NEW between PREV and NEXT.
Here is the program segment for this:

```
C     FIND PLACE TO INSERT NEW VALUE
      PREV=FIRST
      NEXT=LINK(FIRST)
      WHILE(NEXT.NE.NULL)DO
         IF(VALUE.LT.DATA(NEXT))THEN DO
C           SET NEXT TO FORCE EXIT FROM LOOP
            NEXT=NULL
         ELSE DO
            PREV=NEXT
            NEXT=LINK(NEXT)
            END IF
         END WHILE
C     ADJUST LINKS TO MAKE INSERTION
      LINK(NEW)=LINK(PREV)
      LINK(PREV)=NEW
```

The whole subroutine can now be written out. Notice that DATA,
LINK, FIRST, AVAIL and NULL are COMMON to this subroutine:

```
C INSERT NEW VALUE INTO LINKED LIST
      SUBROUTINE INSERT(VALUE)
      CHARACTER*10 VALUE
      COMMON/LIST/DATA,LINK,FIRST,AVAIL,NULL
      CHARACTER*10 DATA(30)
      INTEGER LINK(30),FIRST,AVAIL,NULL
      INTEGER NEW,PREV,NEXT
C     OBTAIN STORAGE ELEMENT FOR NEW VALUE
      NEW=AVAIL
      AVAIL=LINK(AVAIL)
C     PLACE NEW VALUE IN STORAGE ELEMENT
      DATA(NEW)=VALUE
C     SEE IF NEW VALUE GOES FIRST IN LIST
      IF(FIRST.EQ.NULL)THEN DO
         LINK(NEW)=FIRST
         FIRST=NEW
      ELSE DO
         IF(VALUE.LT.DATA(FIRST))THEN DO
            LINK(NEW)=FIRST
            FIRST=NEW
         ELSE DO
C     FIND PLACE TO INSERT NEW VALUE
      (copy above program segment here)
         END IF
      RETURN
      END
```

DELETING FROM A LINKED LIST

The process of deletion is very similar. We will just record the final subroutine.

```
C DELETE SPECIFIED VALUE FROM LINKED LIST
      SUBROUTINE DELETE(VALUE)
      CHARACTER*10 VALUE
      COMMON/LIST/DATA,LINK,FIRST,AVAIL,NULL
      CHARACTER*10 DATA(30)
      INTEGER LINK(30),FIRST,AVAIL,NULL
      INTEGER PREV,OLD
C     FIND THE ITEM TO BE DELETED
      OLD=FIRST
      WHILE(DATA(OLD).NE.VALUE)DO
         PREV=OLD
         OLD=LINK(OLD)
         END WHILE
C     REMOVE ITEM FROM LIST
      IF(FIRST.EQ.OLD)THEN DO
         FIRST=LINK(OLD)
      ELSE DO
         LINK(PREV)=LINK(OLD)
         END IF
C     ADD STORAGE ELEMENT TO FREE LIST
      LINK(OLD)=AVAIL
      AVAIL=OLD
      RETURN
      END
```

Before using these two subroutines we must set NULL to 0, set FIRST to NULL, set AVAIL to 1, and LINK(I) to I+1, with the exception of the last element which should have a NULL link.

STACKS

In the last two sections we showed how to insert and delete items for a linked list. The insertions and deletions could be anywhere in the list. In each case, as the list of data items was changed, a second linked list of available storage elements was maintained. A deletion from the list of data items resulted in an addition to the list of available elements; an addition in the data list produced a deletion in the available list. The actions involving the available storage list were much simpler. This is because the additions and deletions for it always were to the beginning of that list. A list that is restricted to having entries to or removals from the beginning only is called a stack. The situation is similar to a stack of trays in a cafeteria. When you want a tray you take it off the top of the stack; when you are through with a tray you put it back on the top. Stacks operate in a "last in first out" order, so they are sometimes called LIFO systems.

When a list is used as a stack, we often call the pointer to the beginning of the list TOP. When an entry is removed from the top we say we have <u>popped</u> an entry off. TOP must then be adjusted to point at the next entry. When we add an entry we say we have <u>pushed</u> it on to the stack.

Because a stack change only occurs at one end, it is convenient to implement a stack without using a linked list; an ordinary array will do. In our examples, a linked list is necessary for our stack of available storage elements because they are scattered all over. Stacks have other uses so we will show how a stack can be implemented using an array. We will call the array STACK. The bottom of the stack will be in STACK(1), the next entry in STACK(2), and so on. Sorry if our stack seems to be upside down! Here is a stack of symbols:

```
TOP                4

STACK(1)           +
STACK(2)           -
STACK(3)           +
STACK(4)           /
```

This sort of stack is often used in Fortran compilers for translating arithmetic expressions into machine language.

Before using the stack we initialize it to be empty by setting TOP to zero:

```
TOP=0
```

To add an item to the stack we can call the subroutine PUSH:

```
SUBROUTINE PUSH(SYMBOL)
CHARACTER*1 SYMBOL
COMMON/LIFO/STACK,TOP
CHARACTER*1 STACK(20)
INTEGER TOP
TOP=TOP+1
STACK(TOP)=SYMBOL
RETURN
END
```

To remove the top item from the stack we can call the subroutine POP:

```
SUBROUTINE POP(SYMBOL)
CHARACTER*1 SYMBOL
COMMON/LIFO/STACK,TOP
CHARACTER*1 STACK(20)
INTEGER TOP
SYMBOL=STACK(TOP)
TOP=TOP-1
RETURN
END
```

The variable TOP and the array STACK must be COMMON to the PUSH and POP subroutines and to the program that initializes the stack.   Stacks may be implemented in other ways than shown here.

QUEUES

Another specialized type of list is a <u>queue</u>. For it, entries are made at the end of the list, deletions are made from the beginning.   Rather than search for the end of the list each time an entry is made, it is usual to have a pointer indicating the last entry. Queues involve using things in a manner referred to as, "First in first out" (FIFO) or, "First come first served" (FCFS). This is the usual way for a queue waiting for tickets at a box office to operate.

It is not as easy to implement a queue using an array. It is always growing at one end and shrinking at the other. If an array is used, when the growth reaches the maximum limit of the array, we start it at the beginning again. Here is a queue of users of a computer waiting for service. We have a maximum of 8 elements. Five people are in the queue. The next person to be served is named SHUM.

```
     FIRST   6                LAST    2

  QUEUE(1)                  GEORGE
  QUEUE(2)                  JOHNSTON
  QUEUE(3)                  —
  QUEUE(4)                  —
  QUEUE(5)                  —
  QUEUE(6)                  SHUM
  QUEUE(7)                  LINNEMANN
  QUEUE(8)                  LOVGREN
```

Here are subroutines used to ENTER or LEAVE this queue. Before using these subroutines the queue can be initialized to be empty by setting FIRST to 1 and LAST to 8.

```
      SUBROUTINE ENTER(NAME)
      CHARACTER*10 NAME
      COMMON/FIFO/QUEUE,FIRST,LAST
      CHARACTER*10 QUEUE(8)
      INTEGER FIRST,LAST
      LAST=LAST+1
      IF(LAST.GT.8)THEN DO
         LAST=1
         END IF
      QUEUE(LAST)=NAME
      RETURN
      END
```

```
SUBROUTINE LEAVE(NAME)
CHARACTER*10 NAME
COMMON/FIFO/QUEUE,FIRST,LAST
CHARACTER*10 QUEUE(8)
INTEGER FIRST,LAST
NAME=QUEUE(FIRST)
FIRST=FIRST+1
IF(FIRST.GT.8)THEN DO
    FIRST=1
    END IF
RETURN
END
```

Queues can be implemented by linked lists as well as by
simple arrays. Queues are used in the programs called <u>operating</u>
<u>systems</u> that operate computer systems. Different jobs requiring
service are placed in different queues, depending on the demands
they are making on the system's resources and the priority that
they possess to be given service. Also, in programs that
simulate other systems such as factories, queues are maintained
to determine the length of time jobs are required to wait to be
served when other jobs are competing for the same production
facilities.

                              TREES

    A linked list is an efficient way of storing a list that is
changing with time, but it introduces an inefficiency in
retrieval of information from the list. In Chapter 15 we saw
that a binary search for an item in a list is much more efficient
for long lists than a linear search. Unfortunately, there is no
possibility of doing a binary search in a linked list; we must
start at the beginning and trace our way through. There is no
direct access to the middle of a linked list. It is for this
reason that a more complicated data structure called a <u>tree</u> is
used. We can get the efficiency of a binary search by having the
elements linked into a <u>binary</u> <u>tree</u> <u>structure</u>.

    To show how a binary tree is formed, we will look at the
example of our list of names of animals:

```
            3--   CAT
         2------  DOG
                  DUCK
      1---------- FOX
                  GOOSE
                  PIG
                  SNAKE
```

To do a binary search we should begin in the middle. We have
added SNAKE to the list so the list has a middle entry. If we
are looking for the name CAT we find that CAT .LT. FOX, so we
then discard the middle entry and the last half of the list. The
next comparison is with the middle entry of the remaining list,

namely with DOG. Since CAT .LT. DOG we eliminate the last half
of the smaller list.   By this time, we are down to one entry,
which is the one we are looking for. It took three comparisons
to get there. A linear search for CAT would, as it happens, have
taken only 1 comparison. On the average, the binary search takes
fewer comparisons than a linear search. A short list is not a
good example for showing off the efficiency of binary searching,
but it is much easier to write out all the possibilities.

We will now look at the binary tree that would be used to
give the same searching technique. Here it is:

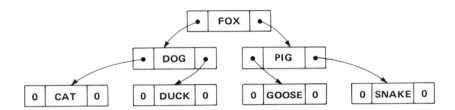

Each data element in the tree structure consists of three
parts, the DATA itself and two links that we designate as LEFT
and RIGHT.   The word FOX is in a special position in the tree,
called the root. From FOX we have branches going to the left to
DOG and to the right to PIG. In a sense, DOG is in the root
position of a smaller tree, what we call the left subtree of the
main tree.   PIG is at the root of the right subtree. The words
CAT, DUCK, GOOSE, and SNAKE are at the end of branches and are
called leaves of the tree. All the data elements are in nodes of
the tree; FOX is the root node and CAT is a leaf node. To search
for an entry in a binary tree, we compare the element in the root
node with the one we are seeking. If the root is the same, we
have found it. If the root is larger we follow the LEFT link to
the next entry; if smaller, we follow the RIGHT link.   We are
then at the root of a smaller tree, a tree with half as many
entries as the original. The process is then repeated until the
looked-for data is found.

Here is our tree structure as it might be stored in three
arrays called DATA, LEFT, and RIGHT. The variable ROOT holds the
link to the root element. We have jumbled up the sequence to
show that the actual order in the DATA array makes no difference.
A zero link is used to indicate the end of a branch.

	ROOT	4
DATA	LEFT	RIGHT
(1) GOOSE	0	0
(2) SNAKE	0	0
(3) DOG	6	7
(4) FOX	3	5
(5) PIG	1	2
(6) CAT	0	0
(7) DUCK	0	0

Starting at ROOT, we find the root is in DATA(4). LEFT(4) leads to DATA(3) which is DOG. RIGHT(3) leads us to DATA(7) which is DUCK. You can see how it works.

A tree structure is a <u>hierarchical</u> <u>structure</u> for data; each comparison takes us one <u>level</u> down in the tree.

ADDING TO A TREE

To add a data item to a tree structure we simply look for the element in the tree in the usual manner, starting at the root. If the element is not already in the tree, we will come in the search to a link that is zero. This is where the element belongs. In our example, if we want to add COW, we would start at FOX, then go to DOG, then to CAT. At this point we would want to follow the right link of CAT, but we find a zero. If we stored the new entry in DATA(8), we would change RIGHT(6) to 8. and set

DATA(8)	LEFT(8)	RIGHT(8)
COW	0	0

As we add items to a tree, the tree becomes lopsided; it is not well balanced. Searching efficiency depends on trees being well balanced, so that in an information retrieval data bank using a tree structure, an effort should be made to keep the tree balanced. We started with a balanced tree and it became unbalanced by adding a new item. If a tree is grown from scratch using the method we have described for adding a new entry, it is unlikely to be well balanced.

DELETING FROM A TREE

Removing an entry from a tree is a more difficult operation than adding an entry. The same method is used to find the element to be deleted, but then the problem comes. It is not difficult if both links of the element to be deleted are zero, that is, if it is a leaf. We just chop it off and make the link

pointing to it zero. If only one link is zero it is similar to
an ordinary linked list and deletion is similar to that. We just
bypass it:

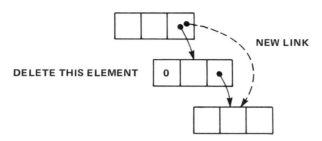

DELETE THIS ELEMENT   NEW LINK

If neither link is zero in the element to be deleted, we must
move another element into its position in the tree.   In our
original tree, if FOX is to be deleted, it must be replaced by an
element that is larger then all other elements in the left
subtree or smaller than all the elements in the right subtree.
This means that either DUCK or GOOSE is the only possible choice.
The one to be moved must be deleted in its present position
before being placed in its new position.

     Remember, in a linked structure, we never move a data item
from its physical location in the data array; we only change the
links to alter its logical position.

                    PRINTING A TREE IN ORDER

     Trees are used where searching and updating are the main
activities. Sometimes we must print out the contents of a tree.
We must be systematic about it and be sure to print every node.
We will show how to print it alphabetically.

     An algorithm for printing a tree alphabetically can be
written in this way:

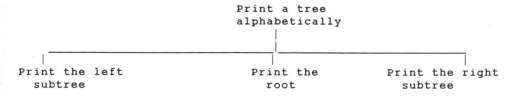

                            Print a tree
                            alphabetically

Print the left   Print the   Print the right
   subtree   root   subtree

We see that we have described our algorithm in terms of three
parts. The middle part, "Print the root," is easy, but the other
two require us to, "Print a tree." This is exactly what our
problem is, to "Print a tree." We have defined the solution to a
problem in terms of the original problem.   This kind of
definition is called a <u>recursive</u> definition of a solution.   It
seems rather pointless, as if we were just going in a circle, but

it really is not. The reason it is not pointless is that the
tree we are attempting to print when we say, "Print the left
subtree," is a smaller tree than the original tree when we said
"Print a tree." When we try to print the left subtree we get
this solution:

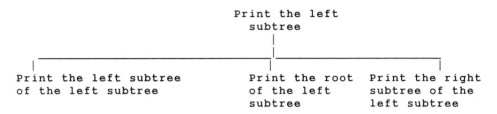

This time the left subtree of the left subtree has to be printed.
It is smaller still. The algorithm is again repeated. Each
application of the algorithm is on a smaller tree, until you
reach a point where there is a zero link and there is no left
subtree at all. Then the action of printing it is to do nothing:
no tree, no printing. That is how recursive algorithms work. In
programming terms, the algorithm calls itself over and over, each
time to do a reduced task, until the task is easy to do.

     In some programming languages, such as PL/1, a subroutine can
call itself. This is not allowed in Fortran, but for the rest of
this paragraph we will assume that Fortran allows such recursive
subroutines. Here is a recursive subroutine for printing a tree
in alphabetic order, given that its root is ROOT and its data and
links are in DATA, LEFT and RIGHT.

```
C A RECURSIVE METHOD OF TREE PRINTING (NOT ALLOWED IN FORTRAN)
      SUBROUTINE OUTPUT(ROOT)
      INTEGER ROOT
      COMMON/TREE/DATA,LEFT,RIGHT,NULL
      CHARACTER*10 DATA(30)
      INTEGER LEFT(30),RIGHT(30),NULL
      IF(LEFT(ROOT).NE.NULL)THEN DO
         CALL OUTPUT(LEFT(ROOT))
         END IF
      PRINT,DATA(ROOT)
      IF(RIGHT(ROOT).NE.NULL)THEN DO
         CALL OUTPUT(RIGHT(ROOT))
         END IF
      RETURN
      END
```

Each time the subroutine is entered for a new subtree, a
different node is referred to by ROOT. For this job, a recursive
subroutine is very easy to program. In a recursive algorithm,
each time a program calls itself, a record must be kept of the
point in the program where the subroutine was called, so that
control can return properly. As the subroutine recursively calls

itself, a list is built of these points of return. Each point of
return is added on top of the stack of other points of return.
Finding the way back involves taking return points, one after the
other, off this stack. For languages such as PL/1, this is all
set up automatically by the compiler. In Fortran, we can still
write a subroutine to print a tree, but since it can not call
itself, it is more difficult to program.

                        CHAPTER 18 SUMMARY

    In this chapter we showed how to build up data structures
using arrays. Some of these data structures use links to give
the ordering of data items. The link (or links) for a given item
gives the array index of the next item. The following important
terms were discussed:

    Linked list - a linked sequence of data items. The next item
        in the list is found by following a link from the
        present item.   The physical order of a collection of
        items, as given by their positions in an array, is
        different from their logical order, as given by the
        links.

    Inserting into a linked list - a new data item can be
        inserted by changing links, without actually moving data
        items.

    Deleting from a linked list - a data item can be deleted by
        changing links, without moving data items.

    Available list - the collection of data elements currently
        not in use.

    Stack - a data structure that allows data items to be added,
        or <u>pushed</u>, on to one end and removed, or <u>popped</u>, from
        the same end.   A stack does not require the use of
        links. A stack handles data items in a last-in-first-
        out (LIFO) manner.

    Queue - a data structure that allows data items to be added
        at one end and removed from the other. A queue handles
        data items in a first-in-first-out (FIFO) manner.

    Binary tree - a data structure in which each item or <u>node</u> has
        two links, a left link and a right link. The left link
        of a node locates another node and with it a subtree.
        Similarly, the right link locates a subtree. There is a
        unique beginning node called the <u>root</u>. If both links of
        a particular node are null, meaning they do not
        currently locate other nodes, then the node is called a
        <u>leaf</u>.

CHAPTER 18 EXERCISES

1. The FLY-BY-NITE Airline company is computerizing its
reservations system. There are four FLY-BY-NITE flights with the
following capacities:

```
FLIGHT #1        5 seats
FLIGHT #2        5 seats
FLIGHT #3        8 seats
FLIGHT #4        4 seats
```

The information for passenger reservations is to be stored in a
linked list. At some point during the booking period, the
following diagram might represent the current passenger bookings.

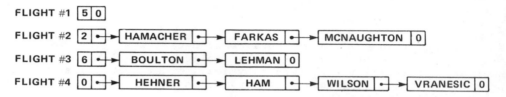

The above diagram shows the first element in each list holding
the number of seats remaining. Each succeeding element holds the
name of a passenger and either points to the next element or
holds a 0 to indicate the end of the linked list.

In order to set up such a linked list system you will need
four arrays. The first will contain the number of seats
remaining. The second array holds the location of the first
passenger of each flight.

The third array called NAME holds all the passengers. If all
seats on all flights are taken, there will be 22 passengers.
Hence NAME will need a maximum of 22 locations. The fourth array
called LINK contains the location of the next passenger, if any.
Before any events happen, the free locations must be linked
together. Initially each LINK(J) contains a value J+1, except
LINK(22) which contains a 0 as end of the list.

A variable AVAIL contains the location of the head of this
chain of available locations. For the example given above, AVAIL
contains 10 and the NAME and LINK arrays could have these values:

```
NAME(1)HAMACHER      NAME(5)LEHMAN        NAME(9)VRANESIC
LINK(1)    6         LINK(5)   0          LINK(9)     0

NAME(2)BOULTON       NAME(6)FARKAS        NAME(10)
LINK(2)    5         LINK(6)   7          LINK(10)   11

NAME(3)HAM           NAME(7)MCNAUGHTON         .
LINK(3)    8         LINK(7)   0               .
```

```
NAME(4)HEHNER        NAME(8)WILSON      NAME(22)
LINK(4)    3         LINK(8)   9        LINK(22)   0
```

The reservation system is to accept four types of transactions:

Type 1 is a request for a reservation. The data card contains the code word RES, name of the passenger, and the flight number.

Type 2 is a request to cancel a reservation. The data card contains the code word CAN, name of passenger, and the flight number.

Type 3 is a request to print out the number of seats remaining on a specified flight. The data card contains the code word SEATS and a flight number.

Type 4 is a request to print out a passenger list for the flight indicated. The data card contains the code word LIST and a flight number.

Each type of transaction is to be handled by a subroutine. Here are descriptions of the subroutines:

ADD(WHO,NUMBER). Adds passenger WHO to flight NUMBER. If that flight is filled, a message is printed to that effect. ADD uses a location in NAME and must update AVAIL.

CANCEL(WHO,NUMBER). Cancels the reservation made in the name of WHO on flight NUMBER. The location in NAME is returned to the free storage pool. AVAIL must be updated.

INFO(NUMBER). Prints out number of seats remaining on flight NUMBER.

LIST(NUMBER). Prints a passenger list for flight NUMBER.

The data cards should simulate a real reservation system in that cards of type 1, 2, 3, 4 should be intermixed. It would seem reasonable to assume that most cancellations would be made by persons holding reservations. However, people being what they are, you should not assume too much. In order to get your system off the ground, several reservation cards should be first.

Write and test each program as a main program before putting the subroutines together. Write LIST first and call it from ADD or CANCEL to help in debugging. If you work in pairs – and this is strongly recommended for this exercise – one person should program ADD and LIST, the other CANCEL and INFO. Turn in several runs which show the capabilities of your system. Be sure to test "odd" situations as well as the obvious ones.

CHAPTER 19

SCIENTIFIC CALCULATIONS

Most of the applications that we have discussed so far in this book are connected with the use of computers in business or in the humanities. We do business applications on computers because of the large numbers of each calculation that must be done. A single payroll calculation is simple, but if a company has thousands of employees, computer processing of the payroll is warranted. Computers were originally developed with scientific and engineering calculations in mind. This is because many scientific and engineering calculations are so long that it is not practical to do them by hand, even with the help of a slide rule or pocket calculator. Fortran as a language was developed to do scientific calculations; it is only by using extensions of it, available in Watfiv, that we can handle character variables. Standard Fortran does not have this facility. You will see that the ability to handle character variables is also very helpful when it comes to plotting graphs of scientific data.

Often the scientific laws describing a physical situation are known in the form of equations, but these equations must be solved for the situation of interest. We may be designing a bridge or aircraft or an air-conditioning system for a building. A computer can be used to calculate the details of the particular situation.

Another important use of computers in science is to find equations that fit the data produced in experiments. These equations then serve to reduce the amount of data that must be preserved. Science as a word means knowledge. The object of scientific work is to gather information about the world and to systematize it so that it can be retrieved and used in the future. There is such a large amount of research activity now in science that we are facing an information explosion. We have talked about retrieving information from a data bank and computers will undoubtedly help us in this increasingly difficult

and tedious   job. But the problem of <u>data</u> <u>reduction</u> is of equal
importance.

    In this chapter we will try to give some of the flavor of
scientific calculations, but we   will   not   be   including   enough
detail for those people who will need to work with them.   We will
give only an overview of this important use of computers.   In the
next   chapter   we   will   present more details and applications of
scientific calculations.

EVALUATING FORMULAS

    To   solve   certain   scientific   problems   we   must substitute
values into formulas and calculate results.   For example, we
could   be   asked   to calculate the distance traveled by a falling
object after it is dropped from   an   airplane.   A formula that
gives   the   distance   in   meters   traveled   in time t seconds,
neglecting air resistance, is

$$d = 4.9t^2$$

Here the   constant   4.9 is one-half   the   acceleration   due to
gravity.   Here is a program to compute the distance at the end of
each second of the first 10 seconds after the drop:

```
C PRINT TABLE OF DISTANCE FALLEN VERSUS TIME
      REAL METERS,TIME
      INTEGER I
      TIME=0.0
C     LABEL TIME-DISTANCE TABLE
      PRINT,'    TIME            DISTANCE'
      DO 10 I=1,10
         TIME=TIME+1.0
         METERS=4.9*TIME*TIME
         PRINT,TIME,METERS
10       CONTINUE
      RETURN
      END
```

The output for this program is

TIME	DISTANCE
0.1000000E 01	0.4900000E 01
0.2000000E 01	0.1960000E 02
0.3000000E 01	0.4410000E 02
0.4000000E 01	0.7840000E 02
0.5000000E 01	0.1225000E 03
0.6000000E 01	0.1764000E 03
0.7000000E 01	0.2401000E 03
0.8000000E 01	0.3136000E 03
0.9000000E 01	0.3969000E 03
0.1000000E 02	0.4900000E 03

This example prints a table of values of METERS for different
times. Printing of tables is an interesting and historic
scientific use of computers. Scientific calculations are usually
done using REAL variables. In the output the distances and times
are printed with seven digits in the fraction part, with a zero
preceding the decimal point. Not all these digits are
significant; the constant in the formula is only expressed with
two digits. We must realize then that only about two digits of
the distance traveled are significant.

The calculations are carried out in the computer keeping 7
digits, but this does not imply that they are meaningful. Even
if the constant in the formula were entered to 7-digit precision,
we would not necessarily have 7 significant digits in the answer.
Because computers represent REAL numbers only to a limited
precision, there are always what are called numerical errors.
These are not mistakes you make but are inherent in the way that
REAL numbers are represented in the computer. When two REAL
numbers are multiplied, the product is rounded off to the same
precision as the original numbers; no more digits in the product
would be significant. As calculations proceed, the rounding
process can erode the significance even of some of the digits
that are maintained. We usually quote numerical errors by saying
that a value is, for example,

19.25 ± 0.05

This means that the value could be as high as 19.30 or as low as
19.20. If the error were greater, say 0.5 instead of 0.05, then
the values could range between 19.75 and 18.75. In this case the
fourth digit in the value is certainly not significant, and you
would say instead that the value was

19.2 ± 0.5

Or we might round it off instead of truncating the insignificant
digit, and write

19.3 ± 0.5

The estimation of errors is an important job that is done by
numérical analysts. If you are doing numerical calculations, you
should be aware of the fact that answers are not exact but have
errors.

BUILT-IN FUNCTIONS

Scientific calculations require mathematical functions that
are not commonly used in business calculations. For many of
these functions, subprograms have already been written for
Fortran; they are built into the compiler. For example, suppose
for our falling-body calculation we wanted to compute the times
when the body reached different distances. To calculate the
time, given the distance, we use this form of the same formula:

$$t = \sqrt{d/4.9}$$

Now we need to be able to calculate a square root. This can be
done by using the built-in function for square root, which is
called SQRT. We would write in the program:

    TIME = SQRT(METERS/4.9)

Other built-in functions available to Fortran for scientific
calculations are connected with trigonometry. They include SIN
and COS. These give the values of the sine and cosine, when the
argument of the function is in radians. ATAN(X) gives the angle
in radians whose tangent is X. The natural logarithm is obtained
by using ALOG, the exponential by using EXP. Other more exotic
functions are available in full Fortran but are not in SF/k.

GRAPHING A FUNCTION

Frequently a better understanding of a scientific formula can
be had if you draw a graph of the function. In the first example
of this chapter we evaluated a function at regular intervals. It
is possible to use these values to plot a graph on the printer.
We could, for instance, plot a distance-time graph for the
falling object. We will show one way to plot a graph on the
printer, but there are lots of other ways.

When you draw a graph of X versus Y you usually make the X-
axis horizontal and have the Y-axis vertical. The values of X,
which is the independent variable, increase uniformly; the
corresponding values of Y are obtained by substituting X into the
function Y=f(X). When we plot a graph on the printer the lines
of printing are uniformly spaced, so we will use the distance
between lines to represent the uniform interval between the Xs.
This means that the X-axis will be vertical and the Y-axis
horizontal. To see the graph in the normal orientation, just

rotate the page 90 degrees counterclockwise.   Here   is   a   graph
for $Y=X^2-X-2$ plotted between X=-2 and X=3:

```
GRAPH OF Y            VERSUS X
MINIMUM OF Y     -0.2240000E 01
MAXIMUM OF Y      0.4000000E 01
-0.20000E 01                       I                                    *
-0.18000E 01                       I                              *
-0.16000E 01                       I                          *
-0.14000E 01                       I                    *
-0.12000E 01                       I       *
-0.10000E 01                       *
-0.80000E 00                   *   I
-0.60000E 00                *      I
-0.40000E 00             *         I
-0.20000E 00           *           I
 0.00000E 00          *            I
 0.20000E 00         *             I
 0.40000E 00        *              I
 0.60000E 00        *              I
 0.80000E 00         *             I
 0.10000E 01          *            I
 0.12000E 01           *           I
 0.14000E 01             *         I
 0.16000E 01                *      I
 0.18000E 01                   *   I
 0.20000E 01                       *
 0.22000E 01                       I     *
 0.24000E 01                       I         *
 0.26000E 01                       I              *
 0.28000E 01                       I                    *
 0.30000E 01                       I                                    *
```

We represent the Y-value corresponding to the X of a
particular printed line by printing an asterisk in the print
position that approximates its value. We use 51 columns to print
the range of Ys. If the lowest Y-value that we must represent is
YMIN and the highest is YMAX, then the 51 print positions must
represent a range of

        YRANGE = YMAX - YMIN

To find the print position for a value Y we compute an integer
variable YPRINT from

        YPRINT=50*(Y-YMIN)/YRANGE+1.5

The value 1.5 is added to round to the nearest integer and put
YMIN in the first position. We are assuming YRANGE is not zero
so that we can divide by it.

We use an array of single characters called LINE to hold each line of the graph to be printed. First, all the characters of LINE are set to be blanks. Next, we put an X-axis on our graph if it is in the proper range. To do this we place a capital I into the line of blanks at the position where a zero value of Y would be placed. Here is the program segment for putting in the capital I for the X-axis.

```
    XAXIS=50*(0-YMIN)/YRANGE+1.5
    IF(XAXIS.GE.1.AND.XAXIS.LE.51)THEN DO
        LINE(XAXIS)='I'
        END IF
```

Before printing the line we place an asterisk in position YPRINT. After printing the line we must replace the asterisk by a blank. If the asterisk was an X-axis, we must again mark the X-axis using a capital I. Here is the program segment for doing this.

```
        LINE(YPRINT)='*'
        PRINT 20,X(I),LINE
20      FORMAT(' ',E12.5,51A1)
        IF(YPRINT.EQ.XAXIS)THEN DO
            LINE(YPRINT)='I'
        ELSE DO
            LINE(YPRINT)=' '
            END IF
```

We do not print a Y-axis, but we list the X-values corresponding to each line opposite the line.

A SUBROUTINE FOR PLOTTING GRAPHS

Here is the complete subroutine for plotting a graph from N pairs of REAL values of X and Y stored in arrays of those names. The values of X are uniformly spaced. The actual names of the variables to be plotted will be given as arguments XNAME and YNAME, which are character variables. The calling statement would be of the form

```
    CALL GRAPH(X,Y,N,XNAME,YNAME)
```

We will call a subroutine to find YMAX and YMIN. It will be called MINMAX.

```
C SUBROUTINE TO PLOT A GRAPH
      SUBROUTINE GRAPH(X,Y,N,XNAME,YNAME)
      INTEGER N
      REAL X(N),Y(N)
      CHARACTER*8 XNAME,YNAME
      CHARACTER*1 LINE(51)
      REAL YMIN,YMAX,YRANGE
      INTEGER COLUMN,XAXIS,YPRINT,I
C     FIND RANGE OF Y TO BE PLOTTED
      CALL MINMAX(Y,N,YMIN,YMAX)
      YRANGE=YMAX-YMIN
C     CLEAR LINE TO BLANKS
      DO 10 COLUMN=1,51
         LINE(COLUMN)=' '
10       CONTINUE
C     PLACE X-AXIS MARK IN LINE
      XAXIS=50*(0-YMIN)/YRANGE+1.5
      IF(XAXIS.GE.1.AND.XAXIS.LE.51)THEN DO
         LINE(XAXIS)='I'
         END IF
C     LABEL THE GRAPH
      PRINT,'GRAPH OF',YNAME,'VERSUS',XNAME
      PRINT,'MINIMUM OF',YNAME,YMIN
      PRINT,'MAXIMUM OF',YNAME,YMAX
C     PREPARE AND PRINT LINES OF GRAPH
      DO 30 I=1,N
         YPRINT=50*(Y(I)-YMIN)/YRANGE+1.5
         LINE(YPRINT)='*'
         PRINT 20,X(I),LINE
20       FORMAT(' ',E12.5,51A1)
         IF(YPRINT.EQ.XAXIS)THEN DO
            LINE(YPRINT)='I'
         ELSE DO
            LINE(YPRINT)=' '
            END IF
30       CONTINUE
      RETURN
      END
C FIND SMALLEST AND LARGEST VALUES IN ARRAY
      SUBROUTINE MINMAX(NUMBER,N,MIN,MAX)
      INTEGER N
      REAL NUMBER(N),MIN,MAX
      INTEGER I
      MIN=NUMBER(1)
      MAX=NUMBER(1)
      DO 10 I=2,N
         IF(NUMBER(I).LT.MIN)THEN DO
            MIN=NUMBER(I)
            END IF
         IF(NUMBER(I).GT.MAX)THEN DO
            MAX=NUMBER(I)
            END IF
10       CONTINUE
      RETURN
      END
```

USING THE GRAPH SUBROUTINE

We will now give the program that was used to plot the function of x,

$$y = x^2 - x - 2$$

between the values x=-2 to x=3. We plot it at intervals of x that are 0.2 wide. There are 26 points in all. Here is the program:

```
$JOB     MARK NAIRN
C PLOT THE FUNCTION Y=X*X-X-2
      REAL X(26),Y(26)
      INTEGER I
C     COMPUTE VALUES FOR X AND Y ARRAYS
      DO 10 I=1,26
         X(I)=-2.0+(I-1)*0.2
         Y(I)=X(I)*X(I)-X(I)-2.0
10       CONTINUE
      CALL GRAPH(X,Y,26,'X       ','Y       ')
      RETURN
      END
(include here the GRAPH and MINMAX subroutines)
$ENTRY
```

The output for this program was shown earlier in this chapter. You will notice that as the graph crosses the X-axis the capital I is replaced by an asterisk. It crosses twice, at

```
x = -1.0
x = +2.0
```

We say that x=-1 and x=2 are the roots of the equation

$$x^2 - x - 2 = 0$$

The function (x^2-x-2) becomes zero at these values of x. This graphical method is one way of finding the roots of an equation. We will look later in this chapter at another way of finding roots that is numerical rather than graphical.

FITTING A CURVE TO A SET OF POINTS

In the last sections we have seen how to compute a set of points of corresponding X and Y values from a formula and then to plot a graph of these points. In some scientific experiments we measure the value of a variable Y as we change some other variable X in a systematic way. The results are displayed by plotting X and Y. If there is a theory that relates the values of X to Y in a formula or equation, then we can see how well the results fit the theoretical formula.

One way would be to compute the values of Y for each X from the formula. The measured values could be called Y(experimental) and the calculated ones Y(theoretical). The differences between corresponding values

Y(experimental) - Y(theoretical)

are called <u>deviations</u> of experimental from theoretical values.

We have spoken so far as if it were possible to compute the proper theoretical value that corresponds to each experimental value. This is the case if the formula has no other variable in it. Frequently there are other variables in the formula that can change. For example, here is the formula for V, the velocity of an object at time T, given that its initial velocity is VINIT and its acceleration is A.

V = VINIT + A*T

If we measured the velocity of an object that has a uniform acceleration we could plot a graph between V and T:

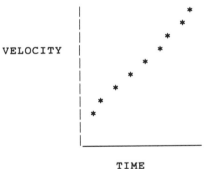

Theoretically, the graph should be a straight line, but the experimental points are scattered. It is possible to draw a line by eye that is placed so that the deviations of points from the line are small. Since some deviations, V(experimental)-V(theoretical), are positive and some negative their sum might be small even though individual deviations were large. To get a good fit we minimize the sum of the squares of the deviations rather than the sum of the deviations. The squares of the deviations are always positive. We choose as the best straight line the one that makes the sum of the squares of the deviations the least. This is called <u>least-squares fitting</u> of a curve (here a straight line) to experimental points. This process can be done very efficiently by a computer. Most computer installations

provide standard subroutines for least-squares fitting, so that
scientists do not have to write their own.

Sometimes no theoretical curve is known. We can still fit
our data to an equation. We choose an equation that has a form
resembling our data. If there is no theory we say it is an
empirical fit, meaning that it is an equation based on the
observations.

SOLVING POLYNOMIAL EQUATIONS

The graph that we plotted as an example was of the function

$$y = x^2 - x - 2$$

This is a polynomial function of x. The places where the graph
crosses the x-axis are the roots of the equation

$$x^2 - x - 2 = 0$$

This is a second-degree equation since the highest power of the
unknown x is the second power. It is a quadratic equation.
There are general formulas for the roots of a quadratic equation.
For the equation

$$ax^2 + bx + c = 0$$

the two roots x1 and x2 are given by the formulas

$$x1 = (-b + \sqrt{b^2 - 4ac})/(2a) \quad \text{and}$$

$$x2 = (-b - \sqrt{b^2 - 4ac})/(2a)$$

Most students of mathematics know these formulas. If the
quantity $(b^2 - 4ac)$ inside the square root sign is positive, all is
straightforward. If it is negative, then the formula requires us
to find the square root of a negative number, and we say the
roots are imaginary. This means, in graphical terms, that the
curve does not cross, or touch, the X-axis anywhere. It is
either completely above or completely below the X-axis. There is
no use looking for values of x where the function is zero.

Here is a subroutine for finding the roots of a quadratic
equation.

```
C FIND ROOTS OF A*X*X + B*X + C
      SUBROUTINE ROOTS(A,B,C)
      REAL A,B,C,TEST,SQROOT,ROOT1,ROOT2
      TEST=B*B-4*A*C
      IF(TEST.GE.0.0)THEN DO
         SQROOT=SQRT(TEST)
         ROOT1=(-B+SQROOT)/(2*A)
         ROOT2=(-B-SQROOT)/(2*A)
         PRINT,'ROOTS ARE',ROOT1,ROOT2
      ELSE DO
         PRINT,'ROOTS ARE IMAGINARY'
         END IF
      RETURN
      END
```

For equations that are polynomial in x of degrees higher than two, the method for finding the roots is not as easy. For an equation of degree three, there is a complicated formula for the three roots. For large degrees there are no formulas and we must look for the roots by a numerical method.

The secret of any search is first to be sure that what you are looking for is in the right area, then to keep narrowing down the search area. One method of searching for roots corresponds to the binary search we discussed in Chapter 15. First we find two values of x for which the function has different signs. Then we can be sure that, if it is continuous, the graph will cross the x-axis at least once in the interval between these points. The next step is to halve the interval and look at the middle. If there is only one root in the interval, then in the middle the function will either be zero, in which case it is the root, or it will have the same sign as one of the two end points. Remember they have opposite signs. We discard the half of the interval that is bounded by the middle point and the end with the same sign and repeat the process. After several steps we will have a good approximation to the location of the root. We can continue the process until we are satisfied that the error, or uncertainty, in our root location is small enough. There is no point in trying to locate it more accurately than the precision with which the numbers are stored. A numerical analyst could determine the accuracy of the calculated answer.

SOLVING LINEAR EQUATIONS

Computers are used to solve sets of linear equations. If we have two unknowns, we must have two equations to get a solution. We can solve the set of equations

$$x-y=10$$
$$x+y=6$$

to get the result x=8, y=-2. To solve the equations we first
eliminate one of the unknowns. From the first equation we get

    x=y+10

Substituting into the second eliminates x. It gives

    (y+10)+y=6 or 2y=-4 or y=-2

Then substituting back gives

    x=-2+10 or x=8

This process of elimination can be carried out a step at a time
for more equations in more unknowns. Each step lowers the number
of unknowns by one and the number of equations by one. A
computer program can be written to perform this job, and can be
used to solve a set of linear equations. What we must provide is
the coefficients of the unknowns and the right-hand sides of the
set   of   equations.   A common method is called the Gauss
elimination method.

AREAS UNDER CURVES

    Another   numerical   method   that   is   relatively easy to
understand is the calculation of the area under a curve by the
trapezoidal method.   Suppose we have a curve of y=f(x) and we
want to find the area between the curve and the X-axis and
between lines at x=X1 and x=Xn.

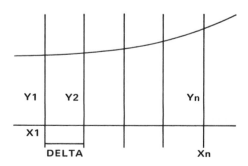

We will divide the distance between X1 and Xn into intervals of
size DELTA. In the drawing we have shown four intervals.   The
area of the first section, thinking of it as a trapezoid, is

    (Y1+Y2)*DELTA/2

The total area under the curve is approximated by the sum of all
the trapezoids. The total area of the trapezoids is

    (Y1+Y2)*DELTA/2+(Y2+Y3)*DELTA/2+...(Y(n-1)+Yn)*DELTA/2

If we factor out DELTA the formula becomes

```
((Y1+Yn)/2+Y2+Y3+... +Y(n-1))*DELTA
```

This is half the sum of Y1 and Yn plus the sum of the other Ys multiplied by the width of the trapezoids. As DELTA is made smaller, the sum of the areas of the trapezoids comes closer and closer to the area under the curve. It is a better and better approximation. There is, however, a limit to the accuracy that can be obtained, due to the precision of the REAL numbers. Here is a program segment to compute the area if the Ys are stored in an array:

```
      SUM=(Y(1)+Y(N))/2.0
      FINAL=N-1
      DO 10 I=2,FINAL
         SUM=SUM+Y(I)
10       CONTINUE
      AREA=SUM*DELTA
```

CHAPTER 19 SUMMARY

This chapter has given an introduction to the use of computers in scientific calculations. Generally, these calculations are done using REAL numbers. The scientist needs to know the accuracy of the final answers. The answers may be inaccurate because of:

Measurement errors – the original data was collected by measuring physical quantities, such as length or speed. These measurements can never be perfect and an estimate of the measurement error should be made.

Round-off errors by the computer – a given computer stores REAL numbers with a particular precision, typically 7 decimal digits of accuracy. Calculations using REAL numbers will be no more accurate than the number of digits of precision provided by the computer. They could even be less accurate due to the cumulative effect of round-off. (Note: sometimes the programmer can choose between "single-precision" REAL, giving typically 7 digits of accuracy and "double-precision" REAL, giving typically 16 digits accuracy.)

Truncation errors in repeated calculations – some calculations, such as searching for the roots of a polynomial equation, produce approximations that are successively closer to the exact answer. When the repeated calculation stops, we have a truncation error, which is the difference between the final approximation and the exact answer (ignoring errors due to measurement and round-off).

The number of digits of accuracy in a particular answer is called its number of <u>significant figures</u>. The scientist needs to know that the computer produces a particular answer with enough significant figures for his purposes.

Fortran provides built-in functions that are useful in solving scientific or mathematical problems. The function SQRT takes the square root of a non-negative number. The functions SIN, COS and ATAN (arctan) operate on or return angles in radians. ALOG takes the natural logarithm of a number, and EXP raises e to a specified power.

This chapter presented the following typical scientific and mathematical uses of computers.

>   Evaluating formulas - a computer can produce tables of numbers, for example tables of navigational figures used on sailing boats.

>   Graphing functions - a computer can plot a particular function; sometimes a special <u>plotter</u> machine is attached to the computer so it can draw continuous lines as well as printing characters.

>   Fitting a curve to a set of points - data points from an experiment can be read by a program and used to determine an equation (a curve) that describes the data.

>   Solving polynomial equations - a polynomial equation such as

$$X^3 + 9X^2 + 6X - 23 = 0$$

>   can be solved by a program that reads the coefficients (1, 9, 6 and -23).

>   Solving linear equations - a set of equations such as

$$2X + 9Y = 7$$
$$10X - 4Y = 2$$

>   can be solved by a program that reads the coefficients of the unknowns (2, 9, 10 and -4) and the right-hand sides of the equations (7 and 2).

>   Areas under curves - a program can find the area under a given curve by using the heights of the curve at many points. Essentially, the program slices the area into narrow strips and adds up the areas of the strips. This process is sometimes called numerical integration or quadrature.

CHAPTER 19 EXERCISES

1. One jet plane is flying 1083.7 kilometers per hour; another jet plane, chasing it from behind, is flying 1297.9 kilometers per hour. What is the relative speed of the second plane, that is, how fast is it catching up to the first plane? The speed of the first plane is known to an accuracy of ±5 km/hr and the speed of the second is known to an accuracy of ±0.5 km/hr. How accurately can we calculate the relative speed? How many significant figures are there in the first plane's speed, the second plane's speed and the relative speed?

2. Use the graphing subroutine given in this chapter to plot the function SIN(X) for X varying from 0 to 3 in steps of one-tenth.

3. Use the graphing subroutine given in this chapter to plot the function X*SIN(X) for X varying from 0 to 12 in steps of 0.25E0.

4. A moon rocket has an instrument that measures the rocket's acceleration every second and transmits the measurement to an on-board minicomputer. A program in the minicomputer estimates the speed of the rocket, assuming a speed of zero at launch time. Essentially, this program determines the area under the curve of acceleration plotted against time. Using the trapezoidal method the speed at time Tn will be approximately

$$((A1+An)/2+A2+A3+ \,.. + A(n-1))* DELTA$$

In this case, DELTA is 1 second and each acceleration is measured in kilometers per second per second. The formula to give the speed in kilometers per second n seconds after blast-off is

$$(A1+An)/2+A2+A3+...+A(n-1)$$

Write a program that reads in the accelerations and prints out the speeds after each second. If you are clever you can avoid recalculating the entire series for each acceleration reading, and you can avoid using an array.

5. A polynomial such as $Y=AX^3+BX^2+CX+D$ can be evaluated more efficiently by writing it as $Y=(((A*X+B)*X+C)*X+D)$. Write a subroutine called POLY to evaluate polynomials of degree N by this method. Assume that the coefficients of the various powers of X are stored as an array. Test your subroutine by tabulating values for $Y=X^2-X-2$ using it.

6. In evaluating formulas care must be taken to avoid illegal calculations such as taking the square root of a negative number or dividing by zero. Tabulate values for the formula

$$Y=(X^2-6X+2)/(X-3)$$

for values of X going in steps of 1 from x= -10 to +10 where Y has a defined value.

CHAPTER 20

NUMERICAL METHODS

In the last chapter we outlined some of the important types of calculations used in scientific and engineering computing. In this chapter we will look at some of the methods which have been devised for doing these numerical calculations. In any calculations, for example those for evaluating functions such as the trigonometic functions sin and cos or finding the area under a curve, the calculation can be carried out to varying degrees of accuracy. Usually the more calculating you do, the more accurate the answer you get. But some methods are better than others; for the same amount of work you get greater accuracy. We will for instance be looking at a way of finding areas under curves that is usually superior to the trapeziodal rule described in the last chapter. As well we will show a general method of solving linear equations and a method for least-squares fitting of a straight line to a set of experimental points. But first we will look at an efficient way of evaluating a polynomial.

EVALUATION OF A POLYNOMIAL

In doing numerical calculations we should be concerned with getting the best calculation we can for the least cost in terms of computer time. This is one of the concerns of people who design what are called numerical methods. They are not just concerned about getting an answer but about whether the cost of getting the answer can be decreased.

As an example of how different methods giving apparently the same result can have different costs, we will look at the calculation of the value of a polynomial. We will look at a third-degree polynomial and then generalize the result later for a polynomial of degree N. A third-degree polynomial has the form

$$Y(X) = A3 \ X^3 + A2 \ X^2 + A1 \ X + A0$$

One way of evaluating this in Fortran is to write

```
Y = A3*X**3 + A2*X**2 + A1*X**1 + A0
```

When the exponent of an exponentiation operation is a positive integer the result is obtained by repeated multiplications so that X**2 is the same as X*X. So our polynomial evaluation is the same as

```
Y = A3*X*X*X + A2*X*X + A1*X + A0
```

In this evaluation there are 6 multiplications (count the asterisks) and 3 additions. For a fourth-degree polynomial there would be 10 multiplications and 4 additions. For an Nth-degree polynomial there would be $N+(N-1)+(N-2)+...+1=N(N+1)/2$ multiplications and N additions.

Now we will look at a different method of evaluating the third-degree polynomial. It is

```
Y = ((((A3)*X+A2)*X+A1)*X+A0)
```

Here there are 3 multiplications and 3 additions. (Just count the asterisks.) For an Nth-degree polynomial there would be N multiplications and N additions. This method is called Horner's rule and is certainly much more efficient, particularly for polynomials of higher degree.

We will now write a function subprogram that will evaluate a polynomial of degree N by this method given that the coefficients of the powers of X namely the As are stored in a one-dimensional array. In a Fortran array the index of the variables goes from 1 to the length of the array. We will store A0 as A(1), A1 as A(2) and AN as A(N+1). Here is a program segment which would work for the third-degree polynomial

```
      POLY=A(4)
      DO 10 I=1,3
         POLY=POLY*X+A(4-I)
10       CONTINUE
```

If we extend this now to work for an Nth degree polynomial we would write

```
      POLY=A(N+1)
      DO 10 I=1,N
         POLY=POLY*X+A(N+1-I)
10       CONTINUE
```

The complete function subprogram would be

```
C FUNCTION SUBPROGRAM FOR EVALUATING POLYNOMIAL OF DEGREE N
      REAL FUNCTION POLY(A,N,X)
      INTEGER N
      REAL A(50),X
      INTEGER I
      POLY=A(N+1)
      DO 10 I=1,N
         POLY=POLY*X+A(N+1-I)
10       CONTINUE
      RETURN
      END
```

ROUND-OFF ERRORS

When a real number is represented in a computer by a finite string of bits an error is usually introduced. This error is called a round-off error. The last bit in the string may be inexact. In decimal notation if the fraction 0.132762 is to be represented by a string of decimal digits of length 4 then the four digits will be either .1327 or .1328. The string may simply be chopped off after the 4th digit, which is called rounding by chopping, or 5 may be added to the 5th digit and the sum then chopped to 4 digits. This latter form of round of is probably somewhat better and is the method that you usually are thinking of if you ask that a number be rounded off.

As numbers are combined in the arithmetic operations of addition, subtraction, multiplication and division, the round-off error may increase. We say that a further error is generated. As operations continue, the generated error may grow and is said to be a propagated error.

In adding, or subtracting two numbers, the error in the sum, or difference is equal to the sum of the errors in the two numbers. Suppose for instance that the number 0.132762 is represented as the 4-digit string 0.1328. The error in this representation due to rounding off is 0.000038. If the number 0.521689 is represented as 0.5217 the error is 0.000011. The sum of the numbers will be 0.6545 as compared with the result of adding the two 6-digit representations which gives 0.654451. The error in the sum is 0.000049 which is the sum of 0.000038 and 0.000011.

In multiplication the relative (or percentage) error introduced in the product is equal to the sum of the relative (or percentage) errors of the two factors. In division the relative error of the quotient is the difference between the relative errors of the dividend and divisor. In any event all arithmetic operations serve to propagate errors due to rounding.

We found that Horner's rule was more efficient for evaluating polynomials than the straightforward method because there were fewer multiplications. Now we can see that it is also more accurate since the propagation of round-off error is less when there are fewer arithmetic operations. This is why we can say that it is a better method; it is more accurate and costs less.

LOSS OF SIGNIFICANT FIGURES

We have seen that arithmetic operations result in errors and these cause the rounding due to the finite representations of real numbers in a computer to grow larger. The number of digits in our final result that are significant gradually decreases as errors are propagated.

There are more drastic ways of losing significant figures. One place where this occurs is in the situation where two nearly equal numbers are subtracted. When 0.3572 is subtracted from 0.3581 the answer is 0.0009 which is normalized to 0.9???E-03. The digits that are written as question marks could be anything; only the 9 is significant. We had 4 significant figures in each of the original numbers and now we have only 1 significant figure in the difference. One way to cope with this loss of precision is to avoid calculations of this sort. Often by regrouping or resequencing operations the offending subtraction can be eliminated. If it is not possible then it may be necessary to work to greater precision, say double precision, during the part of a calculation where this can occur. Loss of significant figures can also occur when divisions are small or multipliers large.

EVALUATION OF INFINITE SERIES

Many mathematical functions can be represented by an infinite series of terms to be added. For example,

$$\exp(x) = 1+(x/1!)+(x^2/2!)+(x^3/3!)+\ldots$$

$$\sin(x) = (x/1!)-(x^3/3!)+(x^5/5!)-\ldots$$

$$\cos(x) = 1-(x^2/2!)+(x^4/4!)-\ldots$$

$$\log(1+x) = (x/1)-(x^2/2)+(x^3/3)-\ldots$$

The series for sin and cos are for angles x in radians. The series for log(1+x) is valid only for values of x whose magnitudes are less than 1.

If we evaluated the infinite series for say sin(x) for a value of x=PI/4 we would get terms that alternately are positive and negative and decrease in magnitude as successive terms are calculated. Here is a program that prints the value of the sum of the sine series up to a given term as well as the value of the latest term added for eight terms.

```
$JOB   TAYLOR
C COMPUTE THE SERIES FOR SIN(X) TERM BY TERM
      REAL PI,X,SQX,SINE,TERM
      INTEGER I
      PI=3.141592
      X=PI/4.
      SQX=X*X
      PRINT,'SIN(X)            ','TERM'
      TERM=X
      SINE=TERM
      DO 20 I=2,16,2
         PRINT,SINE,TERM
         TERM=-1*(TERM*SQX)/((I)*(I+1))
         SINE=SINE+TERM
20       CONTINUE
      PRINT,'VALUE OF SIN(PI/4) IS',1./SQRT(2.)
      RETURN
      END
$ENTRY
```

The output for this program is

```
SIN(X)                TERM
   0.7853980E 00     0.7853980E 00
   0.7046525E 00    -0.8074546E-01
   0.7071429E 00     0.2490392E-02
   0.7071063E 00    -0.3657614E-04
   0.7071066E 00     0.3133609E-06
   0.7071066E 00    -0.1757242E-08
   0.7071066E 00     0.6948429E-11
   0.7071066E 00    -0.2041018E-13
VALUE OF SIN(PI/4) IS     0.7071069E 00
```

You can see that the terms become progressively smaller right from the start. This is because x is less than 1. The ratio of the one term to the next term is $x^2/(i(i+1))$. This ratio becomes smaller as i becomes larger. The terms are decreasing faster and faster. Terms after the 5th do not make any difference. This series for sin(x) can be used even when x is greater than 1. Here is the output if we run the previous program again with the statement X=PI/2 instead of X=PI/4 and print the value of sin(PI/2) which is 1.

```
SIN(X)                TERM
   0.1570796E 01     0.1570796E 01
   0.9248325E 00    -0.6459635E 00
   0.1004524E 01     0.7969242E-01
   0.9998425E 00    -0.4681736E-02
   0.1000003E 01     0.1604404E-03
   0.9999993E 00    -0.3598822E-05
   0.9999993E 00     0.5692136E-07
   0.9999993E 00    -0.6687983E-09
VALUE OF SIN(PI/2) IS     0.1000000E 01
```

This time the terms do not decrease as rapidly; but they are not affecting the result after the 6th term. The accuracy obtained from the evaluation of a fixed number of terms depends on the value of the argument x.

If the series is stopped after 3 terms the value of sine differs from the true value of sin(PI/2) which is 0.100000E01 by 0.0004524E01 which is 4/10 of 1 percent. We say that this error is partly due to truncating the series. If truncation occurs after 4 terms the error is 0.0001575E01 which is 1/10 of 1 percent. The more terms we calculate, the smaller is the truncation error. By taking sufficient terms we can make the truncation error as small as we want.

One way of deciding how many terms of a series are enough is to stop when the absolute value of the most recent term is less than a certain amount. The amount we usually choose is such that it will not change the value of the sum in a noticeable way. It is useless to evaluate more terms because they do not matter.

Even when we have evaluated enough terms so that the contribution of the last term is insignificant, there still remain errors due to round off. In our example, the round-off error would be present even in the first term of the series; as each term is added another round off occurs. These errors may tend to cancel each other; sometimes the number is rounded up, sometimes down. It is possible that all errors are in the same direction so that the total possible error introduced in this way grows larger with the number of terms. We must expect the worst. The round-off error in the sine of PI/4 seems to be 0.0000003, that in sine of PI/2 seems to be 0.0000007. In each case the last figure printed is dubious.

One way of avoiding the accumulation of round-off errors is to work in double precision. In double precision each number is represented by a string of bits that is twice as long as in single precision. The round-off error will then accumulate in the least significant bits of the double precision number. When the result is finally reduced to single precision, a single round off occurs.

A relationship between the functions sine and cosine may be used to improve the accuracy of the result for a given number of terms in the series. This relationship is

    SIN(X)=COS((PI/2.)-X)

This means that for angles greater than PI/4 but less than PI/2 we can compute the sine by using the series for cosine with the argument ((PI/2.)-X). This will be equal to or less than PI/4 and comparable accuracy can be obtained using the same number of terms in the series.

When a fixed number of terms has been decided on, say six, the evaluation of the series becomes the evaluation of a polynomial. We can take advantage of the efficiencies of

Horner's method. In the series for sine and cosine not every power of X is present so the polynomial is really like one in X^2 rather than X. For example, the series for sine to 5 terms can be written as

$$sin(X)=((((X^2/9!)-(1/7!))X^2+(1/5!))X^2+1)X$$

The coefficients (1/9!), (1/7!), and (1/5!) can all be evaluated once and for all and stored as constants in the program.

All values of angles greater than PI/2 must be reduced to be related to either the sin or cos series for X less than or equal to PI/4.

ROOT FINDING

In the last chapter we looked at one method for finding the value of X where a polynomial in X has a zero value.   This same method applies to any function of one variable, say f(X). If there are two values, say X1 and X2, of X at which f(X) has opposite signs then, provided the function is continuous, there must be at least one point in between these values where the function has a zero value. We described a search technique that halved the interval between the given values of X and determined in which half the zero of the function lay. This process can then be repeated in a manner similar to a binary search.

This interval-halving method can be improved upon and numerous other methods for finding zeros or roots of a function of one variable have been devised. The purpose of these methods is to provide a faster way of homing in on a root once it has been located between two values of X.

A technique called the secant method uses, instead of the mid-point, the point at which a line drawn between the point (X1,f(X1)) and (X2,f(X2)) cuts the X-axis. This will be at a point X given by solving the equation

$$f(X2)/(X2-X)=f(X1)/(X-X1)$$

or $X = (f(X1)X2+f(X2)X1)/(f(X2)+f(X1))$

If you have studied analytical geometry you can see this from the diagram.

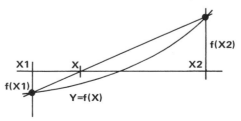

This process is repeated using the point X as a replacement for either X1 or X2. The choice depends on which gives a value to the function opposite to the value at X. As the iteration proceeds the interval is always being narrowed down.

Both the interval-halving method and the secant method will converge on the root. The rate of the convergence depends on the particular function whose zero is being sought. The rate of convergence can sometimes be improved at the cost of the guarantee of convergence. In the secant method, instead of using one of the end points all the time, two intermediate points can be used. Of course, there may not be a zero between these points but the search interval is much smaller.

A method called the Newton-Raphson method is useful for simple functions, like polynomials, whose slopes can be computed using calculus. The iteration formula for approximating the root is

$$X(N+1) = XN - f(XN)/S(XN)$$

where X(N+1) is the approximation to the root at the (N+1)th iteration, XN is the Nth approximation, f(XN) is the value of the function at XN, and S(XN) is the value of the slope of the function at XN.

For those who have studied calculus if, for example,

$$f(X) = 3X^2 + 2X + 1 \text{ then}$$

$$S(X) = 6X + 2$$

S(X) is the derivative of f(X).

The Newton-Raphson method has very rapid convergence, but convergence is not always guaranteed.

SUBROUTINE FOR ROOT FINDING

We will give a program for a subroutine which uses the interval-halving method. It is perhaps slow, but safe. For the function evaluations it will call on a function FUNC. The parameter EPS stands for the Greek letter epsilon. In mathematics, we use epsilon to stand for the small difference between an approximation and a true value. We will use as a stopping condition the fact that two successive approximations to the root differ from each other by less than EPS. When you use the subroutine SOLVE you must decide what accuracy you want. Of course there is no use asking for greater accuracy than is permitted by the finite representation of the numbers.

```
C FIND ROOTS OF FUNC(X) = 0 BY INTERVAL HALVING
      SUBROUTINE SOLVE(LEFT,RIGHT,ROOT,EPS)
      REAL LEFT,RIGHT,ROOT,EPS
      REAL FUNC
      REAL X1,X2,F1
      X1=LEFT
      X2=RIGHT
      F1=FUNC(X1)
      ROOT=(X1+X2)/2.
      WHILE(ROOT-X1.GT.EPS)DO
         IF(F1*FUNC(ROOT).GT.0.)THEN DO
            X1=ROOT
         ELSE DO
            X2=ROOT
            END IF
         ROOT=(X1+X2)/2.
         END WHILE
      RETURN
      END
```

To use this subroutine in a program we must call the function
whose root is sought by the name FUNC and be sure to declare its
type in the main program. We will use it to find the zero of

$$f(X) = X^2 - X - 2$$

that is between X=0 and X=3 to an accuracy of 0.00005E00.

```
$JOB     ART SEDGWICK
C FIND ONE ROOT OF F(X)=X*X-X-2
      REAL FUNC,ANSWER
      CALL SOLVE(0.,3.,ANSWER,5E-5)
      PRINT,'ROOT BETWEEN 0 AND 3 IS',ANSWER
      RETURN
      END
      REAL FUNCTION FUNC(X)
      REAL X
      FUNC=(X-1.)*X-2.
      RETURN
      END
(include definition of SOLVE here)
$ENTRY
```

The output for this program is

```
 ROOT BETWEEN 0 AND 3 IS     0.2000015E 01
```

Notice that the polynomial is being evaluated by Horner's method.
We do not need to use this kind of method of root finding for a
quadratic but it illustrates the method in a case where we can
compute the correct answer which is

```
    0.2000000E01
```

NUMERICAL INTEGRATION

In calculus, we find that the area under a curve can be calculated by evaluating the definite integral of the function that represents the curve between the two limiting values of the independent variable. Not every function can be integrated analytically but a numerical approximation can be obtained for any continuous function. In the last chapter we presented the trapezoidal rule for calculating areas under curves; the function is evaluated at uniformly spaced intervals between the limiting values and the function values are used to find the area. The accuracy of the result improves as smaller intervals are chosen and more function evaluations made.

For the same number of function evaluations it is possible to have an integration formula that combines the values to give a better approximation to the area.

One formula which is often better than the trapezoidal formula is called Simpson's rule. The trapezoidal formula assumes that each little slice of the area has the shape of a trapezoid; Simpson's rule assumes that the curved boundary of two adjacent slices has the shape of a parabola (a second-degree polynomial). It uses the area under such a parabola that can be found using calculus to give a way of finding the area under the curve. The area must be divided into an even number of slices. The area of any pair of slices is the slice width DELTA, mutiplied by one-third of the sum of the values of the function at the outsides together with four times the value in the middle. If the complete area is divided into 2 pairs of slices then the area is

        DELTA*(f(X1)+4*f(X2)+2*f(X3)+4*f(X4)+f(X5))/3.

You can see how to extend this for more pairs of slices.

We will write a program to compare the accuracy of the result obtained with the same number of function evaluations (slices) using the trapezoidal rule and Simpson's rule. We will calculate the area for a simple curve so that a calculus result can give the exact area for comparison. We will compute the area under the curve

        f(X)=sin (X)

between the values of X=0 and PI. From calculus we know the answer should be 2.0000000. We will use 6 slices so that DELTA will be PI/6.

```
$JOB      COROT REASON
C COMPARE SIMPSON'S AND TRAPEZOIDAL RULE
        REAL PI,DELTA,X,TRAP,SIMP,ODD,EVEN,MIDDLE,F(7)
        PI=3.141592
        DELTA=PI/6.
C       EVALUATE SIN(X) AT 7 VALUES OF X
        X=0.
        DO 5 I=1,7
          F(I)=SIN(X)
          X=X+DELTA
5         CONTINUE
C       COMPUTE AREA BY TRAPEZOIDAL RULE
        MIDDLE=F(2)+F(3)+F(4)+F(5)+F(6)
        TRAP=DELTA*(F(1)+2*MIDDLE+F(7))/2.
C       COMPUTE AREA BY SIMPSON'S RULE
        EVEN=F(2)+F(4)+F(6)
        ODD=F(3)+F(5)
        SIMP=DELTA*(F(1)+4*EVEN+2*ODD+F(7))/3.
C       PRINT RESULTS FOR COMPARISON
        PRINT,'TRAPEZOIDAL METHOD GIVES',TRAP
        PRINT,' SIMPSON''S  METHOD GIVES',SIMP
        RETURN
        END
$ENTRY
```

Here is the output

```
TRAPEZOIDAL METHOD GIVES      0.1954096E 01
 SIMPSON'S  METHOD GIVES      0.2000861E 01
```

You can see that the error in the trapezoidal method is 0.04590, that in Simpson's rule is 0.00086. This shows that Simpson's rule is a superior one here, the error is smaller.

LINEAR EQUATIONS USING ARRAYS

We have looked at the problem of solving two linear equations in two unknowns. We do not use computers to solve such simple systems. But computers are useful when we have many equations in many unknowns. In handling these problems we store the coefficients of the unknowns in an array. If we had four equations in four unknowns the equations might be written as

$$A(1,1)X1+A(1,2)X2+A(1,3)X3+A(1,4)X4=B1$$

$$A(2,1)X1+A(2,2)X2+A(2,3)X3+A(2,4)X4=B2$$

$$A(3,1)X1+A(3,2)X2+A(3,3)X3+A(3,4)X4=B3$$

$$A(4,1)X1+A(4,2)X2+A(4,3)X3+A(4,4)X4=B4$$

where A is a two-dimensional array of the coefficients. We can write the Bs, the right-hand sides of these equations, as part of

the A array by letting B1=A(1,5), B2=A(2,5) and so on. To solve
the equations we must reduce these equations in turn to three
equations in three unknowns, two equations in two unknowns, and
then one equation in one unknown. This method eliminates all the
unknowns except one. Then by substituting back you can find the
value of all the unknowns. If the array of coefficients was of
the form

```
A(1,1)  A(1,2)  A(1,3)  A(1,4)  A(1,5)
   0    A(2,2)  A(2,3)  A(2,4)  A(2,5)
   0       0    A(3,3)  A(3,4)  A(3,5)
   0       0       0    A(4,4)  A(4,5)
```

then we could see from the last line that X4=A(4,5)/A(4,4). Then
using this we could substitute back into the equation represented
by the second last line namely

A(3,3)X3+A(3,4)X4=A(3,5)

and solve for X3, and so on to get X2 and X1.

     What we have to do is move from the original array of
coefficients to the one with all the zeros in the lower left
corner. We do this by dividing each element of the first row by
A(1,1) and storing it back in the same location. This makes the
new value of A(1,1) a 1. Next multiply this row by A(2,1) and
subtract it from each element of row two, storing the result back
in the same location. The new value of A(2,1) will be zero. The
process will eventually result in an array with zeros in the
lower left.

     Certain problems of loss of precision can arise if the
element that is currently to be reduced to 1 is small.   This
element, referred to as the pivot element, should be as large as
possible. Various ways of rearranging the array can help prevent
difficulties but trouble is always possible. This sort of
problem provides great interest to numerical analysts.

                    LEAST SQUARES APPROXIMATION

     Very often in scientific experiments, measurements of a
quantity Y are made at various values of an independent variable
X.   It may be known from theory that the relationship between Y
and X is a linear one, for example

     Y=AX+B

If the various corresponding values of X and Y were plotted on a
graph these would be a number of points, say N. A straight line
drawn through any two of these points would not pass exactly
through the others.   We want to choose the values of the
constants A and B so that they define a straight line in such a
way that the sum of the squares of deviations of the actual
points from the straight line is a minimum, that is, the sum of

squares is least.   For   the   Ith   point,   say   at   (XI,YI),   the
deviation squared is

$$(YI-(A*XI+B))^2$$

To   have   something   a   minimum   implies,   in   calculus, that the
derivatives with respect to   the   variables   are   zero.   We   can
differentiate   a   sum   of   squares   of   this   type partially with
respect to A and B, the values that can be varied,   and   set   the
derivatives   equal   to   zero.   This gives two equations. One is the
sum of N terms of the form

YI-(A*XI+B)

set   equal   to zero.   The value of I goes from 1 to N.   The other
is the sum of N terms of the form

(YI-(A*XI+B))*XI

set   equal   to   zero.   These two equations can be written as two
equations in two unknowns, A and B.   These are

C1*A + C2*B = C3

C4*A + C5*B = C6

where C1 is the sum of values XI with I going from 1 to N.   C2 is
N and C3 is the sum of values YI with I going from 1 to N.   C4 is
the   sum   of XI*XI from 1 to N, C5 the sum of XI from 1 to N, and
C6 the sum of XI*YI from   1   to   N.   The   solution   to   the   two
equations can easily be found once they are formed.

   This same technique can be used for points that in theory lie
on a higher degree curve than a straight line but the calculation
is more complex.

MATHEMATICAL SOFTWARE

   We   have   been   describing   a   few   of   the   simpler numerical
methods used in scientific calculations.   Over   the   years   these
methods   have been changed and made more reliable, more efficient
and more accurate.   Nowadays   we   usually   rely   on   a   packaged
program   for   carrying out this type of calculation.   We call the
program packages mathematical software, to distinguish them   from
the   programs that operate the system or compile programs.   These
latter are called systems software and compilers respectively.

   Packages in Fortran exist for almost every standard numerical
calculation.   All that you must do is to find   out   how   to   call
them   in   your   program,   and   what their limitations are.   Every
piece of software should be documented so that you do not need to
read   it   to   be   able   to   use it.   You must know what each input
parameter of the subprogram is   and   what   range   of   values   is

permitted.   You must know also how the output is stored so that
you can use it.

      Frequently   software packages are   stored   in the secondary
memory of the computer and may be included   in   your   program by
using special control cards.   In any event if a deck of cards for
a package exists this can be included with your   own   deck   in   a
position appropriate to a subprogram.

      One of the great things about science is that we build on the
work of others and using subprograms prepared by others   is   good
scientific   practice.   Of   course   these   must be of the highest
standards.

                    CHAPTER 20 SUMMARY

      In   this chapter we have been examining numerical methods for
evaluating polynomials and   infinite   series,   calculating   areas
under   curves,   solving systems of linear equations and obtaining
least squares approximations.   We   were   concerned   particularly
with certain properties of the methods.

Efficiency   of   a   method – the   amount   of   work, as measured in
      number of basic arithmetic operations required   to   obtain   a
      certain   numerical   result.   Horner's   rule   for   polynomial
      evaluation is more efficient than the straightforward method.
      It   is   more   efficient   because   it   requires   fewer
      multiplications.

Horner's   rule – a method for computing the value of a polynomial
      that is efficient.   The polynomial

            $Y=5X^2+2X+3$

      is   evaluated   by   the   Fortran   statement   which   represents
      Horner's rule

            Y = (5*X+2)*X+3

      rather than either

            Y = 5*X*X+2*X+3

      or the equivalent

            Y = 5*X**2+2*X+3

Round-off   error – error   in   real   numbers introduced basically
      because a computer represents the numbers by a finite   string
      of   bits.   When   real   numbers   are   added or subtracted the
      round-off error of the sum or difference is the   sum   of   the
      round-off   errors   of   the   two   individual   numbers.   In
      multiplications the relative errors add.

Generated error - round-off errors produced due to arithmetic operations. The fewer the arithmetic operations the smaller the round-off error generated.

Propagated error - generated round-off errors that grow as calculations proceed.

Significant digits - digits in the representation of a real number that are not in error. Numbers are often quoted with a final decimal digit that may be in error by as much as unity. Digits that are not significant should not be quoted in an answer.

Loss of significant digits - This may occur as the result of subtraction of nearly equal numbers, or division by very small numbers, or multiplication by very large numbers.

Infinite series - many mathematical functions such as sin, cos, exp and log can be written as a sum of an infinite series of terms. These series may be used to evaluate the functions. Because the terms in the series eventually decrease in magnitude a good approximation can be obtained by stopping the addition after a certain number of terms.

Convergence of series - the way in which the terms of an infinite series become smaller and smaller.

Rate of convergence - the ratio of the magnitude of two adjacent terms of an infinite series. For $sin(X)$ the ratio is $X^2/(i(i+1))$. If X is less than 1 then this ratio is always less than one. If X is greater than 1 the terms might initially get larger but eventually get smaller. A series is non-convergent if the term ratio never becomes less than 1.

Double precision - keeping twice the normal number of bits to represent a number in the computer. Calculations carried out to double precision maintain a larger number of significant figures.

Interval-halving method - for finding a root of an equation $f(X)=0$ by a method similar to binary search. The method is guaranteed to converge on a root since the root is always kept between the end points of the interval and the interval is constantly decreasing in size.

Secant method - a method that sometimes has better convergence properties than interval halving for finding a root of an equation.

Newton-Raphson - a method for finding a zero of a function whose derivative can be computed. Convergence is rapid but not guaranteed.

Stopping criterion - the size of error that is to be tolerated in a result due to truncating such as in evaluating an infinite series term by term or iterating to find a root.

Numerical   integration - approximation   of   the   value   of   the definite integral which represents the   area   under   a   curve between two limits.

Simpson's   rule - for   numerical integration assumes each pair of slices of area under a curve is bounded by a   parabola.   The trapezoidal   method   assumes   each   slice   is   bounded   by   a straight line.   Simpson's rule often gives   greater   accuracy for the same number of slices (function evaluations).

Array   of   coefficients - for   linear   equations.   This   is manipulated so as to be transformed into   an   array   that   is triangular,   that   is, has zero elements on the lower left of the diagonal.   This is accomplished   by   operations   such   as multiplying   a row by a constant and subtracting one row from another.   Neither of these operations alters   the   values   of the unknowns.

Back   substitution - evaluating the unknowns once the transformed set of linear equations can be represented   by   a   triangular array.

Least   squares   approximation - finding   an equation to represent experimental information so that the sum of   the   squares   of the   deviations   is   a   minimum.   We investigated the case of fitting a straight line to a set of experimental points.

Mathematical   software - prefabricated subprograms embodying good numerical methods for getting standard results.   The software should   be documented to alert the user to the accuracy to be expected, the cost of the result, and   any   limitations   that must be respected.

CHAPTER 20 EXERCISES

1. Write   a   function   subprogram   that   will give the sine of an angle whose value in radians is between   0   and   PI/2.   Use   the series   for   sine   for   angles   between 0 and PI/4 and for cosine between PI/4 and PI/2.   Use the same   number   of   terms   in   each series.   Test   your   program   and compare the results with those obtained by using the built-in function SIN.   Try   varying   the number of terms in the series.

2. Compute   the   value   of   exp(1.)   using   the series.   Find the values as each term is added up to a maximum of 8 terms.

3. Use   the   built-in   function   for   exp(X) to tabulate values of this function for X going from -10. to +10.   Sketch the graph   of the   function   for   this   range.   You   might   think of using the program for graph plotting on the printer.

4. Use   the   interval-halving   subroutine   to   find a root of the equation

   2X-tanX=0

given that there is at least one between 0 and PI radians.

5. Use Newton's method of finding roots to find a root of the polynomial

   $X^4+6X^2-1=0$

6. Use Simpson's rule to find the area under the curve

   $Y=X^2-2X-1$

from X=0 to 3. Does it matter how many slices you have? Test this.

7. Write a subroutine that keeps doubling the number of slices in an area calculation using Simpson's rule until two successive results for the area under a curve agree to within an accuracy EPS. Make sure you do not have to reevaluate the function at places already computed.

8. Compare Simpson's rule and the trapezoidal rule for finding areas under a curve for Y=exp(X) between X=0 and X=1. Do you know the answer from calculus?

9. Write a subroutine that will solve a set of N equations in N unknowns. Do not include any form of pivoting. Would you expect this to be a good piece of mathematical software?

10. Write a subroutine that will solve two linear equations in two unknowns. Do you encounter any problems about loss of accuracy with such a small system of equations? What happens when there is no solution, for example, if the two equations represent parallel lines?

11. Write a subroutine that accepts two arrays X and Y of N values that represent N points and prints out the equation of the straight line that gives the sum of the squares of the deviations of the points from the straight line a minimum value.

CHAPTER 21

ASSEMBLY LANGUAGE AND MACHINE LANGUAGE

In this book we have presented programming in terms of the extended Fortran language. Fortran is a <u>high-level</u> <u>language</u>; it provides us with a convenient means for directing a computer to do work. The computer cannot execute Fortran programs directly; it can only execute programs in machine language, a <u>low-level</u> <u>language</u>. Before a Fortran program can be executed by a computer, the program must be <u>translated</u> or <u>compiled</u> to machine language. In this chapter we will explain how a computer carries out instructions. We will present features of machine languages and their associated assembly languages.

MACHINE INSTRUCTIONS

In Chapter 2 we gave a brief introduction to machine language. We explained that the instructions a computer can execute are much more basic than Fortran statements. These <u>machine instructions</u> use a special location, called the <u>accumulator</u>, when doing arithmetic or making assignments. For example, the assignment of J to I, written as the Fortran statement

    I=J

could be translated to the instructions

    LOAD J   (copy J into the accumulator)
    STORE I   (copy the accumulator into I)

As another example, the Fortran statement

    I=J+K

could be translated into the three instructions

```
LOAD   J    (copy J into the accumulator)
ADD    K    (add K to the accumulator)
STORE  I    (copy the accumulator into I)
```

Different kinds of computers have different machine languages. Some computers have many accumulators and some have few. Some computers have many instructions and some have few. We will introduce common features of machine languages by inventing a very simple computer. We will call our computer VS, for <u>very</u> <u>simple</u> computer.

The machine instructions for the VS computer are designed to be convenient for representing programs written in a subset of SF/k. The VS computer has never been built; it is just a hypothetical machine that we will use to illustrate points about computer languages.

The instructions for the VS computer have the form

        operator operand

for example,

        STORE I

The <u>operator</u> of an instruction tells the computer what to do; the <u>operand</u> tells the computer what to do it to.

After the computer executes one instruction, it continues to the next, unless the executed instruction directs the computer to jump to another instruction or to skip an instruction. We can translate the SF/k statements

```
        IF(I.LE.K)THEN DO
           K=I+J
           END IF
        I=J
```

into the VS computer instructions

```
    LOAD    K    (copy K into the accumulator)
    SKIPLE  I    (if I .LE. accumulator, skip next instruction)
    JUMP    L    (jump to instruction labeled L)
    LOAD    I    (copy I into the accumulator)
    ADD     J    (add J to the accumulator)
    STORE   K    (copy the accumulator into K)
  L:LOAD    J    (copy J into the accumulator)
    STORE   I    (copy the accumulator into I)
```

In this example, L is the <u>label</u> of an instruction; instructions are labeled so they can be jumped to. In full Fortran, but not in SF/k, there is a GO TO statement that is analogous to the JUMP machine instruction. The following statements are equivalent to the example we just gave:

```
      IF(I.GT.K)THEN DO
         GO TO 5
         END IF
      K=I+J
5     I=J
```

GO TO statements were purposely left out of SF/k because careless use of them leads to unreadable programs.   One of the reasons that low-level languages are inconvenient to use is that they do not directly provide looping constructs, such as the WHILE statement, and selection constructs, such as the IF statement. The programmer must build up these constructs using instructions like jumps and skips. When an SF/k program is translated into a low-level language, the loop and selection constructs appear as jumps and skips.

INSTRUCTIONS FOR A VERY SIMPLE COMPUTER

The VS computer has an instruction to print the value in the accumulator:

      PUTINT

This instruction needs no operand because the accumulator's value is always printed. There is an instruction to print messages:

      PUTSTR   operand

The operand represents a string to be printed.   There is an instruction that directs the machine to stop executing a program:

      HALT

The HALT instruction has no operand.

Altogether the VS computer has nine instructions; most real computers have many more instructions, typically around 100. This table lists the VS instructions.

	Operator	Operand	Action by Computer
1	LOAD	variable	Assign variable to accumulator.
2	STORE	variable	Assign accumulator to variable.
3	ADD	variable	Add variable to accumulator.
4	SUB	variable	Subtract variable from accumulator.
5	JUMP	label	Jump to labeled instruction.
6	SKIPLE	variable	If variable .LE. accumulator then skip next instruction.
7	PUTINT	(none)	Print the integer in the accumulator.
8	PUTSTR	string	Print the string.
9	HALT	(none)	Halt, the program is finished.

We have purposely kept the VS computer simple by leaving out
instructions that might normally be part of the instruction set
of a computer. We have left out a whole set of skip
instructions, such as SKIPGT (skip when greater than). We left
out instructions for doing REAL arithmetic and for reading from
data cards. We left out instructions for manipulating character
strings, indexing arrays, and calling and returning from
subroutines. These additional instructions are important in an
actual computer; if you like, you can design a "super" VS
computer that includes them.

TRANSLATION OF AN SF/k PROGRAM

If we use some care in picking our example, we can translate
an entire SF/k program into VS instructions. This example SF/k
program requires only the types of instructions available on the
VS computer:

High-Level Language		Low-Level Language
INTEGER I		
PRINT,'POWERS OF 2'	PUTSTR	TITLE
I = 1	LOAD	ONE
	STORE	I
WHILE(I.LE.8)DO	L1:LOAD	EIGHT
	SKIPLE	I
	JUMP	L2
PRINT,I	LOAD	I
	PUTINT	
I=I+I	LOAD	I
	ADD	I
	STORE	I
END WHILE	JUMP	L1
RETURN	L2:HALT	
END		

The first VS instruction in this example has as its operand
TITLE; TITLE gives the location of the string 'POWERS OF 2'.
Similarly, ONE and EIGHT give the locations of the values 1 and
8.

MNEMONIC NAMES AND MACHINE LANGUAGE

Up to this point we have written VS instructions using names
such as LOAD, STORE, I and J. These names are not present in the
machine language that a computer executes; they are replaced by
numbers. We will now show how these names can be translated into
appropriate numbers.

As you may recall from Chapter 2, the main memory of the
computer consists of a sequence of words. The words of memory
are numbered; the number that corresponds to a particular word is

called the <u>location</u> or <u>address</u> of the word. Words can be used to represent variables. For example, the variables I, J and K could be represented by the words with locations 59, 60 and 61.   Here we show these three words after I, J and K have been assigned the values 9, 0 and 14.

59	9
60	0
61	14

There is no special significance to 59, 60 and 61. We could just as well represent I, J and K by locations 42, 3 and 87; the important thing is to remember which location corresponds to which variable.

If I, J and K correspond to location 59, 60 and 61, we can write the instructions

```
LOAD    J
ADD     K
STORE   I
```

as

```
LOAD   60        (copy contents of word 60 into accumulator)
ADD    61        (add contents of word 61 to accumulator)
STORE  59        (copy accumulator into word 59)
```

The VS instruction operators, LOAD, STORE and so on, are numbered. LOAD is operator number 1, STORE is 2, ADD is 3 and so on. The names LOAD, STORE and ADD as used in the VS instructions are <u>mnemonic</u> <u>names</u>; a mnemonic name is an "easy-to-remember" name.   We can choose the names of the operands so that they too are easy to remember.

Using the numbers of the operators we can write

```
LOAD   60
ADD    61
STORE  59
```

as

```
1    60
3    61
2    59
```

Instructions that consist only of numbers are in <u>machine</u> <u>language</u>. Instructions that contain mnemonic names, such as LOAD and I, are in <u>assembly</u> <u>language</u>.

```
Assembly Language          Machine Language

     LOAD  J                  1   60
     ADD   K                  3   61
     STORE I                  2   59
```

As you can see, there is a simple translation from assembly
language to machine language. Writing programs in machine
language is even more inconvenient than writing programs in
assembly language. People almost always prefer assembly language
over machine language; they use a program called an <u>assembler</u> to
translate mnemonic names in assembly language programs to
corresponding numeric operators and operands. Although we do not
show it here, assemblers allow the programmer to reserve and
initialize memory for variables and constants. For example,
location 59 would be reserved for I, and location 98 could be
reserved for EIGHT and initialized to 8.

STORING MACHINE INSTRUCTIONS IN WORDS

The values of variables of a program are stored in words of
the computer's memory. In a similar manner, the instructions of
the program are stored in words of memory. We can use two words
to hold each VS instruction; one word for the operator and one
word for the operand. Here we show three instructions stored in
locations 18 through 23:

```
LOAD J    18 [              1]   19 [            60]

ADD K     20 [              3]   21 [            61]

STORE I   22 [              2]   23 [            59]
```

We could have saved space if the VS computer allowed us to pack
the operator and operand into a single word. For example, the
instruction

    1   59

could be packed into a single word as

    1059

with the convention that the rightmost three digits are the
operand and the other digits are the operator. Instructions for
real computers are packed into words to save space, but to keep
things simple, the VS computer uses two words for its
instructions.

A JUMP instruction has as its operand the label of an
instruction. When a JUMP instruction is written in machine
language, the label must be a number. The number used is the

location of the instruction being jumped to. Here is a translation of assembly language into machine language; the label L becomes 48:

JUMP L	40	5	41	48
LOAD I	42	1	43	59
ADD J	44	3	45	60
STORE K	46	2	47	61
L:LOAD J	48	1	49	60

Just as the variables and instructions are stored in words in memory, strings such as 'POWERS OF 2' are stored in memory. In real computers this is done by packing several characters into each word. Since mixing characters and numbers is confusing, we will assume that the VS computer has a separate part of its memory used only for strings. Each string is saved in a different location in the special string memory. If the string 'POWERS OF 2' is in location number 1 in the special string memory, then we translate the statement

        PRINT,'POWERS OF 2'

to the machine instruction

        8   1   (PUTSTR TITLE)

We have now shown how to translate all VS instructions into numbers and thus into machine language. We will return to our program that prints powers of 2 and will translate it to machine language.

A COMPLETE MACHINE LANGUAGE PROGRAM

We will assume that a VS computer always starts by executing the instruction in words 1 and 2. So we will place our machine language instructions in words 1, 2, 3, 4, ... We will continue assuming that variable I corresponds to memory location 59. The integer constants 1 and 8 will be represented by memory locations 91 and 98; these locations are initialized to hold the values 1 and 8 before the program is executed. We show the program as it would appear in memory after having executed instructions in locations 1 through 16. Up to this point the program has printed

        POWERS OF 2
            1

The VS computer has an <u>instruction pointer</u>, presently set to 17, that locates the next instruction to be executed. When an instruction has no operand, we give it a dummy operand of zero; for example, HALT becomes 9 0.

STORAGE OF PROGRAM IN COMPUTER

INSTRUCTION POINTER [17]   ACCUMULATOR [1]

MEMORY

1	8	1	(PUTSTR TITLE)
3	1	91	(LOAD ONE)
5	2	59	(STORE I)
7	1	98	(LI:LOAD EIGHT)
9	6	59	(SKIPLE I)
11	5	25	(JUMP L2)
13	1	59	(LOAD I)
15	7	0	(PUTINT)
17	1	59	(LOAD I)
19	3	59	(ADD I)
21	2	59	(STORE I)
23	5	7	(JUMP L1)
25	9	0	(L2:HALT)
	. . .	. . .	
59	1		(59 CORRESPONDS TO I)
	. . .	. . .	
91	1		(91 CORRESPONDS TO ONE)
	. . .	. . .	
97		8	(98 CORRESPONDS TO EIGHT)

SPECIAL STRING MEMORY

1	'POWERS OF 2'
2	

. . .

SIMULATING A COMPUTER

A VS computer has never been built and undoubtedly never will be built. It might seem that we can never have a VS machine language program executed. But we can, by making an existing computer simulate a VS computer. This is done by writing a program, called a simulator, that acts as if it is a VS computer. We will discuss later in more detail the importance of simulators in computing, but first we will develop an SF/k subroutine that is a simulator for the VS computer.

The VS computer has an accumulator, which can be simulated by a variable declared by

    INTEGER ACCUM

It also has a memory containing 100 words. This can be simulated by an array:

    INTEGER MEMORY(100)

There is a special string memory. Assuming that the VS computer can hold, at most, 10 strings of length 20, we can simulate the string memory by another array:

    CHARACTER*1 STRING(10,20)

We need an instruction pointer to keep track of which instruction is to be executed next.

    INTEGER IP

When the VS computer is executing, the instruction pointer has a particular value, say 10, indicating that word 10 contains the operator of the next instruction to be executed. Word 11 contains the operand. If OPRTOR and OPRAND are declared as integer variables in the simulator, then they should be given values by:

    OPRTOR=MEMORY(IP)
    OPRAND=MEMORY(IP+1)

If the operator is 1, meaning LOAD, the simulator carries out the LOAD machine instruction by executing:

    ACCUM=MEMORY(OPRAND)

If the operator is 2, meaning STORE, the simulator carries out the STORE instruction by executing:

    MEMORY(OPRAND)=ACCUM

Similarly, the simulator can carry out the other VS instructions. After each instruction is carried out, the instruction pointer IP is incremented by 2 and operator and operand are set for the next

instruction. When the instruction is a JUMP or SKIP, then the
instruction pointer IP can be modified so an instruction other
than the next sequential instruction will be selected. For
example, if the operator is 6, for SKIPLE, the simulator executes
this:

```
IF(MEMORY(OPRAND).LE.ACCUM)THEN DO
   IP=IP+2
   END IF
```

To make the simulator more readable, we will use mnemonic
variables for each of the VS instructions:

```
INTEGER LOAD,STORE, ..., HALT
```

We will initialize these variables to their corresponding machine
language numeric values 1, 2, ... 9. These declarations should
be COMMON to the simulator subroutine; the variables should be
initialized before calling the simulator.

Now we give the complete simulator as an SF/k subroutine.
This subroutine assumes that the MEMORY and STRING arrays have
been declared and initialized.

```
C THIS SUBROUTINE SIMULATES A VERY SIMPLE COMPUTER
      SUBROUTINE SIMLTR
      COMMON/CORE/MEMORY,STRING
      INTEGER MEMORY(100)
      CHARACTER*1 STRING(10,20)
      COMMON/OPCODE/LOAD,STORE,ADD,SUB,JUMP,SKIPLE,PUTINT,PUTSTR,HALT
      INTEGER LOAD,STORE,ADD,SUB,JUMP,SKIPLE,PUTINT,PUTSTR,HALT
      INTEGER ACCUM,IP,OPRTOR,OPRAND,COLUMN
      CHARACTER*1 OUTSTR(20)
      IP=1
      OPRTOR=MEMORY(IP)
      OPRAND=MEMORY(IP+1)
      WHILE(OPRTOR.NE.HALT)DO
         IF(OPRTOR.EQ.LOAD)THEN DO
            ACCUM=MEMORY(OPRAND)
            END IF
         IF(OPRTOR.EQ.STORE)THEN DO
            MEMORY(OPRAND)=ACCUM
            END IF
         IF(OPRTOR.EQ.ADD)THEN DO
            ACCUM=ACCUM+MEMORY(OPRAND)
            END IF
         IF(OPRTOR.EQ.SUB)THEN DO
            ACCUM=ACCUM-MEMORY(OPRAND)
            END IF
         IF(OPRTOR.EQ.JUMP)THEN DO
            IP=OPRAND-2
            END IF
         IF(OPRTOR.EQ.SKIPLE)THEN DO
            IF(MEMORY(OPRAND).LE.ACCUM)THEN DO
               IP=IP+2
               END IF
            END IF
         IF(OPRTOR.EQ.PUTINT)THEN DO
            PRINT,ACCUM
            END IF
         IF(OPRTOR.EQ.PUTSTR)THEN DO
            DO 10 COLUMN=1,20
               OUTSTR(COLUMN)=STRING(OPRAND,COLUMN)
10             CONTINUE
            PRINT 20,OUTSTR
20          FORMAT(' ',20A1)
            END IF
         IP=IP+2
         OPRTOR=MEMORY(IP)
         OPRAND=MEMORY(IP+1)
         END WHILE
      RETURN
      END
```

If you want to run a VS machine language program, you can write a main program to put the numbers representing the program and constants into the MEMORY array, initialize the STRING array and then call the SIMLTR subroutine.

USES OF SIMULATORS

We will now discuss some of the uses of simulators. Our simulator for the VS computer can be used to execute VS machine language programs. But it can serve another purpose, too. By reading the SIMLTR subroutine, you can determine the actions carried out for each VS instruction; if you did not know how a VS computer worked, you could find out by studying its simulator. So not only can the simulator direct one computer to act like another, it can also show how a computer works.

Computer simulators are often used to allow programs written for one machine to execute on another machine. For example, a business may buy a new computer to replace an old computer. After the old computer is removed, programs written for the old computer can be executed by a simulator running on the new machine.

Sometimes a hypothetical computer is designed to help solve some particular problem. This is the case with the compiler for the SP/k (not SF/k) subset of the PL/1 programming language. A hypothetical computer was designed to allow easy translation from SP/k programs to the hypothetical computer's machine language. The translated SP/k programs are executed using a simulator for the hypothetical machine. Other compilers, such as the Watfiv compiler, translate programs into the real computer's machine language; then a simulator is not required because the translated program is executed directly by the computer.

CHAPTER 21 SUMMARY

In this chapter we have presented features of machine language in terms of a very simple hypothetical computer called VS. The VS computer has an accumulator that is used for doing calculations. There are VS machine instructions for loading, storing, adding to, subtracting from, and printing the accumulator. There is a machine instruction for printing strings. There are instructions for jumping to instructions, skipping instructions and for halting. The nine VS machine instructions were sufficient for the translation of the example SF/k program given in this chapter. Real computers typically have many more instructions. The following important terms were discussed in this chapter:

    Word - the computer's main memory is divided into words.
             Each word can contain a number. In real computers, a
             word can contain several characters, typically 4
             characters.

    Location (or address) - the number that locates a particular
             word in the computer's main memory.

Operators and operands - most VS machine instructions, such
as,

LOAD I

consist of an operator and an operand; these are LOAD
and I in this example. Some instructions have an
operator but no operand.

Mnemonic name - a name that helps programmers remember
something. For example, STORE is the mnemonic name for
VS machine instruction number 2.

Machine language - the purely numeric language that is
directly executed by a particular type of computer.
Some computer manufacturers sell families of computers,
of various sizes and speeds, that all use the same
machine language.

Assembly language - programs in assembly language use
mnemonic names corresponding to the numeric operators of
machine language. They also permit programmers to
choose mnemonic names for the operands and labels.

Assembler - a program that translates programs written in
assembly language to machine language.

Label - a name that gives the location of a machine
instruction or a statement. The JUMP machine
instruction, as written in assembly language, transfers
control to a labeled instruction. The GO TO statement,
as written in full Fortran, but not in SF/k, transfers
control to a labeled statement.

Simulator - a program that simulates some system such as a
computer. A simulator treats a sequence of numbers as a
machine language program and carries out the specified
operations.

CHAPTER 21 EXERCISES

1. The VS computer described in this chapter does not have an
instruction for reading data. Invent an instruction named GETINT
that reads the next integer in the data into the accumulator.
Show how to translate a read statement such as

READ,K

into VS machine language, as augmented by GETINT. Show how the
SIMLTR subroutine given in this chapter can be modified to
execute GETINT instructions.

2. Translate the following program into VS assembly language and
then into VS machine language.

```
INTEGER I,J
I=1
J=5
IF(I.LE.J)THEN DO
   PRINT,'I IS SMALLER'
ELSE DO
   PRINT,'J IS SMALLER'
   END IF
RETURN
END
```

3. What will the following VS assembly language program print?
Translate the program to both machine language and SF/k.

```
      LOAD    ZERO
      STORE   PREVIOUS
      LOAD    ONE
      STORE   CURRENT
L1:   LOAD    FIFTY
      SKIPLE  CURRENT
      JUMP    L2
      LOAD    CURRENT
      ADD     PREVIOUS
      STORE   NEXT
      LOAD    CURRENT
      STORE   PREVIOUS
      LOAD    NEXT
      STORE   CURRENT
      PUTINT
      JUMP    L1
L2:   HALT
```

4. In this chapter an example program was given that prints
powers of 2. Have this program executed by the VS simulator
given in this chapter. This can be done by writing a main
program that initializes the MEMORY and STRING arrays to hold the
machine language version of the example program, and then calls
the SIMLTR subroutine.

CHAPTER 22

PROGRAMMING LANGUAGE COMPILERS

High-level languages such as Fortran provide a convenient tool to help us use computers. We use a <u>translator</u> or <u>compiler</u> to translate Fortran programs to machine language. For example, the Watfiv compiler translates Fortran programs to IBM 360 machine language.

In this chapter we will show how compilers bridge the gap between high-level languages, which are convenient for people, and machine languages, which can be directly executed by a computer. We will define a simple programming language called PSF/3, and then we will show how programs written in that language can be translated to the machine language for the very simple (VS) computer described in the last chapter.

We will give a compiler that reads cards containing a PSF/3 program and translates the program to VS machine language. Our compiler will be written as a set of subroutines and is about 300 lines long. Since our compiler is longer than any program we have given before, it provides a better example of step-by-step refinement and modular programming. Compilers are usually very large programs.

A SIMPLE HIGH-LEVEL LANGUAGE

We will invent a simple high-level language to illustrate points about compilers and computer languages. We will call our language PSF/3, because it contains <u>part</u> of the features of SF/3.

PSF/3 does not have any of the features of SF/k subsets beyond SF/3: no character string variables, no arrays, no subprograms, and no formatted input-output. PSF/3 allows:

-INTEGER variables named A or B or C ... or Z, but no REAL variables. All INTEGER variables used in a program must be declared via

    INTEGER list of variables separated by commas

- Addition and subtraction, but no multiplication or division, and no parentheses in expressions.

- INTEGER constants 0, 1, 2, ..., 9, but no multiple-digit constants such as 21, no signed constants and no REAL constants.

- Format-free PRINT statement. Exactly one output item must be given. The output item can be a literal such as 'HI THERE' or an integer expression. Literals may not contain an embedded quote, so 'DON''T' is not allowed. READ statements are not allowed.

- Assignment statements.

- WHILE...DO loops. The only allowed comparison is .LE. (the following are not allowed: .GE., .EQ., .LT., .GT., .NE.). No logical operators (.AND., .OR., .NOT) are allowed. Counted DO loops and IF statements are disallowed.

- Every PSF/3 program ends with

    RETURN
    END

This list of restrictions applied to SF/3 defines the PSF/3 language.

Since PSF/3 is a subset of SF/k, a PSF/3 program can be translated by the Watfiv-S compiler. PSF/3 is so limited that it is not particularly useful for solving problems; we impose these limitations so we can develop a complete PSF/3 compiler in this chapter.

Things have been arranged so that it is relatively easy to translate PSF/3 programs to machine language for the very simple (VS) computer described in the last chapter. The program from the last chapter that prints powers of 2 is an example of a PSF/3 program.

SYNTAX RULES

Each programming language has rules that a programmer must follow when writing a program. For example, in SF/k each WHILE...DO must be matched by a following END WHILE. Rules such as these give the grammar or syntax of the language. By now you should know the syntax for SF/k by heart; this means you should be able to tell whether an SF/k statement is correctly formed.

We have described the PSF/3 language by explaining how it
differs from SF/3. We will now describe PSF/3 more directly by
giving its syntax. The syntax for PSF/3 consists of nine rules.
In the syntax rules, the wiggly brackets ¦ ¦ mean that the
enclosed item is optional or can be repeated any number of times.
Thus, the notation

        variable ¦,variable¦

means a list of variables separated by commas.

1. A <u>program</u> is:
                INTEGER variable¦,variable¦
                ¦statement¦
                RETURN
                END

2. A <u>statement</u> is one of the following:
                a. PRINT,output item
                b. variable = expression
                c. WHILE(expression .LE. expression)DO
                    ¦statement¦
                    END WHILE

3. An <u>output item</u> is one of the following:
                a. expression
                b. literal

4. An <u>expression</u> is:
                value ¦operator value¦

5. A <u>value</u> is one of the following:
                a. variable
                b. integer

6. An <u>operator</u> is: + or -

7. A <u>variable</u> is: A or B or C ... or Z

8. An <u>integer</u> is: 0 or 1 or 2 ... or 9

9. A <u>literal</u> is: '¦any non-quote character¦'

    Our syntax rules specify the allowed forms of PSF/3 programs.
Rule 2 specifies that the only allowed statements other than the
final RETURN are PRINT, assignment and WHILE...DO...END WHILE.
Since other statements such as READ and IF are not specified in
the syntax, they are not allowed in PSF/3. Rule 2 specifies that
a WHILE...DO loop contains a list of statements; since a
WHILE...DO loop is itself a statement, rule 2 implies that
WHILE...DO loops can be nested inside WHILE...DO loops. Rule 2
is almost a circular definition, in that a WHILE...DO loop is
specified to be a "statement" and yet a WHILE...DO loop can
contain "statements". We say such a definition is <u>recursive</u>;
recursive definitions provide a concise way of stating that a

particular construct, such as a WHILE...DO loop, can be nested
inside a construct of the same type.

USING SYNTAX RULES TO PRODUCE A PROGRAM

A PSF/3 program is considered to be syntactically correct if
it can be produced or developed using the syntax rules. We start
with rule 1 and produce a "program" of the form

```
INTEGER variable |,variable|
|statement|
RETURN
END
```

The symbols written in small letters, "variable" and "statement",
will not be a part of the final program. Instead, they represent
a set of possibilities. By contrast, symbols such as "INTEGER"
and "END" are a part of the final program. Symbols like
"variable" and "statement" that do not appear in the final
program are called non-terminal symbols. Symbols such as
"INTEGER" and "END" are called terminal symbols because they
appear in the final program.

We can produce a PSF/3 program using our syntax rules by
starting with rule 1 and successively using rules to replace non-
terminal symbols, such as "statement", until we are left with
nothing but terminal symbols. In previous chapters, we have
shown how to develop programs by step-by-step refinement.
Producing programs using syntax rules is analogous to step-by-
step refinement, but serves an entirely different purpose. We
use step-by-step refinement as a method of designing programs.
By contrast, we check the syntax of a given program by trying to
produce it using the syntax rules. We will illustrate this
process by using the PSF/3 syntax rules to verify that an example
program is syntactically correct. We will use as our example the
program from the last chapter that prints powers of 2:


```
INTEGER I
PRINT,'POWERS OF 2'
I=1
WHILE(I.LE.8)DO
    PRINT,I
    I=I+I
    END WHILE
RETURN
END
```

We start with rule 1 and produce

```
INTEGER variable |,variable|
|statement|
RETURN
END
```

In order to produce the desired final program we replace the parts

```
variable |,variable|
```

and

```
|statement|
```

by the corresponding parts

```
variable
```

and

```
statement
statement
statement
```

Our program has now become

```
INTEGER variable
statement
statement
statement
END
```

We can now use rule 7 to produce I from "variable", making the declaration become

```
INTEGER I
```

We can produce the first PRINT statement in our example program by applying rules 2a, 3b and 9 in succession to the "statement" immediately following the declaration:

```
statement
PRINT,output item        (produced using rule 2a)
PRINT,literal            (produced using rule 3b)
PRINT,'POWERS OF 2'      (produced using rule 9)
```

Up to now, we have used the syntax rules to produce

```
INTEGER I
PRINT,'POWERS OF 2'
statement
statement
RETURN
END
```

We   can apply rules 2b, 7, 4, 5b and 8 in succession to transform
the "statement" following the PRINT statement   to   the   desired
form:

```
    statement
    variable=expression        (produced using rule 2b)
    I=expression               (produced using rule 7)
    I=value                    (produced using rule 4)
    I=1                        (produced using rules 5b,8)
```

We   can   now   transform   the   last   "statement"   to   the   desired
WHILE...DO loop:

```
    statement

    WHILE(expression.LE.expression)DO   (rule 2c)
        statement
        statement
        END WHILE

    WHILE(I.LE.8)DO        (rules 2a, 2b, 3a, 4, 5, 6, 7 and 8)
        PRINT,I
        I=I+I
        END WHILE
```

We   have now used the syntax rules to produce the example program
that prints powers of 2.   Since   this   program can be produced
using the syntax rules, it is syntactically correct.

   Syntax   rules provide a concise way of describing a language.
They do not completely describe a language.   For example, the
syntax   rules   for PSF/3 do not imply that every variable used in
the program must   be   declared.   The   syntax   rules   for PSF/3
describe all legal PSF/3 programs, but they describe some illegal
ones as well, in particular the ones with undeclared variables.

   One of the most important uses of syntax rules is for
specifying a high-level language so that a compiler can be
written for the language.   In the next sections we develop a
complete compiler for PSF/3. Because of the level of detail in
these sections, some readers may choose to skim them or to skip
them altogether.

                    ACTIONS OF THE COMPILER

   To keep our compiler simple, we will make several assumptions
about PSF/3 programs. We will assume that PSF/3 programs never
contain errors, so our compiler will not need to check for such
errors.   In the real world of programming, this would be a
disastrous assumption; we are making it only so the example
compiler can be smaller.

   We   will assume that every PSF/3 program is surrounded by the
control cards /JOB and /ENTRY in this manner:

```
/JOB
    PSF/3 program
/ENTRY
```

Our compiler will use the /ENTRY card to detect the end of a PSF/3 job; it will ignore the /JOB card.

To present the compiler we will consider each of the following six types of lines separately; they will appear on separate cards in a PSF/3 program.

```
    INTEGER ...
    PRINT,...
    variable=expression
    WHILE...DO
    END WHILE and END
    RETURN
```

We will assume there are no comment cards and no continuations by punching column 6.

A real Fortran compiler analyzes declarations to determine the attributes of variables and to see that memory space is set aside to represent the variables. Our compiler takes advantage of the fact that all PSF/3 variables are INTEGER and must be named A, B, C, ... or Z. Our compiler always sets aside enough memory for all 26 possible PSF/3 variables, regardless of whether they are used in the particular program. This wastes memory, but it makes our compiler simpler. The only purpose of the declarations in PSF/3 is so that PSF/3 programs are legal SF/k programs.

The PSF/3 compiler can simply ignore the first two cards:

```
/JOB
      INTEGER ...
```

Having skipped these two cards, the compiler must translate each of the following five types of cards to machine language:

```
    PRINT,...
    variable=expression
    WHILE...DO
    END WHILE and END
    RETURN
```

When the compiler reads each of these cards, it should take these actions:

Type of Card	Action by Compiler
PRINT,output item	If the output item is a literal, then an instruction is generated to print the literal. Otherwise instructions are generated to find the value of

the expression and print it.

variable=expression

Instructions are generated to find
the value of the expression and to
store it in the variable's memory
location.

WHILE(expr.LE.expr)DO

Instructions are generated to find
the values of the two expressions.
Then instructions are generated to
compare their values, and either to
execute the body of the loop or
to jump beyond the body of the loop.

END WHILE and END

If the END is for a WHILE...DO loop,
then a JUMP instruction is generated
to repeat the loop. If it is the
final END of the program, the card
is simply ignored.

RETURN

A HALT instruction is generated.

We can modularize our compiler by defining five subroutines to
compile these five kinds of cards:

```
COMPRT (Compile PRINT)
COMASN (Compile Assignment)
COMWHL (Compile WHILE...DO)
COMEND (Compile END)
COMRET (Compile RETURN)
```

After reading a card, the compiler can decide which of these
subroutines to call by inspecting the first word on the card. We
will define the subroutine:

SCANWD (scan word) - skips blanks and finds the length and
first letter of the first word on the card. These will be used
to determine the kind of card as follows:

First letter	Length	Type of card
P	5	PRINT,output item
any	1	variable=expression
W	5	WHILE...DO
E	3	END WHILE or END
R	6	RETURN

Since each PSF/3 identifier consists of one letter, our compiler
can recognize an assignment statement by seeing if the length of
the first word on the card is 1. Using these subroutines, we can
now give the structure of our compiler:

```
Do any required initialization
Read and print two cards (/JOB and INTEGER...)
WHILE(card is not /ENTRY)DO
    Read and print a card
```

```
      CALL SCANWD
      Call the appropriate subroutine among
         COMPRT,COMASN,COMWHL,COMEND and
         COMRET to compile the card
      END WHILE
   RETURN
   END
```

SCANNING WORDS AND CHARACTERS

Within a compiler, it is often necessary to determine the next word or character on a card. The part of the compiler that does this work is called the <u>scanner</u>. Our scanner includes the SCANWD subroutine and the two subroutines:

SCANCH - sets NEXTCH to the next character on the card. (NEXTCH may be set to a blank).

SCANNB - sets NEXTCH to the next non-blank character on the card

COMPILING ASSIGNMENT STATEMENTS

We will now explain how the COMASN (Compile Assignment) subroutine works. Given a card such as

    I=1

this subroutine must generate machine language:

```
1   91   (LOAD ONE)
2   59   (STORE I)
```

We set aside memory locations 51 through 76 to hold variables A through Z, so variable I corresponds to 59. We set aside memory locations 90 through 99 to hold the allowed PSF/3 constants 0 through 9. There is no special significance to locations 51 to 76 and 90 to 99; we could have used other locations.

If PSF/3 allowed constants other than 0 to 9, our compiler would need to reserve locations for each new constant it encountered. We have avoided this complication by allowing only constants 0 to 9. If you wish, you can augment our compiler so it could accept other constants.

To generate machine language for assignment statements, the COMASN subroutine uses three other subroutines:

EXPRSN - generates instructions to find the value of an expression and leave that value in the accumulator.

VARABL - determines the location corresponding to a given variable. For example, 59 is returned for variable I.

> EMIT - places one machine instruction in memory. This subroutine accepts two parameters, an operator and an operand, and places these in two memory locations just after the last generated machine instruction. This subroutine uses a variable called IP (instruction pointer) to keep track of the next location to receive an instruction. IP is initialized to one. Do not confuse this IP with the one used by the simulator in the last chapter. They are two quite different things.

When the COMASN subroutine is entered, its parameter holds the name of the variable to be assigned a value. The subroutine will do the following:

> Skip over the '=' sign
> Find the beginning of the expression
> Generate instructions to place the value of the expression
>   in the accumulator
> Generate a STORE instruction to assign the accumulator
>   to the location corresponding to the variable
>   specified by the parameter.

When we write this in SF/k, we get the COMASN subroutine.

```
C COMPILE AN ASSIGNMENT TO THE VARIABLE 'TARGET'
      SUBROUTINE COMASN(TARGET)
      CHARACTER*1 TARGET
      COMMON/OPCODE/LOAD,STORE,ADD,SUB,JUMP,SKIPLE,PUTINT,PUTSTR,HA
      INTEGER LOAD,STORE,ADD,SUB,JUMP,SKIPLE,PUTINT,PUTSTR,HALT
      INTEGER VARABL
C     SKIP '=' AND FIND BEGINNING OF EXPRESSION
      CALL SCANNB
C     GENERATE CODE FOR EXPRESSION
      CALL EXPRSN
C     GENERATE CODE TO ASSIGN EXPRESSION TO VARIABLE
      CALL EMIT(STORE,VARABL(TARGET))
      RETURN
      END
```

As was done in the last chapter, the names of the machine instructions, LOAD, STORE, and so on are declared as variables and initialized to their appropriate numeric values. This allows us to write STORE in the call to EMIT when we want to specify operator 2.

COMPILING PRINT STATEMENTS

The COMPRT subroutine, which compiles PRINT statements, is not much more complicated than COMASN. If the output item to be printed is an expression, then the EXPRSN subroutine is called to generate instructions to place the expression's value in the accumulator. The PUTINT instruction will print the value in the accumulator; this instruction is generated by executing:

```
CALL EMIT(PUTINT,0)
```

Since the PUTINT instruction uses no operand, a dummy operand of zero is used.

If the output item is a literal, then the characters of the literal are collected and placed in the next available string location in the VS computer's special string memory. Then the PUTSTR instruction is generated by

```
CALL EMIT(PUTSTR,STRNO)
```

The variable STRNO gives the location of the literal.

COMPILING WHILE...DO AND END WHILE

There are two complications in compiling WHILE...DO and END WHILE. The first has to do with using the accumulator to evaluate two different expressions, without losing the value of either. The second has to do with making JUMP instructions transfer control to appropriate locations. We have already faced this second complication in using standard Fortran to translate the WHILE...DO of extended Fortran. We will now consider the first of these complications.

When our compiler encounters a card such as

```
WHILE(I+1.LE.J-K)DO
```

it must see that instructions are generated to evaluate both expressions, I+1 and J-K, before the comparison is made. The difficulty is that both evaluations use the accumulator. After I+1 is evaluated, its result, which will reside in the accumulator, is <u>temporarily</u> saved while J-K is evaluated in the accumulator. The following sequence of instructions performs the evaluations, the temporary saving of one value, the comparison and the conditional jump beyond the end of the WHILE...DO loop.

```
LOAD     I
ADD      ONE
STORE    TEMP        (save value of I+1)
LOAD     J
SUB      K
SKIPLE   TEMP        (compare values of I+1 and J-K)
JUMP     DOEND
```

These instructions are followed immediately by the body of the loop. The value I+1 is saved in the location called TEMP; in our compiler we will arbitrarily make TEMP correspond to location 80.

The COMWHL (Compile WHILE...DO) subroutine can generate the above sequence of instructions by first executing

```
CALL EXPRSN          (generates LOAD I and ADD ONE)
CALL EMIT(STORE,TEMP)
```

Next, .LE. is skipped over and this is executed:

```
CALL EXPRSN   (generates LOAD J and SUBTRACT K)
CALL EMIT(SKIPLE,TEMP)
```

Finally, this is executed:

```
CALL EMIT(JUMP,0)
```

This leads us to the second complication in compiling WHILE...DO and END WHILE. When the JUMP instruction for WHILE...DO is generated, the compiler does not yet know where the end of the loop will be. The operand of the JUMP is temporarily set to the dummy value of zero.

Our compiler records the location of this JUMP instruction, so its operand can be corrected when the END of the loop is found. The COMEND (Compile END) subroutine corrects the operand of this JUMP. It also generates a JUMP instruction to return to the beginning of the loop. The COMEND subroutine must know the location of the beginning of the loop so it can make the JUMP instruction transfer to the correct location.

If PSF/3 programs were allowed to contain at most a single un-nested WHILE...DO loop, then we could easily produce the required JUMP operands by using two variables:

```
START - records location of beginning of loop.
EXIT - records location of operand of JUMP at beginning
       of loop.
```

The COMWHL subroutine would set START to IP, which gives the location of the instruction to be generated next, before generating instructions to evaluate the left expression of the comparison. The COMWHL subroutine would set EXIT to IP+1 just before generating the instruction JUMP 0. The COMEND subroutine would then execute

```
CALL EMIT(JUMP,START)
MEMORY(EXIT)=IP
```

This generates a JUMP to the start of the loop and then corrects the JUMP instruction at the beginning of the loop to transfer control beyond the just generated JUMP instruction.

Things are not this simple in PSF/3, because WHILE...DO loops can be nested inside WHILE...DO loops. Whenever our compiler encounters the END of a loop, it must match it with the nearest preceding WHILE...DO. It needs to keep track of the locations of the WHILE...DOs on a last-in-first-out basis. The last encountered WHILE...DO is the next one to be matched with an END. Once the compiler matches a WHILE...DO to an END and produces the

appropriate   JUMPs,   it   can   discard   the   location   of   that
WHILE...DO.

We need a data structure that allows us to save the locations
of WHILE...DOs until they are needed.   What we need is   a   stack,
as   was described in Chapter 18.   We can establish a stack by the
declaration

```
        INTEGER STACK(20),TOP
```

We   will   initialize   TOP   to   zero to indicate that the stack is
empty.   Before the COMWHL subroutine generates any   instructions,
it   places   the value of the instruction pointer IP on top of the
stack.   Just   before   it   generates   the   JUMP   instruction   that
transfers control beyond the end of the loop, it places the value
of IP+1 on top of the stack.   The COMEND   subroutine   uses   these
stacked locations in this way:

```
C       CORRECT THE OPERAND OF JUMP AT BEGINNING OF LOOP
        MEMORY(STACK(TOP))=IP+2
        TOP=TOP-1
C       EMIT JUMP TO GO BACK TO BEGINNING OF LOOP
        CALL EMIT(JUMP,STACK(TOP))
        TOP=TOP-1
```

Before   executing   these statements, the COMEND subroutine checks
to see if the stack is empty.   If it   is   empty,   this   indicates
that the END does not correspond to a WHILE...DO.   Instead, it is
the   final   END   of   the   PSF/3   program,   and   is   ignored.
Alternatively,   the   COMEND   subroutine could have scanned beyond
the END to see if WHILE appeared later on the card.

COMPILING RETURN

The   easiest   statement   to   compile   is   RETURN.   The COMRET
(Compile RETURN) subroutine simply generates a HALT   instruction,
with   a   dummy   zero operand, to tell the VS computer to stop the
PSF/3 program.   This is accomplished by executing

```
        CALL EMIT(HALT,0)
```

THE COMPILER

We   have   now   described the modules of our compiler.   We can
put these modules together to make a program that compiles   PSF/3
programs.   Our program has this overall structure:

```
SUBROUTINE COMPIL
(COMMON definitions of IP,STRNO,STACK,TOP and CARD)
(declarations of LENGTH and FIRST, used to find first word
    of card)
Initialize an array to hold the variable names (letters of
    alphabet)
Initialize an array to hold the digits and set values of
    digits into locations 90 to 99
Initialize IP, STRNO and TOP
Read and print two cards (/JOB and INTEGER..)
WHILE(CARD(1).NE.'/')DO
    Read and print a card
    CALL SCANWD(FIRST,LENGTH)
    Call the appropriate subroutine among COMPRT,COMASN,
        COMWHL, COMEND, and COMRET to compile the card
    END WHILE
RETURN
END
(the subroutine GETPUT that reads and prints cards)
(the subroutines SETALP and SETDIG that initialize alphabet
    and digit arrays)
(the subroutines for scanning: SCANWD,SCANCH and SCANNB)
(the subroutines for compiling cards: COMPRT,COMASN,COMWHL,
    COMEND and COMRET)
(the subprograms EMIT, VARABL, VALUE and EXPRSN)
```

Our compiler must have access to arrays representing the regular and string memory of the VS computer. These arrays can be declared to be COMMON to the compiler via

```
COMMON/CORE/MEMORY,STRING
INTEGER MEMORY(100)
CHARACTER*1 STRING(10,20)
```

As we have explained, our compiler uses the words in the VS computer's memory as follows:

    Locations 1 to 50 - used for instructions.
    Locations 51 to 76 - used for variables A to Z.
    Location 80 - used for TEMP (saves the value of the left-hand
            expression in a comparison).
    Locations 90 to 99 - used for constants 0 to 9.

The compiler must have access to variables for each of the VS instructions

```
COMMON/OPCODE/LOAD,STORE,ADD,SUB,JUMP,SKIPLE,PUTINT,PUTSTR,HALT
INTEGER LOAD,STORE,ADD,SUB,JUMP,SKIPLE,PUTINT,PUTSTR,HALT
```

These variables must be initialized to their corresponding machine language numeric values:

```
LOAD=1
STORE=2
...
```

```
      HALT=9
```

Here is the complete set of subprograms that translates PSF/3 programs into VS machine language:

```
C THIS SUBROUTINE COMPILES A PSF/3 PROGRAM
      SUBROUTINE COMPIL
      COMMON/SOURCE/CARD
      CHARACTER*1 CARD(80)
      COMMON/CURSOR/IP,STRNO,COLUMN
      INTEGER IP,STRNO,COLUMN
      COMMON/LIFO/STACK,TOP
      INTEGER STACK(20),TOP
      INTEGER LENGTH
      CHARACTER*1 FIRST
C     INITIALIZE ALPHABET AND DIGIT ARRAYS
      CALL SETALP
      CALL SETDIG
C     INITIALIZE INSTRUCTION POINTER, STRING NUMBER AND STACK TOP
      IP=1
      STRNO=1
      TOP=0
C     SKIP CARDS FOR /JOB AND INTEGER...
      CALL GETPUT
      CALL GETPUT
      WHILE(CARD(1).NE.'/')DO
C        READ AND PRINT NEXT CARD
         CALL GETPUT
C        COMPILE ASSIGNMENT, PRINT, WHILE...DO, END WHILE OR RETURN
C           ACCORDING TO LENGTH AND FIRST LETTER OF FIRST WORD
         CALL SCANWD(FIRST,LENGTH)
         IF(LENGTH.EQ.5.AND.FIRST.EQ.'P')THEN DO
            CALL COMPRT
            END IF
         IF(LENGTH.EQ.1)THEN DO
            CALL COMASN(FIRST)
            END IF
         IF(LENGTH.EQ.5.AND.FIRST.EQ.'W')THEN DO
            CALL COMWHL
            END IF
         IF(LENGTH.EQ.3.AND.FIRST.EQ.'E')THEN DO
            CALL COMEND
            END IF
         IF(LENGTH.EQ.6.AND.FIRST.EQ.'R')THEN DO
            CALL COMRET
            END IF
         END WHILE
      RETURN
      END
C
C READ AND PRINT A PSF/3 CARD
      SUBROUTINE GETPUT
      COMMON/SOURCE/CARD
      CHARACTER*1 CARD(80)
      READ 10,CARD
10    FORMAT(80A1)
```

```
         PRINT 20,CARD
20       FORMAT(' ',80A1)
         RETURN
         END
C
C INITIALIZE ALPHA ARRAY TO HOLD THE LETTERS OF THE ALPHABET
         SUBROUTINE SETALP
         COMMON/LETTER/ALPHA
         CHARACTER*1 ALPHA(26)
         ALPHA(1)='A'
         ALPHA(2)='B'
         ALPHA(3)='C'
            ...
         ALPHA(26)='Z'
         RETURN
         END
C
C INITIALIZE DIGIT ARRAY TO HOLD THE DIGITS '0','1','2',...,'9'
C        AND SET MEMORY LOCATIONS 90 TO 99 TO HOLD VALUES 0 TO 9
         SUBROUTINE SETDIG
         COMMON/CORE/MEMORY,STRING
         INTEGER MEMORY(100)
         CHARACTER*1 STRING(10,20)
         COMMON/INTEGR/DIGIT
         CHARACTER*1 DIGIT(10)
         INTEGER LOC
         DIGIT(1)='0'
         DIGIT(2)='1'
         DIGIT(3)='2'
            ...
         DIGIT(10)='9'
C        SET VALUES OF 0 TO 9 INTO 90 TO 99
         DO 10 LOC=90,99
             MEMORY(LOC)=LOC-90
10           CONTINUE
         RETURN
         END
C
C FIND LENGTH AND FIRST LETTER OF FIRST WORD ON CARD
         SUBROUTINE SCANWD(FIRST,LENGTH)
         CHARACTER*1 FIRST
         INTEGER LENGTH
         COMMON/SOURCE/CARD
         CHARACTER*1 CARD(80)
         COMMON/CURSOR/IP,STRNO,COLUMN
         INTEGER IP,STRNO,COLUMN
         INTEGER START
C        MARK END OF CARD SO SCANNB SUBROUTINE WILL STOP AT END
         CARD(73)='$'
         COLUMN=7
         WHILE(CARD(COLUMN).EQ.' ')DO
             COLUMN=COLUMN+1
             END WHILE
         FIRST=CARD(COLUMN)
         START=COLUMN
         WHILE(CARD(COLUMN).GE.'A'.AND.CARD(COLUMN).LE.'Z')DO
```

```
          COLUMN=COLUMN+1
          END WHILE
      LENGTH=COLUMN-START
      CALL SCANNB
      RETURN
      END
C
C SET NEXTCH TO NEXT CHARACTER ON CARD
      SUBROUTINE SCANCH
      COMMON/SOURCE/CARD
      CHARACTER*1 CARD(80)
      COMMON/CURSOR/IP,STRNO,COLUMN
      INTEGER IP,STRNO,COLUMN
      COMMON/SCAN/NEXTCH
      CHARACTER*1 NEXTCH
      NEXTCH=CARD(COLUMN)
      COLUMN=COLUMN+1
      RETURN
      END
C
C SET NEXTCH TO NEXT NON-BLANK CHARACTER ON CARD
      SUBROUTINE SCANNB
      COMMON/SCAN/NEXTCH
      CHARACTER*1 NEXTCH
      CALL SCANCH
      WHILE(NEXTCH.EQ.' ')DO
          CALL SCANCH
          END WHILE
      RETURN
      END
C
C COMPILE A PRINT STATEMENT
      SUBROUTINE COMPRT
      COMMON/CORE/MEMORY,STRING
      INTEGER MEMORY(100)
      CHARACTER*1 STRING(10,20)
      COMMON/CURSOR/IP,STRNO,COLUMN
      INTEGER IP,STRNO,COLUMN
      COMMON/SCAN/NEXTCH
      CHARACTER*1 NEXTCH
      COMMON/OPCODE/LOAD,STORE,ADD,SUB,JUMP,SKIPLE,PUTINT,PUTSTR,HALT
      INTEGER LOAD,STORE,ADD,SUB,JUMP,SKIPLE,PUTINT,PUTSTR,HALT
      INTEGER STRCOL
C     SKIP COMMA AFTER 'PRINT' AND FIND START OF OUTPUT ITEM
      CALL SCANNB
C     SEE IF NEXT CHARACTER IS A QUOTE
      IF(NEXTCH.EQ.'''')THEN DO
C         PUT QUOTED CHARACTERS INTO STRING MEMORY
          CALL SCANCH
          DO 10 STRCOL=1,20
              IF(NEXTCH.EQ.'''')THEN DO
                  STRING(STRNO,STRCOL)=' '
              ELSE DO
                  STRING(STRNO,STRCOL)=NEXTCH
                  CALL SCANCH
                  END IF
```

```
10          CONTINUE
C       GENERATE CODE TO PRINT THE STRING
        CALL EMIT(PUTSTR,STRNO)
        STRNO=STRNO+1
     ELSE DO
C       GENERATE CODE TO PRINT THE EXPRESSION
        CALL EXPRSN
        CALL EMIT(PUTINT,0)
        END IF
     RETURN
     END
C
C COMPILE AN ASSIGNMENT TO THE VARIABLE 'TARGET'
     SUBROUTINE COMASN(TARGET)
     CHARACTER*1 TARGET
     COMMON/OPCODE/LOAD,STORE,ADD,SUB,JUMP,SKIPLE,PUTINT,PUTSTR,HALT
     INTEGER LOAD,STORE,ADD,SUB,JUMP,SKIPLE,PUTINT,PUTSTR,HALT
     INTEGER VARABL
C       SKIP '=' AND FIND BEGINNING OF EXPRESSION
     CALL SCANNB
C       GENERATE CODE FOR EXPRESSION
     CALL EXPRSN
C       GENERATE CODE TO ASSIGN EXPRESSION TO VARIABLE
     CALL EMIT(STORE,VARABL(TARGET))
     RETURN
     END
C
C COMPILE WHILE...DO
     SUBROUTINE COMWHL
     COMMON/LIFO/STACK,TOP
     INTEGER STACK(20),TOP
     COMMON/CURSOR/IP,STRNO,COLUMN
     INTEGER IP,STRNO,COLUMN
     COMMON/OPCODE/LOAD,STORE,ADD,SUB,JUMP,SKIPLE,PUTINT,PUTSTR,HALT
     INTEGER LOAD,STORE,ADD,SUB,JUMP,SKIPLE,PUTINT,PUTSTR,HALT
     INTEGER TEMP
     TEMP=80
C       SKIP '(' AND FIND START OF LEFT EXPRESSION
     CALL SCANNB
C       RECORD LOCATION OF BEGINNING OF LOOP ON TOP OF STACK
     TOP=TOP+1
     STACK(TOP)=IP
C       GENERATE CODE TO STORE LEFT EXPRESSION IN 'TEMP'
     CALL EXPRSN
     CALL EMIT(STORE,TEMP)
C       SKIP OVER .LE.
     CALL SCANNB
     CALL SCANNB
     CALL SCANNB
     CALL SCANNB
C       GENERATE CODE FOR RIGHT EXPRESSION AND CONDITIONAL SKIP
     CALL EXPRSN
     CALL EMIT(SKIPLE,TEMP)
C       RECORD LOCATION OF JUMP SO ITS OPERAND CAN BE CORRECTED
     TOP=TOP+1
     STACK(TOP)=IP+1
```

```
      CALL EMIT(JUMP,0)
      RETURN
      END
C
C COMPILE END WHILE AND END
      SUBROUTINE COMEND
      COMMON/CORE/MEMORY,STRING
      INTEGER MEMORY(100)
      CHARACTER*1 STRING(10,20)
      COMMON/LIFO/STACK,TOP
      INTEGER STACK(20),TOP
      COMMON/OPCODE/LOAD,STORE,ADD,SUB,JUMP,SKIPLE,PUTINT,PUTSTR,HALT
      INTEGER LOAD,STORE,ADD,SUB,JUMP,SKIPLE,PUTINT,PUTSTR,HALT
      COMMON/CURSOR/IP,STRNO,COLUMN
      INTEGER IP,STRNO,COLUMN
C     SEE IF STACK HOLDS LOCATIONS OF ONE OR MORE WHILE...DO'S
C         IF SO, COMPILE END WHILE; OTHERWISE IGNORE FINAL
C         END OF PROGRAM.
      IF(TOP.GT.0)THEN DO
C         CORRECT THE OPERAND OF JUMP AT BEGINNING OF LOOP
          MEMORY(STACK(TOP))=IP+2
          TOP=TOP-1
C         EMIT JUMP TO GO BACK TO BEGINNING OF LOOP
          CALL EMIT(JUMP,STACK(TOP))
          TOP=TOP-1
          END IF
      RETURN
      END
C
C COMPILE A RETURN STATEMENT
      SUBROUTINE COMRET
      COMMON/OPCODE/LOAD,STORE,ADD,SUB,JUMP,SKIPLE,PUTINT,PUTSTR,HALT
      INTEGER LOAD,STORE,ADD,SUB,JUMP,SKIPLE,PUTINT,PUTSTR,HALT
      CALL EMIT(HALT,0)
      RETURN
      END
C
C PUT AN INSTRUCTION INTO THE MEMORY
      SUBROUTINE EMIT(OPRTOR,OPRAND)
      INTEGER OPRTOR,OPRAND
      COMMON/CORE/MEMORY,STRING
      INTEGER MEMORY(100)
      CHARACTER*1 STRING(10,20)
      COMMON/CURSOR/IP,STRNO,COLUMN
      INTEGER IP,STRNO,COLUMN
      MEMORY(IP)=OPRTOR
      MEMORY(IP+1)=OPRAND
      IP=IP+2
      RETURN
      END
C
C FOR IDENTIFIERS A TO Z, THIS WILL RETURN 51 TO 76, RESPECTIVELY
      INTEGER FUNCTION VARABL(IDENT)
      CHARACTER*1 IDENT
      COMMON/LETTER/ALPHA
      CHARACTER*1 ALPHA(26)
```

```
      INTEGER I
      I = 1
      WHILE(IDENT.NE.ALPHA(I))DO
         I = I + 1
         END WHILE
      VARABL=I+50
      RETURN
      END
C
C FIND MEMORY LOCATION OF NEXT VARIABLE OR INTEGER ON CARD
      INTEGER FUNCTION VALUE(CHAR)
      CHARACTER*1 CHAR
      COMMON/INTEGR/DIGIT
      CHARACTER*1 DIGIT(10)
      INTEGER VARABL
      IF(CHAR.GE.'A'.AND.CHAR.LE.'Z')THEN DO
         VALUE=VARABL(CHAR)
      ELSE DO
         VALUE=1
         WHILE(CHAR.NE.DIGIT(VALUE))DO
            VALUE=VALUE+1
            END WHILE
C        INTEGERS 0 TO 9 ARE IN LOCATIONS 90-99
         VALUE=VALUE+89
         END IF
      RETURN
      END
C
C GENERATE CODE FOR NEXT EXPRESSION ON CARD
      SUBROUTINE EXPRSN
      COMMON/SCAN/NEXTCH
      CHARACTER*1 NEXTCH
      COMMON/OPCODE/LOAD,STORE,ADD,SUB,JUMP,SKIPLE,PUTINT,PUTSTR,HALT
      INTEGER LOAD,STORE,ADD,SUB,JUMP,SKIPLE,PUTINT,PUTSTR,HALT
      INTEGER VALUE
      CALL EMIT(LOAD,VALUE(NEXTCH))
      CALL SCANNB
      WHILE(NEXTCH.EQ.'+'.OR.NEXTCH.EQ.'-')DO
         IF(NEXTCH.EQ.'+')THEN DO
            CALL SCANNB
            CALL EMIT(ADD,VALUE(NEXTCH))
         ELSE DO
            CALL SCANNB
            CALL EMIT(SUB,VALUE(NEXTCH))
            END IF
         CALL SCANNB
         END WHILE
      RETURN
      END
```

RUNNING THE COMPILED PROGRAM

We can have a PSF/3 program executed by translating it using
our compiler, and then placing the machine language version of
our program in the memory of a VS computer. The electronic

circuitry of the VS computer would carry out the machine
instructions corresponding to our program. By analogy, the
Watfiv compiler translates Fortran programs to IBM 360 machine
language and then has the IBM 360 computer execute the translated
program. Unfortunately, we do not have a VS computer. But we do
have a simulator for VS machine language, which we developed in
the last chapter, and we could use it to execute our translated
PSF/3 program. This is accomplished by the following job, which
both compiles and executes a PSF/3 program:

```
C COMPILE AND EXECUTE A PSF/3 PROGRAM
(include the definitions of these COMMON blocks:
      CORE and OPCODE
      LETTER and INTEGR
      SOURCE, CURSOR, SCAN and LIFO)
C      FIRST, INITIALIZE THE NAMES OF INSTRUCTION OPERATORS
      CALL SETINS
C      RUN THE COMPILER AND THEN THE SIMULATOR
      CALL COMPIL
      CALL SIMLTR
      RETURN
      END
C
C INITIALIZE THE INSTRUCTIONS LOAD, STORE,...,HALT
      SUBROUTINE SETINS
      COMMON/OPCODE/LOAD,STORE,ADD,SUB,JUMP,SKIPLE,PUTINT,PUTSTR,HALT
      INTEGER LOAD,STORE,ADD,SUB,JUMP,SKIPLE,PUTINT,PUTSTR,HALT
      LOAD=1
      STORE=2
      ADD=3
      SUB=4
      JUMP=5
      SKIPLE=6
      PUTINT=7
      PUTSTR=8
      HALT=9
      RETURN
      END
(include the following subprograms which make up the PSF/3 compiler
      as given in this chapter:
      COMPIL
      GETPUT
      SETALP and SETDIG
      SCANWD, SCANCH and SCANNB
      COMPRT,COMASN,COMWHL,COMEND and COMRET
      EMIT,VARABL,VALUE and EXPRSN)
(include SIMLTR subroutine as given in last chapter)
$ENTRY
/JOB
      INTEGER I
      PRINT,'POWERS OF 2'
      I=1
      WHILE(I .LE. 8)DO
         PRINT,I
         I=I+I
         END WHILE
```

```
      RETURN
      END
/ENTRY
```

If you want to run a PSF/3 program, make sure that your PSF/3
program has no errors. Remember, the compiler was simplified by
ignoring the possibility of errors; it may fail miserably if it
encounters a syntax error in a PSF/3 program.

CHAPTER 22 SUMMARY

In this chapter we showed how a program, called a compiler,
can translate from a high-level language like Fortran to machine
language. A simple language called PSF/3 was defined to
illustrate points about syntax, language specification and
translation. We presented a compiler written in SF/k that
translates error-free PSF/3 programs to the machine language for
the VS computer described in the last chapter. If this compiler
is combined with the VS computer simulator given in the last
chapter, we have a program that compiles and executes PSF/3
programs. The following important terms were discussed in this
chapter:

Syntax (or grammar) - a set of rules that specify the legal
     forms of programs in a particular programming language.

Non-terminal symbol - a symbol such as "statement" used in
     syntax rules to represent a set of possibilities. Non-
     terminal symbols do not appear in the final program.

Terminal symbol - a symbol such as "WHILE", "(" or "I" that
     appears in the final program.

Producing a program - using the syntax rules to create a
     program by successively replacing non-terminal symbols
     until only terminal symbols remain.

Recursive definition - defining a term in a way that uses the
     term. For example, in PSF/3 a WHILE...DO loop is
     defined recursively as a statement with the form

     WHILE(expression.LE.expression)DO
         |statement|
         END WHILE

     This is recursive because a statement inside a
     WHILE...DO loop can be a WHILE...DO loop.

Stack - a data structure providing last-in-first-out
     manipulation of data, as described in Chapter 18.
     Stacks are used in compilers for keeping track of nested
     structures, including WHILE...DO loops and parenthesized
     expressions.

CHAPTER 22 EXERCISES

1. The PSF/3 compiler given in this chapter requires the
following six types of lines to be on single cards:

```
(1) INTEGER...
(2) PRINT,...
(3) WHILE...DO
(4) END WHILE and END
(5) RETURN
(6) variable = expression
```

Modify the PSF/3 compiler so that continuations from card to
card, as indicated by '+' in column 6, are allowed.

2. Modify the PSF/3 compiler and VS simulator so that any
attempt to use an uninitialized variable is detected. For
example, the following job should be stopped by the simulator in
line 3 when the uninitialized value of J is accessed.

```
1   /JOB
2         INTEGER I,J
3         I=J
4         PRINT,I
5         RETURN
6         END
7   /ENTRY
```

The use of an uninitialized variable can be detected in the
following manner. Before the program begins execution, the
values of all variables are set to some special value, say 99999.
When the simulator executes the LOAD instruction, it checks to
see if the loaded value is 99999. If so, the program is stopped
and an error message is printed. (The Watfiv compiler uses a
technique similar to this for detecting the use of uninitialized
variables.)

3. Modify the PSF/3 compiler as given in this chapter so that it
prints an error message if a variable is used but not declared.
This can be done in the following manner. An array having 26
elements is declared and initialized so that all elements are
zero. When the compiler reads the declaration, the elements of
the array corresponding to declared variables are set from zero
to one. Whenever a variable is encountered in the remainder of
the PSF/3 program, a check is made to see if the corresponding
array element is zero or one. If it is zero, an error message is
printed.

APPENDIX 1

SPECIFICATIONS FOR THE SF/k LANGUAGE

SF/k is a sequence of language subsets, called SF/1, SF/2, SF/3, ... that has been designed for teaching programming. Each subset introduces more programming features, while keeping the features of previous subsets. The SF/k sequence is a compatible subset of the Fortran language as extended by the Watfiv-S compiler, so SF/k programs can be run on the IBM 360/370 using Watfiv-S. The following notable extensions to Standard (ANSI) Fortran are included in SF/k: structured control (IF...THEN...ELSE and WHILE...DO loops), character string variables and format-free input-output.

In the interest of making Fortran more suitable for pedagogic purposes, SF/k restricts or eliminates many Fortran features. In SF/k every variable must be declared. Features implied by the following terms are not in SF/k: pause, complex, implicit, equivalence, data block and namelist. Implicit conversions are not allowed among numeric, logical and character types, thereby eliminating anomalies due to value representations.

The SF/k subsets of Fortran are based on the SP/k subsets of the PL/1 language. The SP/k subsets were designed by R.C. Holt and D.B. Wortman at the Computer Systems Research Group, University of Toronto and are supported by specially written SP/k compilers that run on the IBM 360/370 or the Digital Equipment PDP-11 computers.

The Watfiv-S compiler does not enforce the restrictions that SF/k imposes on Fortran. As a result, Watfiv-S will not diagnose errors such as failure to declare a variable (because in full Fortran variables are declared implicitly). See Appendix 4 for more on error handling by the Watfiv-S compiler.

Language features introduced by subsets SF/1 to SF/8 are summarized in the following table.

Subset   Features Introduced

SF/1   Characters: letters, digits and special characters
          Constants: integer, real and character string

```
          Expressions:  +, -, *, /, **, integer to real conversion
          Simple output:  format-free printing
          Mathematical built-in functions:  mod, abs, sin, cos,
                    atan, alog, exp, sqrt
```

SF/2   Identifiers and variables
            Declarations: integer and real
            Assignment statements (with real to integer conversion)
            Simple input: format-free reading

SF/3   Comparisons
            Logical expressions
            Selection: if-then-else
            Repetition: while do loop and counted do loop
            Paragraphing
            Logical constants
            Logical variables

SF/4   Character string variables (fixed length only)
            Character string comparison

SF/5   Arrays (including multiple dimensions)

SF/6   Detailed control of input and output: formats

SF/7   Subprograms: subroutines and functions
            Calling and returning
            Arguments and parameters

SF/8   Files and records
            Initializing and closing off files
            Read and writing records

    The following sections give detailed specifications for each subset. In describing the subsets, we will use this notation:

```
          [item] means the item is optional
          |item| means the item can appear zero or more times
```

When presenting the syntax of language constructs, items written in <u>upper</u> <u>case</u> letters, for example,

```
          RETURN
```

denote keywords; these items must appear in SF/k jobs exactly as presented. Items written in <u>lower</u> <u>case</u> letters, for example,

```
          statement
```

denote one of a class of constructs; each such item is defined below as it is introduced.

SF/1: INTRODUCTION OF EXPRESSIONS AND OUTPUT

We now begin the specification of the first subset.

A <u>character</u> is a letter or a digit or a special character.

A <u>letter</u> is one of the following:

A B C D E F G H I J K L M N O P Q R S T U V W X Y Z

A <u>digit</u> is one of the following:

0 1 2 3 4 5 6 7 8 9

A <u>special</u> <u>character</u> is one of the following:

```
+ - * / ( ) = . , $
b (blank)
' (apostrophe or single quote)
```

An <u>integer</u> <u>constant</u> is one or more digits optionally preceded by a minus sign (without embedded blanks), for example:

4   -19   243   92153

Note that an integer constant must not contain a decimal point.

A <u>real</u> <u>constant</u> can be one or more digits with a decimal point. Alternately, a real constant can be a mantissa (<u>fractional</u> <u>part</u>) followed by an exponent. The <u>mantissa</u> must be one or more digits with an optional decimal point. The <u>exponent</u> must be the letter E, followed by an optional plus or minus sign, followed by one or more digits. A minus sign may optionally precede the real constant. There must not be embedded blanks. The following are examples of real constants.

3.14159   -2.   .0025   5.16E+00   50E0   .9418E24   1.E-2

There is a maximum size for an integer constant. There is a maximum allowed number of digits in the mantissa of a real constant and a maximum allowed magnitude of exponent. (These maximum values will vary from compiler to compiler.)

A <u>literal</u> (or <u>character</u> <u>string</u> <u>constant</u>) is a single quote (an apostrophe), followed by zero or more occurrences of non-single-quote characters or twice repeated single quotes, followed by a single quote. The following are examples of literals:

'FRED'   'X=24'   'MR. O''REILLY'

There is a maximum length of character strings.

In SF/1 an <u>expression</u> consists of integer and/or real constants combined using:

```
+    addition
-    subtraction and negation
*    multiplication
/    division
**   exponentiation
( )  parentheses
```

Built-in functions can also be used in expressions. Two operators (among +, -, *, / and **) cannot be adjacent to each other.

Real and integer values may be combined in expressions. When a integer value is combined with a real value, the result is a real value.

Evaluation of expressions proceeds from left to right, with the following exceptions. Multiplications and divisions have higher precedence than (i.e., are evaluated before) additions subtractions and negations. Parenthesized sub-expressions are evaluated before being used in arithmetic operations. Division (/) can be used only when one or both of the operands are real values. Division of an integer value by an integer value is not allowed. Exponentiation has higher precedence than multiplication and division; exponentiations are evaluated from right to left. The following are examples of legal expressions.

    -4+20   2*8.5E+00   (4.0E+01-12.0E+01)/(-2)

The values of these three expressions are, respectively, 16, 17.0E+00, and 4.0E+01.

Character strings cannot be used in arithmetic operations. In SF/k there are no implicit conversions from numeric values to character string values or vice versa.

An SF/1 built-in function call is one of the following:

```
MOD( expression , expression )
ABS( expression )
SIN( expression )
COS( expression )
ATAN( expression )
ALOG( expression )
EXP( expression )
SQRT( expression )
```

The MOD function accepts two integer expressions as arguments and produces an integer result. The ABS, SIN, COS, ATAN, ALOG, EXP, and SQRT mathematical functions accept a single real expression as an argument and produce a real result. Appendix 3 gives a more detailed description of SF/k built-in functions.

An SF/1 <u>statement</u> is:

>   PRINT, output item ⌐,output item⌐

Each <u>output item</u> must be a literal or an expression.

An SF/1 <u>program</u> is:

>   ⌐statement⌐
>   RETURN
>   END

Remember that the notation ⌐statement⌐ means zero or more statements. The following is an example of an SF/1 program:

>   PRINT,2,'PLUS',3,'MAKES',2+3
>   RETURN
>   END

The output from this example is: 2   PLUS   3   MAKES   5

   Output produced by the PRINT statement is placed in successive "fields" across the print line. The widths of these fields depends upon the compiler. The Watfiv compiler prints integer values in 12-column fields, real values in 16-column fields and character strings in fields as long as the particular string. Fields are separated by a blank column.

   When a literal is printed by a PRINT statement, its enclosing single quotes are removed. In addition twice repeated single quotes in a literal are printed as one single quote.

   SF/1 programs must appear in columns 7 to 72 of punched cards. Continuation from card to card is accomplished by placing a plus sign in column 6 of each continuation card.

SF/2: INTRODUCTION OF VARIABLES, INPUT AND ASSIGNMENT

We now begin the specifications of the second subset, SF/2.

An identifier is a letter followed by more letters and digits. An identifier cannot contain embedded blanks. Most compilers allow identifiers to be at least 6 characters long.

An SF/2 program is:

```
|declaration|
|statement|
RETURN
END
```

A declaration is:

```
type variable |,variable|
```

A type is one of the following:

```
INTEGER
REAL
```

A statement is one of the following:

```
PRINT,output item|,output item|
READ,variable|,variable|
variable = expression
```

In SF/2, each variable is simply an identifier. (There are no arrays in SF/2.) In SF/k all variables must be declared. In SF/2 an expression may be or include a variable.

Real values may be assigned to integer variables. Any non-integer part of such a real value is truncated before the assignment without a warning message. Integer values may be assigned to real variables with automatic conversion.

The items in the data (the input stream) read by READ statements must be separated by one or more blanks. When a READ statement is executed, one data item is read for each variable in the statement. Each READ statement begins reading at the beginning of the next card.

In SF/2 each item in the input stream must be an integer constant or a real constant.

An integer constant can be read (and will be automatically converted) into a real variable. However, a real constant can not be read into an integer variable. There are no automatic conversions from character string values to numeric values or vice versa.

A **keyword** is any of the special identifiers, e.g., REAL, PRINT and END, that are part of the SF/k syntax. A variable must not be given the same name as a keyword.

Any number of blanks can appear between symbols, e.g., between constants, keywords, identifiers, operators +, -, *, /, ** and the parentheses (and). When constants, keywords or identifiers are adjacent, for example, INTEGER and I, they must be separated by at least one blank.

A **comment** consists of the character C in column 1 and any characters (the actual comment) in columns 2 to 72 inclusive. Comments are continued by putting the character C in column 1 of succeeding cards (not by putting a plus sign in column 6). Comments cannot appear in the data.

SF/3: INTRODUCTION OF LOGICAL EXPRESSIONS, SELECTION AND REPETITION

A condition is one of the following:

```
.TRUE.
.FALSE.
.NOT. condition
condition .AND. condition
condition .OR. condition
comparison
(condition)
logical variable
```

A condition is sometimes called a logical expression.

A comparison is one of the following:

```
expression .LT. expression
expression .GT. expression
expression .EQ. expression
expression .LE. expression
expression .GE. expression
expression .NE. expression
```

A type is one of the following:

```
INTEGER
REAL
LOGICAL
```

Logical variables can be operands in the logical operations of and, or and not. Real and integer values cannot be operands in logical operations.

The .AND. operator has higher precedence than the .OR. operator. Logical variables can be assigned but not read, printed or compared.

There is no implicit conversion between numeric values (integer and real) and logical values. Logical values cannot participate in arithmetic operations.

An SF/3 <u>statement</u> is one of the following:

```
PRINT, output item |,output item|
READ, variable |,variable|
variable = expression
IF( condition )THEN DO
   |statement|
[ELSE DO
   |statement|]
   END IF
WHILE( condition )DO
   |statement|
   END WHILE
DO label identifier = start,limit [,step]
   |statement|
label    CONTINUE
```

In the counted DO loop (the last compound statement above) the <u>label</u> must be an unsigned integer that appears after DO and is repeated in the label field (columns 1 through 5) of the CONTINUE. This label must be different from other labels in the program. The counter variable (identifier) must have been declared to be an integer variable. Even after arrays are introduced, the counter variable must still be simple, i.e., not an array element. The step is optional; if omitted it is taken to be 1.

The start, limit and step (if present) must be given by integer constants or integer variables that are strictly positive. If they are variables, they must not be changed inside the loop. The counter variable should not be changed inside the loop.

The body of the counted DO loop is executed at least once, for the counter variable set to the start value. At the end of the loop if the sum of the current value of the counter variable and the step does not exceed the limit then the sum is assigned to the counter variable and the loop body is executed again. Otherwise the loop is terminated, and the value of the counter variable is unspecified.

<u>Paragraphing</u> <u>rules</u> are standard conventions for indenting program lines. Some compilers may provide automatic paragraphing of programs. If this feature is available, it should be used.

A set of paragraphing rules can be inferred from the method used to present SF/k constructs. For example, the WHILE...DO loop was presented in the following form:

```
WHILE( condition )DO
   |statement|
   END WHILE
```

This form means that the statements enclosed in a WHILE...DO group should be indented beyond the level of the opening

WHILE...DO line. The construct END WHILE which closes the group should be indented to the same level as the enclosed statements.

The text of comments should be indented to the same level as their corresponding program lines. The continuation(s) of a long program line should be indented beyond the line's original indentation. If the level of indentation becomes too deep, it may be necessary to abandon indentation rules temporarily, maintaining a vertical positioning of lines.

SF/4: INTRODUCTION OF CHARACTER STRING VARIABLES

A <u>type</u> is one of the following:

    INTEGER
    REAL
    CHARACTER*length
    LOGICAL

Variables declared to have the attribute CHARACTER*length are called <u>character</u> <u>string</u> <u>variables</u>. In the declaration of character string variables, <u>length</u> must be a strictly positive integer constant.

Each character string variable has a fixed length determined by its declaration. If the variable is assigned a string shorter than its declared length then the string is padded with blanks on the right to the required length. If the string is longer than the declared length, it may be truncated on the right to the required length; some compilers may consider such truncation to be illegal.

When character string values of different lengths are compared, the shorter is temporarily padded on the right with blanks to the length of the longer. Character string constants can be read from the data. Character string variables can be printed.

There are no string built-in functions for finding lengths, concatenating or finding substrings. There is no implicit conversion between character string values and numeric or logical values.

SF/5: INTRODUCTION OF ARRAYS

The form of declaration remains as it was:

A <u>declaration</u> is: type variable ⏐,variable⏐

However, the form of <u>variable</u> is now allowed to specify array
bounds. In a declaration, a variable is now:

identifier [(range ⏐,range⏐)]

A <u>range</u> is a strictly positive integer constant; it specifies
that the array index can vary from 1 to the given integer.
(Standard Fortran allows at most three ranges to be specified.)

In an expression, or in a READ statement, a variable has the
form:

identifier [(expression ⏐,expression⏐)]

where each expression is an array index.   Each array index
expression must have an integer value that is within the
specified range.

Array elements may be compared, assigned, read, and printed
on an element by element basis, in the same way as single
variables with similar attributes.   Arrays must be read and
printed an element at a time; the only exception is via the nAw
format item introduced in SF/6.

SF/6: INTRODUCTION OF FORMATTED INPUT AND OUTPUT

Format-free PRINT and READ statements were introduced in SF/1 and SF/2. SF/6 introduces formatted PRINT and READ statements of the form:

```
        PRINT label |,expression|
label FORMAT(control |,format item|)

        READ label,variable |,variable|
label FORMAT(format item |,format item|)
```

In these statements, the label is a strictly positive integer constant that appears after PRINT or READ and is repeated in the label field (columns 1 through 5) of the immediately following FORMAT specification. Within the main program or a particular subprogram, all labels in columns 1 through 5 must be different.

It is possible to use both format-free and formatted READ and PRINT statements in the same program.

The control in a formatted PRINT statement must be one of the following carriage control characters:

```
' '   (blank)   start a new line (single space)
'1'   (one)     start a new page
'0'   (zero)    skip a line then start a new line (double space)
'+'   (plus)    go back to beginning of current line (overprint)
```

The formatted READ statement reads the next data card, skipping any remaining columns of the last read card. Carriage control characters cannot be specified in a formatted READ statement.

A format item is one of the following:

nX   Skips next n columns.

Iw   Prints or reads an integer right justified in a field of w columns.

Fw.d   Prints or reads a real quantity without an exponent, right justified in a field of w columns. The number of digits to the right of the decimal point is given by d.

Ew.d   Prints or reads a real quantity with an exponent, right justified in a field of w columns. The number of digits to the right of the decimal point is given by d.

Aw   Prints or reads w character.

nAw   Prints (reads) n sets of w characters from (into)
                 a one-dimensional array of n CHARACTER*w elements.
                 This is the only format item that transmits an
                 entire array.

    The following restrictions and details should be noted. Each
of n, w and d must be unsigned non-zero integer constants, as in
80A1. REAL quantities are rounded off before printing.

    Numbers read   or printed by the I, F and E format items are
right justified in their fields. The variable   or   literal   that
corresponds to Aw must be w characters long.

    Each variable in a formatted READ or PRINT must correspond to
an I, F, E or A format item. The X format item can precede or be
intermixed with I, F, E and A items, but must not be last in a
list of format items.

    When reading numbers, any blank columns are considered to be
zeros, so that if the data is not right justified in its field,
it is scaled. If data read using Fw.d does not contain a decimal
point, then one is assumed to be d digits from the right of the
field.   If the data read using Fw.d contains a decimal point,
then it overrides the d in the format item. Numbers read using
Fw.d must not have exponents.

    Numbers read using Ew.d can have exponents, but do not need
to. If the decimal point is punched then the d is ignored.   If
it is not punched, it is assumed d digits from the right of the
mantissa.

SF/7: INTRODUCTION OF SUBPROGRAMS

In SF/7 the form of a program is extended to allow the specification of subprograms.

An SF/7 **program** is:

```
        ¦definition¦
        ¦statement¦
        END
        ¦subprogram¦
```

A **subprogram** is one of the following:

```
        SUBROUTINE identifier[(identifier ¦,identifier¦)]
        ¦definition¦
        ¦statement¦
        END

        type FUNCTION identifier(identifier ¦,identifier¦)
        ¦definition¦
        ¦statement¦
        END
```

A **definition** is one of the following:

```
        type variable ¦,variable¦
        COMMON /identifier/ identifier ¦,identifier¦
```

Notice that a "definition" can be a declaration. The CALL statement is introduced:

```
        CALL subroutine name [(expression ¦,expression¦)]
```

As well, RETURN now becomes a statement:

```
        RETURN
```

When a RETURN is executed in the main program, it terminates the entire program's execution. When executed in a subprogram, it causes return to the calling main program or subprogram. Typically each subprogram or main program has one RETURN, just before its END.

All parameters for a subprogram must be declared and must have the same types, ranges and lengths as their corresponding arguments. There is no automatic real/integer conversion for parameters/arguments. A parameter array range may be given as another parameter if that parameter is a simple (non-array) integer. (The Watfiv compiler requires that a parameter giving the range be declared before the array.) Lengths of character string parameters must be unsigned non-zero integer constants.

Assignment of a value to a parameter will cause the value to be assigned to the corresponding argument. If the argument is a constant or an expression containing operators, then an assignment must not be made to the parameter. Similarly if the argument is a DO loop start, limit, step or counter variable, then an assignment must not be made to the parameter. Functions must have at least one parameter but subroutines can have none.

Each definition of a particular COMMON block must specify the same names of variables in the same order. These variables must be declared to have the same types, ranges and lengths as in other specifications of the particular COMMON block. Every COMMON block must be defined in the main program.

A subroutine subprogram is invoked by the CALL statement. A function subprogram is invoked by using its name with argument(s) as required in an expression. Each subprogram (or the main program) that invokes a function must contain a declaration giving the type of the function. For example, if AREA is a function then the declaration

    INTEGER AREA

must be included in the main program and subprograms that invoke AREA. Inside a function, the name of the function acts as a simple variable. This variable must be assigned a value before returning from the function and this provides the function's value. (The Watfiv compiler supports REAL, INTEGER and LOGICAL functions, but not CHARACTER functions.)

Subprograms cannot be recursive meaning they may not invoke themselves directly or indirectly.

Within a particular subprogram, or in the main program, all names of accessible variables, subprograms and common blocks must be unique and labels must be unique. Names and labels need not be unique from subprogram to subprogram to main program.

SF/8: INTRODUCTION OF FILES

SF/8 introduces the use of external files other than card input and printer output. A file is sometimes called a <u>data</u> <u>set</u>. In SF/k, a file is <u>sequential</u> and consists of a sequence of <u>records</u>; each record consists of a sequence of <u>fields</u>. Each field has a value of one of the SF/k types: integer, real, logical or character string of a particular length. The <u>template</u> of a record is the sequence of types of its fields. Each record in a particular file must have the same template.

Before a file can be written on or read from, it must be initialized by the statement:

REWIND file number

Each <u>file</u> <u>number</u> must be an unsigned, non-zero integer constant. Generally, the integers 5 and 6 are not used because they typically correspond to the card reader and line printer. The available file numbers depend on the individual computer center.

Records are sequentially added to the end by the statement:

WRITE(file number)variable,variable

Each transmitted variable must be a simple (non-array) variable or an element of an array. The list of variables constitutes one record that is added to the end of the file. After the final record of a file has been written, the file must be ended by the statement:

ENDFILE file number

Records are sequentially read from a file by the statement

READ(file number)variable,variable

Each variable in the list must be a simple (non-array) variable or an array element. The next record is read into the list of variables. The record template defined by the types of the variables in the list must be the same as the template of the records on the file. Reading must not go beyond the final record written on the file.

Once a file has been initialized (by REWIND) it can be either written or read but not both. A file that is being written can be ended (by ENDFILE), initialized (by REWIND) and then read or re-written in the same program. A file that is being read can be initialized (by REWIND) and then written or re-read. Every time the writing of a file starts (after REWIND), any previous contents of the file are lost, and once the writing is completed, the file must again be ended (by ENDFILE).

(The Watfiv compiler requires that any transmitted record be at least 16 bytes long. Real, integer and logical values each take up 4 bytes and character strings take up one byte per character. For example, a record consisting of two integers, a real value and a CHARACTER*5 value is acceptable because it is 17 bytes long.)

APPENDIX 2

THE STATEMENT SYNTAX OF SF/7

```
A job is:         $JOB
                      program
                      |subprogram|
                  $ENTRY
                      [data]

A program is:     |definition|
                  |statement |
                  END

A definition is one of the following:
        a.        type variable |,variable|
        b.        COMMON /identifier/ identifier |,identifier|

A type is one of the following:
        a.        INTEGER
        b.        REAL
        c.        CHARACTER*length
        d.        LOGICAL

A subprogram is one of the following:
        a.        SUBROUTINE identifier[(identifier|,identifier|)]
                  |definition|
                  |statement |
                  END
        b.        type FUNCTION identifier(identifier|,identifier|)
                  |definition|
                  |statement |
                  END

A statement is one of the following:
        a.        PRINT, expression |,expression|
        b.        READ, variable |,variable|
```

```
c.          PRINT label |,expression|
      label FORMAT( control |,format item| )
d.          READ label, variable |,variable|
      label FORMAT( format item |,format item| )
e.          variable = expression
f.          IF (condition) THEN DO
                 |statement|
            [ELSE DO
                 |statement|]
            END IF
g.          WHILE (condition) DO
                 |statement|
            END WHILE
h.          DO label identifier=start,limit [ ,step]
                 |statement|
      label       CONTINUE
i.          CALL subroutine name [(expression|,expression|)]
j.          RETURN
```

```
Notation:   [item] means the item is optional.
            item| means the item is repeated zero or more times.
```

APPENDIX 3

BUILT-IN FUNCTIONS IN SF/k

a. An <u>integer</u> <u>built-in</u> <u>function</u>.

   MOD(i,j) -remainder of i divided by j; i and j must be integer
        values. The result is integer.

b. <u>Real</u> <u>built-in</u> <u>functions</u>.

   For these functions, the arguments must be real.
   The result is real.

   ABS(x) - absolute value of x.
   SIN(x) - sine of x radians.
   COS(x) - cosine of x radians.
   ATAN(x) - arctangent of x in radians.
   ALOG(x) - natural logarithm of x.
   EXP(x) - e to the x power.
   SQRT(x) - square root of x.

Note: there are no built-in functions for character strings.

APPENDIX 4

THE WATFIV-S COMPILER

The Watfiv-S compiler was developed at the University of Waterloo. It supports a Fortran dialect that includes Standard Fortran features as well as most of the Fortran extensions supported by the IBM System 360/370 compilers. Several other extensions are included, such as IF...THEN...ELSE and WHILE...DO statements, format-free READ and PRINT statements and the allowing of expressions in output items. The SF/k language used in this book is a compatible subset of the Watfiv-S dialect of Fortran. This means that SF/k programs can be run under the Watfiv-S compiler, but programs that can be run under Watfiv-S are not necessarily legal SF/k programs.

Originally, the University of Waterloo developed a compiler called Watfor, short for Waterloo Fortran. This was superceded by the Watfiv compiler, whose name means "the one after Watfor" or perhaps Waterloo Fortran IV. Now this compiler has been extended and called Watfiv-S where the S stands for structured programming.

WATFIV-S CONTROL CARDS

The first card of a Watfiv-S job is called the job card, for example

$JOB   JOHN WALSH

In some computer installations, a different form of job card or cards may be used. For example, on the University of Toronto High Speed Job Stream, $JOB must be replaced by $JOBW. The name JOHN WALSH is used to identify the job and at some computer centers is printed in a header box preceding the printing of the program.

The placement of the name on the job card varies from installation to installation. At the University of Toronto, it should begin in column 9 and can extend to column 23. Some computer centers may require the word WATFIV to precede the name. Other parameters, besides the name, can be given on the job card, as is shown in this example:

```
$JOB    GLEN BONHAM    20 3 4
```

The parameter 20 specifies that the program is to be allowed 2 seconds (20 tenths of a second) of execution time before being terminated for excess running time. The parameter 2 specifies that the program is allowed to print 200 lines before being terminated for excess printing. The parameter 4 specifies that 4 new pages of output can be started without termination for excess pages. At the University of Toronto, the limits for seconds, lines and pages are punched in columns 24-26, 27-28 and 29-30, respectively. Other computer installations may require that the keywords TIME, LINES and PAGES be used as illustrated here:

```
$JOB    PHIL KHAIAT    TIME=20,LINES=2,PAGES=4
```

It is possible to abbreviate TIME as T, LINES as L and PAGES as P. There may be additional job card parameters.

The program must be followed by a $ENTRY card, which precedes any data. In some installations, the University of Toronto in particular, a $DATA card is used instead of $ENTRY. This card and the $JOB card must be punched starting in card column 1.

As an option, the compiler will print warnings for constructs that are allowed in Watfiv-S but are not allowed by IBM Fortran compilers, for example:

```
     PRINT,J+1
*EXTENSION*  OTHER COMPILERS MAY NOT ALLOW EXPRESSIONS IN OUTPUT
```

Since SF/k uses several extensions, these warning messages make programs hard to read. The computer center should set up the compiler so that these warning messages are not printed. If this is not the case, the messages can be deleted by including the following card just after the $JOB card:

```
$NOEXTEN
```

Sometimes it is desirable to delete the printing of all or part of a program. For example, printer paper can be saved by deleting the printing of a well-tested subroutine that is included as a part of a larger program. To turn off the printing, use this card:

```
$PRINTOFF
```

When the printing is to be turned back on, use this card:

```
$PRINTON
```

All of the cards $NOEXTEN, $PRINTOFF and $PRINTON must be punched
starting in column 1.

HANDLING ERRORS IN PROGRAMS

When an error is found in a program, the compiler prints an
error message or messages and then processes more of the program.
We will show how a number of errors are handled. Compilers are
always being modified, and the treatment of these errors by a
particular version of the compiler may differ slightly from what
we present.

Fortran is a column-oriented language, and statements must
appear in columns 7 through 72. In the following example, PRINT
erroneously begins in column 6.

```
      PRINT,I,J
***ERROR*** UNDECODEABLE STATEMENT
```

"Undecodeable statement" is the compiler's way of saying it could
not figure what to do with the card. The next example is more
subtle:

```
        PRINT, 'IT LOOKS LIKE THIS PRINTS 3, BUT IT PRINTS...',1+2
```

Assuming that the expression 1+2 starts in column 72, then the +2
part is beyond column 72 and is ignored so that 1 is printed,
instead of 3. The compiler does not give an error message
because unfortunately it does not consider this to be an error.

In the next example the comma has been forgotten between
PRINT and I:

```
      PRINT I
***ERROR*** VARIABLE FORMAT MUST BE AN ARRAY NAME
```

This is the compiler complaining that there is an error, but
making a misleading diagnosis of the cause. The next example has
an extra comma.

```
      INTEGER,I
***ERROR*** EXPECTING SYMBOL,BUT , BEFORE I WAS FOUND
```

In confusing terminology the message says the comma was not
expected. In the next example a right-hand quote mark has been
forgotten.

```
      PRINT,'HI THERE
***ERROR*** NO CLOSING QUOTE OR NEXT CARD NOT CONTINUATION
```

The programmer misspelled the keyword CHARACTER in the
following:

```
      CHARATER(10)STRING
```

ERROR UNDECODEABLE STATEMENT

The next program does not make sense because it tries to use the value of the variable named INCHES, but INCHES is never given a value.

```
1       REAL CM,INCHES
2       CM=2.54*INCHES
3       PRINT,'LENGTH IS',CM
4       RETURN
5       END
```
ERROR VALUE OF INCHES IS UNDEFINED
PROGRAM WAS EXECUTING LINE 2 IN ROUTINE M/PROG WHEN
  TERMINATION OCCURRED

The error messages say that the main program (M/PROG) is stopped in line 2 due to the error. Now, suppose this example is changed by inserting the following after line 1, so this line becomes the new line number 2.

```
2       PRINT,'INCHES:',INCHES
```

As a result the following is printed:

INCHES: UUUUUUUUUUUU

Since INCHES has no value, the string of U's is printed.

The next two examples show what happens if a variable's name is misspelled.

```
1       REAL WEIGHT
2       WEIGHT=10.0
3       WIEGHT=2.2*WEIGHT
4       PRINT,WEIGHT
5       RETURN
6       END
```

In line 3 WEIGHT is misspelled as WIEGHT. Unfortunately, the compiler assumes the misspelled version is a new variable and assigns 2.2*WEIGHT to it. But the true WEIGHT variable remains with a value of 10.0, and this is printed in line 4. The problem is that in Watfiv-S, but not in SF/k, a new spelling such as WIEGHT is implicitly declared to be a new variable. If the misspelled variable is an array something different happens as the next example shows.

```
1       REAL HEIGHT(4)
2       HEIGHT(1)=8.2
3       PRINT,HEIGTH(1)
```
ERROR SUBPROGRAM HEIGTH USED IN LINE 3 IS MISSING

In line 3 HEIGHT is misspelled as HEIGTH, and the compiler assumes (erroneously) that HEIGTH is a missing function subprogram.

In the next program, it was forgotten to read values of
NUMBER inside the loop. As the program now stands, there is an
infinite loop because NUMBER is not changed inside the loop.

```
1        INTEGER NUMBER,SUM
2        SUM=0
3        NUMBER=0
4        WHILE(NUMBER.NE.-99999)DO
5            SUM=SUM+NUMBER
6            END WHILE
7        PRINT,'SUM IS',SUM
8        RETURN
9        END
***ERROR*** JOB-TIME EXCEEDED
PROGRAM WAS EXECUTING LINE 5 IN ROUTINE M/PROG WHEN
    TERMINATION OCCURRED
```

In the next program the NAME array contains elements NAME(1),
NAME(2), NAME(3) and NAME(4). The program is supposed to read
four names followed by the dummy name ZZZ. When the program
runs, there is an error because an attempt is made to read ZZZ
into NAME(5), but NAME(5) does not exist. The error can be
corrected by increasing the declared upper bound of NAME to 5.

```
1        CHARACTER*20 NAME(4)
2        INTEGER I
3        I=1
4        READ,NAME(I)
5        WHILE(NAME(I).NE.'ZZZ')DO
6            PRINT,NAME(I)
7            I=I+1
8            READ,NAME(I)
9            END WHILE
10       RETURN
11       END
```

After the four names are printed, these error messages appear:

```
***ERROR*** SUBSCRIPT NUMBER 1 OF NAME HAS VALUE 5
PROGRAM WAS EXECUTING LINE 8 OF M/PROG WHEN
    TERMINATION OCCURRED
```

The following program is supposed to print one billion
(1,000,000,000), two billion, and then three billion.

```
         INTEGER I
         DO 10 I=1,3
             PRINT,I*1000000000
10           CONTINUE
         RETURN
         END
```

It seems incredible, but the following is actually printed.

    1000000000
    2000000000
    -1294967296

The problem is that the largest value allowed in a Watfiv-S
integer is 2,147,483,647 so when three is multiplied times a
billion the answer does not fit and there is an overflow.
Unfortunately this condition is not detected and the final wired
number is printed instead of three billion. By contrast, if an
overflow occurs with REAL numbers (maximum value is about 10 to
the 78), this is detected and an error message is printed.

BIBLIOGRAPHY

1. Moore, John B., Watfiv: Fortran Programming with the Watfiv Compiler, Reston Publishing Co., Reston, Virginia, 1975.

2. Cress, Paul, Dirksen, Paul and Graham, J. Wesley, Fortran IV with Watfor and Watfiv, Prentice-Hall, Inglewood Cliffs, New Jersey, 1970.

3. Hume, J.N.P. and Holt, R.C., Structured Programming Using PL/1 and SP/k, Reston Publishing Co., Reston, Virginia, 1975.

4. USA Standard Fortran, United States of America Standards Institute, 10 East 40th Street, New York, N.Y. 10016, 1966.

5. Holt, Richard C. and Wortman, David B., "Structured Subsets of the PL/1 Language", Technical Report CSRG-55, Computer Systems Research Group, University of Toronto, May 1975.

INDEX